INDIA'S POLICY TOWARDS WEST ASIA

The Modi Era

INDIA'S POLICY TOWARDS WEST ASIA

The Modi Era

Editors

Sujan Chinoy

Prasanta Kumar Pradhan

First published in 2024 by

PENTAGON PRESS LLP
206, Peacock Lane, Shahpur Jat
New Delhi-110049, India
Contact: 011-26490600

Typeset in Palatino, 11 Point
Printed by Aegean Offset Printers, Greater Noida, U.P.

ISBN 978-81-968722-2-9 (HB)

www.pentagonpress.in

Contents

Preface

India's policy towards West Asia has undergone a massive transformation under the leadership of Prime Minister Narendra Modi. There has been more proactive engagement with the countries of the region, with new fronts of engagement having been opened and existing interactions being substantially strengthened. India considers the West Asian region as its 'extended neighbourhood'. India's 'Think West' policy is commensurately focused on deepening engagements with the region. Prime Minister Modi's 'neighbourhood first' policy also emphasises the West Asian neighbourhood.

West Asia remains a highly sensitive region as recent events have shown in the context of the Israel-Gaza war and the Houthi attacks on merchant shipping traversing the Red Sea through the narrow choke-point of the Bab-el-Mandab, and even beyond, in the Arabian Sea.

During the last ten years, several issues such as the Arab Spring, the emergence and spread of the Islamic State of Iraq and Syria (ISIS), the COVID-19 pandemic, oil price fluctuations, and the parlous situation in Yemen, Syria and the Strait of Hormuz, as well as the Israel-Palestine conflict, have severely challenged the politics, economy and security of the region. India's West Asia policy has been shaped by a nuanced understanding of these complex political and security dynamics of the region. India has endeavoured to protect its national interests against the rising tide of regional geopolitical challenges while adhering to fundamental principles such as condemnation of terrorism, resolution of disputes through peaceful dialogue, humanitarian assistance to affected people, and, the importance of a rules-based international order that provides for freedom of navigation and overflight, unimpeded commerce along critical sea lines of communication and security of the global commons.

Modi's pragmatic approach has focused on maintaining a delicate balance between various competing centres of power without getting involved in regional conflicts. India's neutrality and strategic autonomy have given credibility to its image as an influential regional power that stands ready to provide assistance during pandemics, natural disasters and economic downturns.

Bilateral trade and energy are key elements that shape India's cooperation with countries of West Asia. Modi has actively interacted with the nine-million strong Indian diaspora during his frequent visits to the region. Alongside his hosts, Modi has lauded their contributions to the economic development of the region. Modi's government has taken a keen interest in their safety, security and well-being. Under Modi, the needs of the Indian diaspora have received greater consideration on the part of the host governments, including the fulfillment of their social and cultural aspirations. For example, it would have been inconceivable a decade ago that the UAE would grant permission for the construction of a Hindu temple in Abu Dhabi. These developments have their roots in the close personal relationship between Prime Minister Modi and his counterparts. It is also a manifestation of the changing outlook towards India as it courses its way to the top ranks of the global economy, offering myriad opportunities to West Asian investors.

In recent years, India has strengthened its economic partnership with the West Asian region. Countries such as the UAE and Saudi Arabia have consolidated their positions as top trading partners of India. Modi has invited entrepreneurs and business houses in West Asia to invest in India to boost mutual economic growth and prosperity. With a view to moving beyond the buyer-seller relationship in the energy sector, India has encouraged the establishment of joint ventures. Indian companies are now increasingly acquiring stakes in the Gulf energy sector. Besides, India is also engaged with a number of countries in its efforts to achieve net zero carbon emission and to transition towards cleaner fuels such as green hydrogen.

India's defence and security cooperation with West Asian countries has undergone a major transformation in recent years. There is a noticeable increase in the visits of high-level military officials and joint military exercises. Some West Asian countries have expressed interest in procuring arms and equipment from India in keeping with the latter's thrust on "Make in India" in the defence sector and the new emphasis on defence exports. Partnerships in this field are being explored. Enhanced cooperation on terrorism and maritime security are visible expressions of closer security ties under the Modi government.

The India, Israel, the UAE and the USA (I2U2) format has emerged as a key forum for collaboration in the fields of food, energy, agriculture and technology. During the G20 Summit in New Delhi in September 2023, India together with Saudi Arabia, the UAE, the European Union, France, Germany, Italy and the USA signed a MoU to establish the India–Middle East–Europe Economic Corridor (IMEC). The proposed mega-connectivity project intends to connect India, West Asia and Europe through rail and sea routes to enhance trade and economic interconnectedness.

The Gulf region is a key fulcrum in India's ties with West Asia, given its geographical proximity and the history of close engagement over centuries. The six Arab Gulf Cooperation Council (GCC) countries and Iran are key partners in the economic and security issues. People-to-people contacts have left a deep and indelible imprint on both sides.

In recent years, India's engagements with Israel have also deepened significantly. Under Prime Minister Modi, both countries have strengthened defence, security and strategic cooperation. India's commitment towards the establishment of an independent Palestinian State remains undiluted. India continues to support the Palestinian people bilaterally and through the United Nations Relief and Works Agency for Palestine Refugees in the Near East (UNRWA) as well. Elsewhere in the region, the prolonged regional conflicts in Iraq, Syria and Yemen have hampered closer links despite the historical connect.

This book, titled *India's Policy Towards West Asia: The Modi Era*, presents a comprehensive analysis of Indian foreign policy towards West Asia since Prime Minister Narendra Modi took office in 2014. It covers key dimensions of India's West Asia policy.

Sujan Chinoy, in his chapter "India's West Asia Policy Under Modi", provides a detailed analysis of the progress and achievements made in India's relationship with West Asia. He avers that Modi came to the helm in 2014 at a time when the West Asian region was experiencing tumult, with the ISIS on the rampage and a rash of civil wars erupting in Syria, Yemen and Libya. While Modi's government joined hands together with the countries of the region to fight terrorism, it refrained from getting bogged down in the internal affairs of countries in the region. Chinoy argues that Modi's outreach and endeavours at deepening economic engagement and strengthening the defence and security dimensions of India's strategic partnerships in the region have been reciprocated by many in West Asia.

Prasanta Kumar Pradhan, in his chapter "India and the GCC States: A Growing Engagement", argues that since Prime Minister Modi came to power, India's engagement with the GCC countries has increased exponentially. Modi has adopted a proactive approach towards the countries of the region and has engaged with them in multiple fields. Moving beyond the traditional areas of cooperation, Modi has visualised and implemented stronger and multifaceted strategic partnerships with the GCC countries. Modi's engagement has resulted in creating new nodes of engagement with the GCC States.

Deepika Saraswat, in her chapter "India-Iran Connectivity Partnership: Opportunities and Challenges", analyses the geo-economic dimension of the India-Iran relationship focusing primarily on the connectivity partnership. She highlights the fact that despite facing challenges such as the re-imposition of US sanctions on Iran in 2018 and the Taliban takeover in Afghanistan in 2021, India and Iran have made progress in establishing stable North-South connectivity in the wake of the historic Chabahar Agreement. Geopolitical events, including the US withdrawal from Afghanistan, Iran's accession to the Shanghai Cooperation Organisation (SCO) and the Ukraine War have highlighted the need for continued commitment to the connectivity partnership.

Jatin Kumar, in his chapter "India-Israel Ties Under Prime Minister Narendra Modi", analyses different aspects of the strengthening relationship between India and Israel. He postulates that since 2014, India-Israel ties have entered a new phase of significantly expanded relations. The bilateral engagement has expanded significantly, encompassing defence, innovation, trade, agriculture and cybersecurity. Under Modi, both nations have strengthened their defence collaboration through joint military exercises, procurement of security equipment and technology sharing. Notably, the transformation in India-Israel relations since 2014 was underscored by a shift in the perception of Israel among Arab countries, evident in the signing of the Abraham Accords, the recent conflict in Gaza, notwithstanding.

Md. Muddassir Quamar, in his chapter "India's Approach to Conflicts in West Asia and North Africa", analyses how India under Modi has adopted a balanced approach towards the regional conflicts. He has examined India's responses to conflicts such as the Israel-Palestine issue, civil wars in Syria, Libya and Yemen, as well as the friction between Saudi Arabia and Iran and the irreconcilable differences between Iran and Israel. Emphasising India's vital interests in the region – such as energy security, expatriates, business, trade, investments, maritime security in the Western Indian Ocean, and counterterrorism efforts – the government of Prime Minister Modi has intensified its diplomatic outreach and expended considerable political capital to secure better relations with regional countries.

Rajeev Agarwal, in his chapter "Security in West Asia and India: Shared Concerns and Converging Interests", delves into the convergence of security interests of India and West Asian countries and advocates stronger defence and security cooperation. He states that India's security collaboration with the region is rapidly expanding, with a growing number of countries acknowledging India as a dependable security ally. Under Prime Minister Modi, West Asia has become a critical part of India's extended neighbourhood. This is evident in the significant number of defence and security arrangements concluded with regional countries over the past decade.

Saman Ayesha Kidwai, in her chapter "India's Counter-Terror Cooperation with West Asia and North Africa", states that the issue of terrorism has emerged as a dominant and recurring theme in India's engagements with the countries of the region. India's thrust on the imperative need for global efforts to combat terrorist networks has found resonance among the West Asian and North African countries.

Counter-terror collaboration between India and this region encompasses crucial aspects such as disrupting the financial networks of terrorist organisations, de-radicalisation, education, military training, and intelligence sharing. Given the rising spectre of terrorism in different parts of WANA, there is a significant potential for collaboration in future on counter terrorism.

Finally, we, the editors, convey our gratitude to all the contributors to this volume. We acknowledge the effort put in by Abhishek Yadav, Research Analyst at the West Asia Centre, in poring over all the chapters in a timely manner and providing feedback to help refine the contents. We also extend our appreciation to Vivek Kaushik, Associate Editor of *Strategic Analysis*, for his unstinted support, and to Rajan Aryaa and Virender Negi of Pentagon Press LLP for bringing out this volume.

We are confident that this compendium of writings on a region at the centre of a world in flux will prove to be invaluable for scholars, students, academicians and policymakers alike, offering them a comprehensive insight into India's policy towards West Asia during the Modi era.

February 2024

Sujan Chinoy
Prasanta Kumar Pradhan

About the Contributors

Amb. Sujan Chinoy is the Director General of the Manohar Parrikar Institute for Defence Studies and Analyses (MP-IDSA), New Delhi since 2019. A career diplomat from 1981-2018, he was Ambassador to Japan and Mexico and the Consul General of India in Shanghai and Sydney, besides serving at India's Missions at the UN and Saudi Arabia. A specialist on China, East Asia and politico-security issues, he anchored confidence-building measures (CBMs) with China on the boundary dispute from 1996-2000. At the National Security Council Secretariat (NSCS) from 2008-2012, he handled external and internal security policy, including in the extended neighbourhood of the Indo-Pacific. He was the Chair of the Think20 engagement group for India's G20 Presidency. He is the author of *World Upside Down: India Recalibrates Its Geopolitics* published in July 2023 by Harper Collins. He writes regularly for newspapers and journals and has a well-known presence on the international think-tank circuit.

Dr. Prasanta Kumar Pradhan is a Research Fellow and Coordinator of the West Asia Centre at the Manohar Parrikar Institute for Defence Studies and Analyses (MP-IDSA), New Delhi. He holds a doctorate degree from Jawaharlal Nehru University, New Delhi. Since joining MP-IDSA in 2008, he has been researching on foreign policy, security and strategic issues in West Asia, and India's relationship with West Asia and the wider Arab world. Dr. Pradhan is the author of *India and the Arab Unrest: Challenges, Dilemmas and Engagements* (Routledge, London 2022), *Arab Spring and Sectarian Faultlines in West Asia: Bahrain, Yemen and Syria* (Pentagon Press, New Delhi, 2017) and the monograph *India's Relationship with the Gulf Cooperation Council: Need to Look beyond Business* (MP-IDSA, New Delhi, 2014). He is also the editor of the book *Geopolitical Shifts in West Asia: Trends and Implications* (Pentagon

Press, New Delhi, 2016) and co-edited (with Sujan Chinoy) *India's Approach to West Asia: Trends, Challenges and Possibilities,* (Pentagon Press, New Delhi, 2024).

Dr. Deepika Saraswat is an Associate Fellow at the West Asia Centre, Manohar Parrikar Institute for Defence Studies and Analyses (MP-IDSA), New Delhi. Her research focuses on Iran's foreign policy and geopolitical developments in West Asia and Eurasia, and Indian Foreign Policy. Her research project at MP-IDSA is on 'Iran's Asian Orientation: Quest for Status and Regional Cooperation.' Saraswat has a PhD in Political Geography from the Centre for International Politics, Organisation and Disarmament, School of International Studies, Jawaharlal Nehru University, New Delhi. Earlier, she was a Research Fellow at the Indian Council of World Affairs (ICWA). She has authored a book *Between Survival and Status: The Counter-hegemonic Geopolitics of Iran* (ICWA & Macmillan: 2022). Her commentaries on Iran's foreign policy and domestic policy have featured in national dailies and periodicals such as *The Indian Express, The Hindustan Times* and the *Open Magazine* among others.

Dr. Jatin Kumar is an Assistant Professor at the Department of Political Science, Ram Lal Anand College, University of Delhi. Before joining the University of Delhi, he was working as a Research Analyst in the West Asia Centre at Manohar Parrikar Institute for Defence Studies and Analyses (MP-IDSA). He holds a PhD degree from the Centre for West Asian Studies, Jawaharlal Nehru University, for his doctoral thesis on "Israel's National Security Policy Making after Oslo." His areas of interest are the contemporary Middle East, especially Israel. He is a frequent contributor on various strategic issues to online publications and newspapers. He has published articles with *Contemporary Review of Middle East* and *Strategic Analysis* and contributed chapters in various edited books. In July 2017, he was awarded the Council for Higher Education's Scholarship (CHE), Israel, to participate in an International Summer Programme on Identity-Based Conflict Resolution at Bar Ilan University, Israel.

Dr. Md. Muddassir Quamar is an Associate Professor at the Centre for West Asian Studies, School of International Studies in Jawaharlal

Nehru University (JNU), New Delhi. Dr. Quamar was earlier an Associate Fellow at the Manohar Parrikar Institute for Defence Studies & Analyses (MP-IDSA), New Delhi. He specialises on Middle East strategic affairs, political Islam, and India's relations with the region. Among other issues, he is interested in society, politics and foreign policy of Saudi Arabia and Turkiye. Dr. Quamar has authored and edited several books, published research articles in reputed academic journals and contributed chapters in edited volumes on contemporary developments in the Middle East. He serves as Associate Editor of the *Contemporary Review of the Middle East* (Sage, India) and served as Book Review Editor of *Strategic Analysis* between July 2018 and March 2023. In 2014-15, he was a Visiting Fellow at the King Faisal Centre for Research and Islamic Studies in Riyadh.

Col. Rajeev Agarwal was commissioned into the Artillery in June 1990. He has been Director Military Intelligence at the Army HQ and a Military Observer with the UN. He holds a Master's degree in Defence and Strategic Studies from Madras University. He was also Director in the Ministry of External Affairs, New Delhi and is currently Assistant Director, MP-IDSA. His major published works include the Monograph *Turkey and its Quest for Leadership Role in the West Asian Region*, IDSA, 2014; IDSA Occasional Papers "Threat of Israel's Regional Isolation and Imperatives for the Future", June 2014 and "Egypt's Uneasy Transition: Internal and External Dynamics and Challenges for India", August 2014; and "India's Strategic Partnership with the UAE: A Key Pillar of India's Outreach in West Asia", *Indian Foreign Affairs Journal*, Vol. 17, No.1-2, June 2022.

Ms. Saman Ayesha Kidwai is a Research Analyst (Counter Terrorism Centre) at MP-IDSA. She joined the Institute in August 2021. She holds a Master's degree in Conflict Analysis and Peacebuilding from the Nelson Mandela Centre for Peace and Conflict Resolution, Jamia Millia Islamia, New Delhi. Her areas of interest include political violence, counter-terrorism, and geopolitics, primarily within South Asia, West Asia and the Horn of Africa. Among her publications across different forums, her notable works include, "The Rise of Iran as a Regional Power" and "Rivalry Between the Taliban and ISKP: The Collision of Terror" in the *India Quarterly* journal.

1

India's West Asia Policy Under Modi

Sujan Chinoy

Introduction

India's policy towards West Asia has received renewed attention since Prime Minister Narendra Modi assumed power in 2014. Moving beyond the traditional spheres of interaction such as trade, energy and diaspora, India has now established strategic partnerships with many of the countries of the region. Defence and security cooperation has emerged as a key component of India's West Asia policy under Modi. In the energy sector, India is moving beyond the buyer-seller relationship and engaging in strategic partnerships with the key energy producers in the Gulf. India's bilateral trade with the regional countries has been amplified further and India has revived engagement with the Gulf Cooperation Council (GCC) to sign a Free Trade Agreement (FTA) with the organisation. Cooperation during the COVID-19 pandemic was significant as India sent medicines, equipment and healthcare professionals to a number of countries to help them fight the pandemic in 2020. Later in 2021, when India went through the worst phase of the pandemic, it also received some assistance from a number of these countries. Further, Prime Minister Modi appealed to the Gulf rulers to look after the safety, security and well-being of the nine-million strong Indian expatriate workers in the region as many of them were stranded due to the lockdown, some had lost their jobs and had exhausted their savings during the prolonged pandemic. The number of high-level visits and interactions between India and West Asia has significantly increased in recent years which was found lacking in the previous decades. Besides, Prime Minister Modi is regarded as a close and trusted friend by many regional leaders which is reflected in the several civilian awards of the highest order that he has been conferred with.

When Modi came to power in 2014, the West Asian region was undergoing a period of deep turbulence with the aftereffects of the Arab Spring. The region was dealing with the removal of leaders like Ben Ali in Tunisia, Hosni Mubarak in Egypt, Muammar Gaddafi in Libya and Ali Abdullah Saleh in Yemen. A civil war-like situation was unfolding in Syria, Libya and Yemen. The humanitarian situation in these three countries was deteriorating by the day. After a great deal of internal turmoil, Egypt was slowly limping back towards normalcy following Sisi's advent to power in June 2014. The tension between Iran and Saudi Arabia, often called as a proxy war, was at its peak with the involvement of both countries in different regional conflicts. After establishing the so-called caliphate in Iraq and Syria, the Islamic State of Iraq and Syria (ISIS) was spreading its terrorist activities throughout the region and beyond. The ISIS targeted Indian nationals in Iraq and Libya, thus posing a direct threat to India. Thus, the situation in West Asia and the wider Arab world was one of the most challenging foreign policy issues for Prime Minister Modi. The ISIS became the most pressing challenge for the Modi government. It kidnapped Indians in Iraq and the Indian government had to negotiate hard with it for their rescue and release.

India maintained neutrality in the domestic affairs of the countries. It also chose to refrain from interfering in the conflicts and civil wars in the region. India has adopted a neutral stance in the internal and regional political affairs in West Asia. India firmly believes that there are no military solutions to the crises in the region and has emphasised the need for dialogue and negotiation within the respective countries. India has demonstrated its commitment to this approach by providing humanitarian assistance, including food and medicines, to nations such as Syria, Libya and Yemen at various stages.

From "Look West" to "Think West" Policy

India's foreign policy towards West Asia has undergone significant transformations in recent years. In 2005, then Prime Minister Manmohan Singh announced the "Look West" Policy of India to prioritise India's engagements with the West Asia region. But over the course of the next few years, the pace of engagement and cooperation in India's relationship with West Asian countries was slow. Prime Minister Modi adopted the "Think West" policy to emphasise India's engagement with the West Asian countries and to deepen engagement in economic, defence, security and strategic cooperation. While recognising the historical and civilisational connection between India and West Asia, Modi's Think West policy envisions forging strategic partnerships which would be mutually beneficial. It also aims to promote trade, investment, energy cooperation and people-to-people contacts. The "Think West" policy has since been an important pillar of India's West Asia policy.[1]

The West Asian region is a part of India's extended neighbourhood where India has significant economic, political, security and strategic interests. The rise of religious extremism, terrorism, maritime security and the continuing civil wars in the region significantly challenge India's interests in West Asia. India's Think West policy, therefore, is not only aimed at safeguarding and promoting its national interests but also designed to play a proactive role in maintaining peace and stability in the region.

India and the Gulf Region

The Gulf region is important for India for a number of reasons. Prime Minister Modi's outreach to the Gulf region has been a core element in his overall policy towards the wider Arab and Islamic world. He has made several visits to a number of countries in the Gulf region. During the last ten years, Prime Minister Modi has made four official visits to the UAE. Besides, Saudi Arabia is another important strategic partner for India in the Gulf. For his rich contributions to the strengthening of ties, Modi has been conferred with the highest civilian awards by Saudi Arabia "the King Abdulaziz Sash", the UAE "Order of Zayed" and Bahrain's "King Hamad Order of the Renaissance" among the Gulf countries.

Modi has fundamentally transformed India's relationship with the Gulf region. India's bilateral trade with the GCC countries alone stands at around US$ 184.5 billion.[2] He has engaged with the countries of the region beyond the traditionally dominant spheres of energy and trade. Today, the India-Gulf relationship encompasses a wide range of issues including cooperation in defence, security, food security, climate change, health, renewable energy, to name a few. Recognising their significance in the fields of energy, geopolitics and economy, Prime Minister Modi has focused on building strategic partnerships with the GCC countries. He has attached priority to bilateral dialogues, high-level visits and joint initiatives with the GCC countries in order to deepen political, defence and security cooperation.

Energy

The Gulf countries are the most important source of energy given the fact that India imports around 60 per cent of its oil from the region. Iraq is the largest supplier of crude oil to India followed by Saudi Arabia and the UAE. Presently, there exists a significant alignment of interests between India and the Gulf nations regarding collaboration in the energy sector. India sees the Gulf countries as a dependable supplier of energy, while the Gulf nations perceive India as a secure and enduring market for their oil and gas resources. Around half of India's LNG imports come from Qatar alone. India has established a Strategic Petroleum Reserve (SPR) to meet the requirements of energy in case of exigencies. In its initial stages, India has successfully established an SPR of five MMT (Million Metric Tons) at Visakhapatnam, Mangalore and Padur. The government is moving forward with the second phase, planning to extend the SPR to two additional locations in Odisha and Padur. Collaborating with the Gulf nations holds critical importance for India in reaching the targeted storage capacity within these reserves. In recent times, India has moved the traditional buyer-seller dynamics with Gulf nations, forging strategic alliances and making substantial investments in the energy domain. Indian public sector entities have ventured into the oil and gas sectors of the UAE, Oman and Iraq, actively participating in exploration, production activities and pivotal pipeline projects.

India is deepening its engagement with the Gulf countries in the green and renewable energy sectors as well. There is a convergence of interests and initiatives between India and the Gulf countries to reduce carbon emissions. India is looking to investing more in solar energy, hydropower and green hydrogen. This was highlighted at the recently concluded G20 Leadership Summit in New Delhi. Earlier in 2021 India invited the GCC countries to invest in the sustainable energy sectors.[3] The UAE and Saudi Arabia are two key players which have taken a keen interest and significantly deepened collaboration with India. In June 2023, during Prime Minister Modi's visit to Abu Dhabi, India and the UAE issued a joint statement on climate change. In October 2023, both countries agreed to collaborate on energy storage technologies, Smart Grids, renewable energy and energy efficiency.[4] Earlier in January 2023, India and the UAE signed a MoU on collaboration in Green Hydrogen. Similarly, India and Saudi Arabia signed a MoU on Electrical Interconnections, Green Hydrogen and supply chains in October 2023. Both countries have also agreed to promote investment in the new and renewable energy sector.[5]

Indian Expatriates in the Gulf

There are more than nine million Indians living in the Gulf region contributing to the economic development and progress of these countries. For many decades, the Indian expatriate workers in the Gulf have served as a bridge connecting India and the Gulf region. The contribution of India's expatriate workers to the development and progress of their economies has been acknowledged by the leaders in the Gulf. Their safety, security and well-being are matters of serious concern for the Government of India. India also benefits from substantial remittance inflows, a result of expatriates sending a significant portion of their earnings back to their families in the country. These remittances form a significant portion of India's foreign exchange receipts, contributing to financial stability. In 2022, India received foreign remittances of US$ 111 billion.[6] Around half of the total remittances received by India flow from the Gulf region.

Defence and Security Cooperation

Under Prime Minister Modi, defence and security cooperation with the Gulf region has significantly been strengthened. Defence and security cooperation between India and the Gulf countries has been a constant point of discussion between Modi and the Gulf rulers in bilateral meetings and discussions. The number of military-to-military interactions such as joint training and exercises which help in sharing their experiences and skills has increased substantially. Traditionally, the Indian Navy was at the forefront of engagement with the navies of the Gulf region. But in recent years, the Indian Air Force and the Indian Army as well as the Coast Guard have been engaging with their counterparts in the Gulf.

Modi has invited the Gulf countries to invest in the 'Make in India' defence initiatives. In order to strengthen defence ties, India seeks joint manufacturing and co-production of arms and weapons with the GCC states. This would require investment, technology and the highest level of trust between the countries. Besides, some of the Gulf countries have expressed their interest in buying arms and equipment from India. The UAE has expressed interest in buying Brahmos missiles from India. In 2019, the Ordnance Factory Board (OFB) signed a contract with the UAE worth US$ 45.75 million for the supply of 50,000 Bofors 155 mm shells. Prior to that in 2017, OFB had signed a deal with the UAE for the Bofors Shells.[7]

Terrorism is a common issue of concern between India and the GCC countries. Prime Minister Modi has emphasised the importance of joint efforts and cooperation with the GCC countries to fight the menace together. India believes that as terrorist organisations have established transnational networks, it is necessary for the concerned states to build consensus and join hands together to fight the menace. Both India and the GCC countries have joined hands together and taken initiatives to address the shared challenges of extremism and terrorism. Counter-terror cooperation between India and the Gulf region has been an important aspect of cooperation between the two.

Iran

Due to Pakistan's obstruction of India's overland connectivity to Afghanistan and Central Asia, New Delhi has turned its attention to Iran. Recognising Iran's strategic geographical position between the Persian Gulf and the Caspian Sea, India views it as a crucial hub for inter-regional connectivity between South and Central Asia. Iran is seen as a valuable land bridge, linking India's West coast to Central Asia and the wider Eurasian region. The 2003 New Delhi Declaration, which was signed during President Mohammed Khatami's visit to India, committed to developing the Chabahar port with an eye to facilitating regional trade and transit, especially with Afghanistan. The New Delhi Declaration also underscored the mutual interest of India and Iran in fully utilising the North-South transit routes and enhancing infrastructure connectivity.[8]

However, significant progress on the Chabahar Port and the development of the International North-South Transport Corridor could only be achieved after the signing of the Joint Comprehensive Plan of Action (JCPOA) in 2015. This led to the lifting of UN-mandated economic sanctions in January 2016. In May 2016, Prime Minister Modi's visit to Tehran presented an opportunity to forge strategic ties with Iran. The highlight of the visit was the signing of the India, Iran and Afghanistan Trilateral Agreement, also known as the Chabahar Agreement, on the establishment of an International Transit and Transport Corridor, also called the Chabahar Agreement. Under this agreement, India committed itself to building and taking operational responsibility for the Chabahar Port. The agreement also highlighted the significant interests shared by Tehran and New Delhi in the development and stability of Afghanistan.

As part of the Chabahar Agreement, India pledged a US$ 500 million credit line to build, equip and operate two berths at Chabahar Port in the Gulf of Oman. To operationalise the hinterland potential of the port, Indian Railway Construction Limited (IRCON) signed a MoU with Iran's Construction, Development of Transport Infrastructure Company (CDTIC) that will enable IRCON to provide requisite services for the construction of the Chabahar-Zahedan railway line which forms part of the transit and transportation corridor in the Chabahar Agreement. In January 2018, India's Exim Bank operationalised a US$ 150 million line of credit to Iran's Maritime and Ports Organisation for making jetties and berths at Chabahar. India Ports Global Pvt Limited, a joint venture between the Jawaharlal Nehru Port Trust (JNPT) and Deen Dayal Port Authority made a capital investment of US$ 85.21 million under a deal with an Iranian company to equip and operate the container and multi-purpose terminals at Shahid Beheshti Chabahar Port Phase-I. In December 2018, just before the US sanctions on Iran were to take effect, India took over operations at the Shahid Beheshti Port.

Notably, India's development of Chabahar Port has a regional dimension, rectifying India's sub-optimal level of trade and economic ties with Central Asian republics, while helping these landlocked countries diversify their connectivity to international markets including South Asia. India's ascension into the multilateral initiative Ashgabat Agreement, which was signed in 2011 by Uzbekistan, Turkmenistan, Iran, Oman and Qatar, was a key milestone in the development of North-South connectivity in Eurasia. In order to mutually reinforce the development of the INSTC and Chabahar, especially given the latter's significance for Central Asia, both Tehran and New Delhi have been keen to interlink the two infrastructure projects. In March 2021, marking 'Chabahar Day' at the Maritime India Summit 2021, External Affairs Minister S. Jaishankar proposed its inclusion in the INSTC trade corridor. While welcoming the interest of Uzbekistan and Afghanistan in joining the 12-member multimodal corridor project, the minister noted that an 'eastern corridor through Afghanistan' would maximise the potential of the project.[9] In a nutshell, Chabahar Port, despite the challenges posed to its development by the US sanctions and the Taliban takeover in Afghanistan, has emerged as a flagbearer of India's connectivity with Central Asia and a key symbol of Indo-Iranian cooperation.[10]

As the US began negotiating peace with the Taliban securing its military withdrawal from Afghanistan, both India and Iran maintained that any initiative on the country should be centred on the Afghan government. Furthermore, both favoured a regional approach to stabilise Afghanistan and tackle counter-terrorism in the region. In December 2019, Tehran convened a six-nation "Regional Security Dialogue" attended by national security officials of Russia, China, Pakistan, Tajikistan, Uzbekistan, and India.[11] In November 2021, New Delhi hosted the Regional Security Dialogue on Afghanistan with senior security officials from Iran, Kazakhstan, Kyrgyzstan, Russia, Tajikistan, Turkmenistan and Uzbekistan.[12] At the meeting, Prime Minister Modi emphasised four aspects that countries in the region need to focus on, namely, the need for an inclusive government, a zero-tolerance stance about Afghan territory being used by terrorist groups, a strategy to counter trafficking of drugs and arms from Afghanistan and addressing the increasingly critical humanitarian crisis in Afghanistan.[13] Both countries also support the use of regional organisations such as the Shanghai Cooperation Organisation to tackle challenges emerging from Afghanistan.

India and the Israel-Palestine Issue

India has historically upheld a nuanced approach towards the Israel-Palestine conflict. While strengthening ties with Israel, India has called for a two-state solution, respecting the aspirations of the Palestinian people. The diplomatic relations between India and Israel witnessed significant improvement following the normalisation of ties in 1992. Initially, the focus of cooperation was primarily on the defence and agriculture sectors. However, over a period of time, the engagement expanded to encompass a broader range of areas, including defence, agriculture, cybersecurity, trade, tourism and scientific development. Under the leadership of Prime Minister Modi, the bilateral ties between India and Israel have reached new heights, highlighting the mutual recognition of the importance of strengthening and broadening their mutually beneficial partnership. Modi's emphasis has been on expanding cooperation beyond the defence sector, particularly in areas such as science and technology, drinking water and sanitation, agricultural cooperation, space research, innovation and cyber security.

This shift in focus was clearly evident during Prime Minister Modi's visit to Israel in July 2017, which marked the first-ever visit by an Indian Prime Minister to the country. The visit represented a significant departure from India's previous foreign policy approach towards Israel, as Modi chose not to visit Palestine during the tour, breaking with convention and symbolising a "de-hyphenation" of India's relations with them. In reciprocation, Israeli Prime Minister Benjamin Netanyahu visited India in January 2018. During this visit, Modi and Netanyahu reaffirmed their commitment to strengthening the bilateral relationship, expressing a shared vision for the future.

On 15 January 2018, both leaders shared a joint statement and said that both countries share a common vision for the relationship.

Israeli Defence Minister Benjamin Gantz visited India in June 2022. During his visit, both countries reiterated their commitment to further deepening and expanding defence cooperation. In recent years, high-level visits from the military have taken place which have provided a fillip to the defence ties between India and Israel. The Chief of the Air Staff Air Chief Marshal Rakesh Kumar Singh Bhadauria visited Israel in August 2022 and the then Chief of Army Staff General Manoj Mukund Naravane visited Israel in November 2022.

The expansion of ties in the areas of Health and Medicine is another milestone in India-Israel ties. Since the onset of the COVID-19 pandemic, India and Israel have been closely cooperating with each other in this sector. On 21 December 2020, both countries signed an Agreement on Cooperation in the fields of Health and Medicine.

Since the beginning of the Israel-Palestine conflict, India has overall maintained a supportive stance towards the Palestinian issue. In 1974, India became the first non-Arab state to recognise the Palestine Liberation Organisation (PLO) as the sole and legitimate representative of the Palestinian people. Furthermore, India was among the early nations to acknowledge the state of Palestine in 1988. In 1996, India inaugurated its Representative Office in Gaza, which later shifted to Ramallah in 2003. These actions indicate India's traditional support for the Palestinian cause.

Palestinian President Mahmoud Abbas visited India in May 2017 on his third State Visit and overall, his fifth visit to India during his Presidency. The visit was reciprocated by the historic first-ever visit by Prime Minister Modi to Palestine on 10 February 2018. India signed six MoUs focusing on the construction of a hospital, school, the India-Palestine Centre for Empowering Women and the procurement of equipment and machinery for the New National Printing Press. India also promised to provide "one-time project assistance worth US$ 42.1 million for Palestinian nation-building in education, health, women empowerment and capacity building."[14] During the visit, Prime Minister Modi was conferred with the "Grand Collar of the State of Palestine" – the highest civilian honour of Palestine – in recognition of India's constant support for the Palestinian cause.

India has deepened its engagement with both Israel and Palestine while at the same time 'de-hyphenating' the two. While continuing its traditional support for the Palestinian cause, India has steadily expanded its cooperation with Israel on a wide range of issues. India's moral principle of supporting Palestinian statehood has continued alongside the strengthening of the relationship with Israel in the areas of defence, security, technology, health, innovation and other fields.

India has maintained a balanced position towards the Israel-Hamas war that broke out after the 7 October terrorist attack on Israel. India expressed solidarity with Israel and condemned the Hamas attack on Israel. While India hasn't formally designated Hamas as a terrorist organization, it labelled the 7 October 2023 attack as an act of terrorism. Prime Minister Modi spoke with Palestinian President Mahmoud Abbas following the tragic blast at the Al Ahli hospital in Gaza, expressing concern for the loss of lives. India was one of the first countries to supply humanitarian aid to Gaza after the Rafah border crossing was opened. Modi reiterated India's position on the longstanding Israel-Palestine issue, advocating for direct negotiations between the two parties to resolve the conflict.

Revitalising Ties with Jordan

For the most part of history, the India-Jordan relationship has remained low-key. The visit by King Abdullah II and Queen Rania to India in December 2006 created an opportunity for both countries to share views on all aspects of their bilateral relations.[15] The first-ever visit by an Indian Head of State took place after 65 years of establishment of diplomatic ties, when then President of India, Pranab Mukherjee, visited Amman in October 2015.[16] During the visit, both countries inaugurated the US$ 860 million Jordan India Fertiliser Company (JIFCO) joint venture and signed six agreements focusing on various areas of cooperation.

Prime Minister Narendra Modi visited Jordan in February 2018 which was described as the beginning of a new chapter in the bilateral ties by King Abdullah II. Later in the same month, King Abdullah II visited India. During the visit, both countries signed 12 MoUs, focusing on areas such as defence, trade, investment, industry, education, agriculture, mineral exploration and IT. The agreement on defence cooperation will be vital for India to "have a strategic imprint in the region of the Red Sea and the Eastern Mediterranean through the Levant."[17] Later, India's National Security Adviser, Ajit Doval, visited Jordan in 2020. Jordan is a stable country in the turbulent West Asian region and holds significant geostrategic value for fostering collaboration with India in the areas of counter-terrorism and security cooperation.

Both countries have also engaged in fighting against the COVID-19 pandemic. During the difficult COVID-19 situation in Jordan, India helped the Kingdom by providing supplies of essential medicine and equipment.[18] Furthermore, a two-week long training for 15 medical experts of the Jordanian Armed Forces on COVID-19 intensive care units was organised by the Indian government in February and March 2021.[19] The bilateral trade between the two countries stands at US$ 2.8 billion in 2021-2022.[20] Both countries aim to reach bilateral trade of US$ 5 billion by 2025 and agreed to diversify the trade basket.[21] To further enhance the commercial ties, India and Jordan launched a trade and business forum in 2021.

Exploring New Space with Egypt

India and Egypt shared strong political and military ties during the 1950s and 1960s during the leadership of Jawaharlal Nehru and Gamal Abdel Nasser. Both countries were the champions of the Non-Aligned Movement (NAM) during the turbulent times of the Cold War. However, in the subsequent decades, the bilateral relationship between India and Egypt remained on a low ebb as the earlier momentum could not be sustained due to a number of factors. Both Prime Minister Modi and President Sisi came to power in 2014. Since then, both leaders have expressed their desire to strengthen the bilateral relationship in different spheres. Sisi has made three visits to India as President. He first came to India in 2015 to participate in the India–Africa Forum Summit held in Delhi, undertook a State visit to India in 2016 and in January 2023 he participated in India's Republic Day celebrations as the Chief Guest. From India's side, there have been frequent ministerial and official visits to Cairo, including a visit by Defence Minister Rajnath Singh in September 2022 and one by the External Affairs Minister S. Jaishankar in October 2022. Prime Minister Modi visited

Egypt on June 24-25, 2023. During the visit, both countries signed a strategic partnership agreement agreeing to elevate their relationship to a strategic level.

Some important areas of convergence such as trade and investment, counter-terrorism, defence and security issues have emerged between India and Egypt since 2014. Egypt, like India, confronts significant terrorism challenges, with various extremist groups operating in the Sinai Peninsula. These include ISIS, Al Qaeda, and local militant organisations, forming networks across Western Asia and North Africa. The Egyptian government faces a major security concern, as these groups frequently target security forces and minority communities. Therefore, both countries have announced 'zero tolerance' for terrorism and have committed themselves to forging comprehensive counter-terrorism cooperation.[22]

Under the leadership of Modi, defence and security cooperation with Egypt has received significant attention. India is eager to enhance its partnership in these areas with Egypt. In recent years, there has been intensified military cooperation, including regular visits and port calls by India and Egypt. The Indian and Egyptian navies have conducted joint exercises, training programs, and port calls. India and Egypt conducted their first-ever air exercise 'Desert Warrior' in Egypt, while the Indian Air Force participated in the Tactical Leadership Programme of the Egyptian Air Force Weapons School.[23] Additionally, the Indian and Egyptian armies conducted their inaugural joint exercise, 'Exercise Cyclone-I,' in Rajasthan.[24] Given their extensive experience in combating terrorism, collaborative efforts in strategy and skills sharing will prove mutually beneficial.

As prominent countries in the Global South, India and Egypt share common interests and concerns regarding global challenges. As part of India's G20 presidency, Egypt has been invited as a guest country, showcasing the alignment between the two nations. Egypt has expressed its backing for collaborative efforts with India on G20 issues, emphasising the importance of addressing Global South issues adequately within the G20 framework.

Challenges Remain in India-Turkiye Relationship

The relationship between India and Turkiye has historically been limited by global and regional geopolitical factors. Although diplomatic ties were established in 1948, soon after Indian independence, the Cold War geopolitical dynamics prevented any political warmth from taking root despite the two being secular republics. India's leadership of the Non-Aligned Movement (NAM), and later, its proximity with the Soviet Union and Turkiye's close security ties with the US and membership of the North Atlantic Treaty Organisation (NATO) in 1952 put them in different camps during the Cold War. Furthermore, Turkiye developed close fraternal and ideological proximity with Pakistan and sided with Islamabad on critical issues between India and Pakistan making it difficult for bilateral relations to gain any traction. The post-Cold War recalibration in Indian and Turkish foreign policies generated some opportunities for moving beyond geopolitics to develop bilateral relations. However, the Pakistan factor as well as Turkiye's position on Jammu and Kashmir has prevented any meaningful progress.

Prime Minister Modi has endeavoured to overcome the geopolitical hurdles that prevented the full realisation of the potential in bilateral ties, particularly by giving greater thrust to practical cooperation as well as political and diplomatic engagement. As a result, a number of important bilateral visits have taken place in recent years, including by then External Affairs Minister Sushma Swaraj on 15-16 January 2015 and a return visit by Turkish Foreign Minister Mevlut Cavusoglu on 19 March 2015. These were followed by the participation in April 2015 of an Indian delegation led by the then Minister of State for External Affairs, Gen. (Retd.) V.K. Singh in the 100th anniversary ceremonies of the Canakkale Land and Sea battles of 1915. In November 2015, Modi attended the G20 Summit held in Antalya and also held bilateral talks with President Erdogan on the sidelines. Cavusoglu paid a visit to India on 18-19 August 2016. Modi and Erdogan also met on the side-lines of other multilateral summits leading to hopes for improvement in ties. This was followed by the visit of President Erdogan to India in April-May 2017. These efforts led to improved trading and business ties leading to bilateral trade reaching US$ 7.22 billion in 2017-18.[25]

However, the Pakistan factor has repeatedly come in the way and impacted adversely on the further deepening of ties. Turkiye's support for Pakistan on the Kashmir issue, especially since India's decision in August 2019 to abolish the special status of Jammu and Kashmir, has created serious political friction in bilateral relations. President Erdogan has been one of the most vocal supporters of Pakistan over the Kashmir issue in the United Nations General Assembly (UNGA). The Turkish position is anchored in both its historically friendly relations with Pakistan as well as a broad convergence on contemporary geopolitical issues as fellow members of the Organisation of Islamic Cooperation (OIC). The ideological and Islamist leanings of the Justice and Development Party (AKP) and Erdogan himself clearly lead Turkiye to place fraternal religious ties with Pakistan above trade and business transactions with India. This has diminished any hopes for improvement in bilateral relations even though, as large middle powers with growing regional influence, India and Turkiye should find more common space to work together at the multi-lateral level.

New Delhi, in response, has begun to be more assertive in dealing with Ankara and has started taking more vocal positions on conflicts between Turkiye and its neighbours including Greece, Cyprus and Syria. It is in Turkiye's interest to improve bilateral economic ties with India as the country faces a deepening economic crisis. On the other hand, Turkiye's defence manufacturing industry is quite advanced and holds some opportunities for the two sides to cooperate in manufacturing of equipment. However, political challenges remain especially given the intransigent position adopted by Turkiye on the Kashmir issue. This issue clearly casts a long shadow. Hence, going forward, it would require more than just improved economic relations for the relationship to progress. For the foreseeable future, bilateral ties are likely to remain frosty and continue to pose a challenge for the Modi government.

Mini-lateral and Plurilateral Engagements in West Asia

Given the polarised nature of geopolitics in the West Asian region, India has traditionally preferred to engage with each of the countries of West Asia at the bilateral level. Even regional organisations like the OIC and the Arab League have remained divided over different issues. With the changing times, India has opted to engage with the region by forming mini-lateral groupings taking like-minded countries on board. The India, Israel, the UAE and the US (I2U2) has emerged as an important mini-lateral in the region. It has announced six major areas of cooperation. The I2U2 group is intended to "encourage joint investments in six mutually identified areas such as water, energy, transportation, space, health, and food security."[26] The issues agreed upon are non-controversial, devoid of suspicion about ulterior motives and unilateral advantages to member states. Furthermore, they actively promote private sector involvement, encourage technological collaboration, enhance investments and facilitate infrastructure improvements.

In July 2022, the inaugural summit of the I2U2 was conducted virtually, with the participation of Prime Minister Narendra Modi, Israeli Prime Minister Yair Lapid, Emirati President Mohammed bin Zayed Al Nahyan and American President Joe Biden. The leaders engaged in discussions concerning two critical issues, namely food security and the energy crisis. A significant outcome of the meeting was the agreement for the UAE to invest US$ 2 billion in India, specifically towards the establishment of food parks and the implementation of smart technology for water conservation and the utilisation of renewable energy sources. Notably, this initiative will leverage American and Israeli technology while involving their respective private sectors. The primary objective is to foster a collaborative approach to address the challenges posed by food insecurity. Additionally, the leaders at the summit concurred with one another on the establishment of hybrid renewable energy projects in Gujarat, India, with active participation from the UAE, Israel and the US in terms of investment and technology. The private sector will also play a crucial role in the field of clean energy projects to advance renewable energy targets.

In another development, in May 2023, the National Security Advisers of India, Saudi Arabia, the UAE and the US met in Riyadh. Without elaborating further details, US National Security Advisor Jake Sullivan stated that the officials met "to advance their shared vision of a more secure and prosperous Middle East region interconnected with India and the world."[27] It is widely reported that they discussed, among other issues, the development of a joint railway connectivity infrastructure project that would connect the Gulf with other Arab countries in the Levant. This will be connected to India via the shipping lanes.[28] Although this project has yet to take off, it has the potential to provide economic and connectivity benefits to the whole region and India. It will provide India with further opportunities in trade, energy and connectivity access to West Asia. Beyond the stated objective of establishing connectivity, the cooperation between these four countries could deepen their convergence on the geopolitical situation.

During the G20 Leaders' Summit held in New Delhi in September 2023, India along with Saudi Arabia, the UAE, the USA, France, Germany, Italy and the EU announced the formation of the India-Middle East-Europe Economic Corridor (IMEC). This is an economic and transport corridor which will connect India to Europe through West Asia. It is believed that this corridor will significantly bolster trade and connectivity between these regions using both sea and rail routes.

Managing Complex Regional Rivalries

The complex regional security dynamics, involvement of external powers and protracted conflicts in the region bring fresh challenges to India's engagement in the region. Keeping in mind its long-term interests, India has engaged all the regional powers while avoiding any involvement in any regional disputes. For instance, India maintains strong relations with both Iran and Saudi Arabia who have had an adversarial relationship with one another in the past. Similarly, India has simultaneously been engaging with Iran and Israel despite acrimony between the two. In the aftermath of the Qatar crisis which led to its boycotting in 2017 by the quartet of Saudi Arabia, Bahrain, the UAE and Egypt, India also treaded a fine line without taking sides. India appealed to the GCC States to resolve the crisis amicably. Similarly, India has adopted a nuanced policy towards the long-standing Israel-Palestine conflict.

Cooperation during the COVID-19 Pandemic and *Vande Bharat Mission*

In 2020, India demonstrated its support to countries in the region by offering assistance in various ways. It supplied hydroxychloroquine tablets to Bahrain, Oman, Qatar, Saudi Arabia, Israel and the UAE. Additionally, India responded to Kuwait's request by dispatching a 15-member medical team,[29] while also deploying a team of 88 medical and healthcare professionals to the UAE to aid in their fight against the pandemic.[30] These proactive measures have consolidated India's reputation as a reliable and steadfast friend, providing timely assistance during crises. In 2021, when the dangerous Delta variant of the COVID-19 virus spread across India, there was an acute shortage of liquid oxygen in India. At the time, the Gulf countries such as the UAE, Saudi Arabia and Kuwait quickly stepped in to supply liquid oxygen to help India in its struggle against the pandemic.[31] Israel too emerged as a key partner in fighting the COVID-19 pandemic as it supplied liquid oxygen, medical equipment and Artificial Intelligence (AI) based technologies to the All India Institute of Medical Sciences (AIIMS), New Delhi.

During the pandemic, India reached out to a number of countries in the world supplying medicines, professionals and equipment. This was widely known as India's "COVID diplomacy." Later, as the vaccines gradually became available, India supplied vaccines to several countries despite its heavy domestic requirements. India sent millions of doses of Covishield and Covaxin vaccines to countries all over the world, including the West Asian countries.

In April 2020, India initiated a registration process for its nationals abroad who wished to return home, as many expatriates expressed a desire to come back as the pandemic continued to spread. Responding to this, a significant number of Indian citizens in various Gulf countries registered themselves for repatriation. To address this situation, India launched the *Vande Bharat Mission* in May 2020, with the aim of bringing back stranded Indian nationals from different parts of the world. India engaged in discussions with GCC countries to facilitate repatriation and established air bubbles to enable phased repatriation. The Gulf countries responded positively to India's efforts, resulting in the successful repatriation of expatriates. The *Vande Bharat Mission* emerged as one of the largest peacetime repatriation initiatives ever undertaken globally. In December 2021, the Indian Government announced that over 700,000 Indians had been repatriated from the Gulf region during the pandemic through the *Vande Bharat Mission*.[32]

Conclusion

India's approach towards West Asia has undergone significant change under Prime Minister Modi. His multiple visits to the region filled the void of high-level visits which was necessary keeping in mind India's enormous stakes and interests in West Asia. Engagement at a personal level among the top leadership on both sides has increased significantly. This has, to a large extent, bridged the earlier trust deficit between India and the countries of the region.

Modi came to power at a time when the West Asian region was going through a period of turmoil with ISIS on the rampage and civil wars in Syria, Yemen and Libya. Intelligence sharing and cooperation in countering terrorism has been accelerated under Modi. The rise of ISIS and other terrorist organisations in the region amid the Arab unrest has propelled India-West Asia cooperation in dealing with the common challenge of global terrorism. While Modi's government joined hands together with the countries of the region to fight terrorism, it refrained from getting dragged into the internal affairs of countries in the region. Instead, India chose to use its resources to provide humanitarian support to the countries experiencing the ravages of civil wars.

Moving beyond the traditionally dominant areas of cooperation such as trade, energy and diaspora, Prime Minister Modi has engaged the countries of the West Asian region on defence, security and strategic issues. He has adopted a long-term approach towards West Asia and focused on building strategic partnerships with the regional powers. In the energy sector, India is now redefining the traditional buyer-seller relationship and seeking investments and partnerships in both upstream and downstream activities. India has invested in the energy sector in the Gulf in terms of human resources and technology in the exploration and production of oil and gas.

The 'neighbourhood first' policy of Modi has proved to be very successful in West Asia. His priority on deepening economic engagement and on strengthening the defence and security dimensions of its strategic partnerships in the region has been reciprocated by many in West Asia. India's image as a Good Samaritan during the COVID-19 pandemic has left a deep and indelible impression on the people of the region. India's efforts to promote the interests of the Global South have burnished India's, and Prime Minister Modi's, credentials at the government and popular levels. The change and dynamism introduced by Modi to India's West Asia policy will have a lasting impact on the India-West Asia relationship.

NOTES

1 "Committed to Global Order Based on Rules in Post-Covid-19 World", *Hindustan Times*, 21 September 2020, at https://www.hindustantimes.com/india-news/committed-to-global-order-based-on-rules-in-post-covid-19-world-harsh-shringla-on-foreign-policy-priorities/story-zC7ohdSW5Qy9S5XDRc6RwJ.html (Accessed 13 May 2022).

2 Export-Import Data Bank, Department of Commerce, Ministry of Commerce and Industry, Government of India.

3 "India invites GCC Nations to invest in sustainable energy sectors", *Business Standard*, 10 November 2021, at https://www.business-standard.com/content/press-releases-ani/india-invites-gcc-nations-to-invest-in-sustainable-energy-sectors-121111000524_1.html (Accessed 22 January 2022).

4 "UAE-India MoU to drive investment and collaboration in industry and advanced technologies", Press Information Bureau, 5 October 2023, at https://pib.gov.in/PressReleaseIframePage.aspx?PRID=1964714#:~:text=In%20the%20energy%20space%2C%20the ,renewable %20energy% 20and%20energy%20efficiency (Accessed 22 November 2023).

5 "India and Saudi Arabia decide to promote investment in New & Renewable Energy", Press Information Bureau, 10 October 2023, at https://pib.gov.in/PressReleaseIframePage.aspx?PRID=1966200 (Accessed 22 November 2023).

6 Vandana Chandra, "Remittance flows reached an all-time high in 2022 in South Asia", World Bank Blog, 10 October 2023, at https://blogs.worldbank.org/peoplemove/remittance-flows-reached-all-time-high-2022-south-asia (Accessed 27 November 2023).

7 "In its largest ever export order, OFB to supply 50,000 Bofors shells to UAE", *Economic Times*, 3 August 2019, at https://economictimes.indiatimes.com/news/defence/in-its-largest-ever-export-order-ofb-to-supply-50000-bofors-shells-to-uae/articleshow/70501461.cms?from=mdr (Accessed 12 March 2023).

8 The Republic of India and the Islamic Republic of Iran, "The New Delhi Declaration", Ministry of External Affairs, Government of India, 25 January 2003, at https://www.mea.gov.in/other.htm?dtl/20182/The+Republic+of+India+and+th#1 (Accessed 2 March 2023).

9 Dipanjan Roy Chaudhury, 'India proposes inclusion of Iran's Chabahar Port in International North South Transport Corridor', *The Economic Times*, 5 March 2021, at https://economictimes.indiatimes.com/news/politics-and-nation/india-proposes-inclusion-of-irans-chabahar-port-in-international-north-south-transport-corridor/articleshow/81336893.cms?from=mdr (Accessed 22 February 2023).

10 Philip Reid, "Makaran Gateways: A Strategic Reference for Gwadar and Chabahar", *IDSA Occasional Paper no. 53*, August 2019, at https://idsa.in/system/files/opaper/makran-gatways-op-53.pdf (Accessed 22 February 2023).

11 Alireza Noori, "Tehran convenes allies against threats that include US", *Al Monitor*, 24 December 2019, at https://www.al-monitor.com/originals/2019/12/iran-tehran-allies-threats-security-conference-afghanistan.html (Accessed 12 February 2023).

12 Prime Minister's Office, "Joint Call on Prime Minister by National Security Advisers / Secretaries of Security Councils attending the "Delhi Regional Security Dialogue on Afghanistan", Press Information Bureau, 10 November 2021, at https://pib.gov.in/PressReleaseIframePage.aspx?PRID=1770732 (Accessed 22 February 2023).

13 "Joint Call on Prime Minister by National Security Advisers / Secretaries of Security Councils attending the "Delhi Regional Security Dialogue on Afghanistan", Press Information Bureau, 10 November 2021, at https://pib.gov.in/PressReleaseIframe Page.aspx?PRID=1770732 (Accessed 22 February 2023).

14 "India-Palestine Bilateral Relations", Ministry of External Affairs, Government of India, at https://mea.gov.in/Portal/ForeignRelation/Bilateral_Brief-Sept_2019.pdf (Accessed 4 December 2022).

15 "India-Jordan Relations", Ministry of External Affairs, Government of India, at https://mea.gov.in/Portal/ForeignRelation/Jordan2020New.pdf (Accessed 4 December 2022).

16 "Visit of President to Jordan", Ministry of External Affairs, Government of India, at https://mea.gov.in/press-releases.htm?dtl/25890/Visit_of_President_to_Jordan_October_1012_2015 (Accessed 4 December 2022).

17 Ibid.

18 "India ambassador lauds Jordan-India ties, as country celebrates independence", *Jordan News Agency*, at https://petra.gov.jo/Include/InnerPage.jsp?ID=40477&lang=en& name= en_news (Accessed 4 December 2022).

19 Ibid.

20 Department of Commerce, Ministry of Commerce and Industry, Government of India, at https://tradestat.commerce.gov.in/eidb/iecnt.asp (Accessed 4 December 2022).

21 Ibid.

22 "India-Egypt Joint Statement during the State Visit of the President of Egypt to India", Ministry of External Affairs, Government of India, 26 January 2023, at https://mea.gov.in/bilateral-documents.htm?dtl/36148/indiaegypt+joint+ statement + during + the+state+visit+of+the+president+of+egypt+to+india+ january+2427+2023 (Accessed 24 April 2023).

23 "IAF Participation in Tactical Leadership Programme in Egypt", Press Information Bureau, Government of India, 8 July 2022, at https://pib.gov.in/PressReleaseIframe Page.aspx?PRID=1840177 (Accessed 22 March 2023).

24 "Inaugural Edition of Indo-Egypt Joint Training Exercise Cyclone-I Commences in Rajasthan", Press Information Bureau, Government of India, 20 January 2023 at https://pib.gov.in/PressReleasePage.aspx?PRID=1892377#:~:text= The%20 first %20ever%20joint%20exercise, Rajasthan %20since% 2014%20January%202023 (Accessed 22 March 2023).

25 Export-Import Data Bank, Department of Commerce, Ministry of Commerce and Industry, Government of India.

26 "First I2U2 (India-Israel-UAE-USA) Leaders' Virtual Summit", Ministry of External Affairs, Government of India, 12 July 2022, at https://mea.gov.in/press-releases.htm?dtl/35489/First_I2U2_IndiaIsraelUAEUSA_Leaders_Virtual_Summit (Accessed 12 May 2023).

27 "Readout of National Security Advisor Jake Sullivan's Meeting on Regional Integration", White House, 7 May 2023, at https://www.whitehouse.gov/briefing-room/statements-releases/2023/05/07/readout-of-national-security-advisor-jake-sullivans-meeting-on-regional-integration/ (Accessed 12 June 2023).

28 "Doval in Saudi to discuss US rail link plan for West Asia", *Indian Express*, 8 May 2023, at https://indianexpress.com/article/india/doval-in-saudi-to-discuss-us-rail-link-plan-for-west-asia-8596962/ (Accessed 12 June 2023).

29 "India rushes Covid-19 medical team to Kuwait, says ready to help Gulf countries", *Hindustan Times*, 11 April 2020, at https://www.hindustantimes.com/india-news/india-rushes-covid-19-medical-team-to-kuwait-says-ready-to-help-gulf-countries/story-q2at5ekUpOdC0h62ix57VL.html (Accessed 12 May 2023).

30 "Combating coronavirus: 88 medics from India arrive in UAE to assist in war against pandemic", *Khaleej Times*, 9 May 2020, at https://www.khaleejtimes.com/uae/combating-coronavirus-88-medics-from-india-arrive-in-uae-to-assist-in-war-against-pandemic (Accessed 2 March 2023).

31 "UAE, Kuwait send oxygen to India amid second coronavirus wave", *Arabian Business*, 4 May 2021, at https://www.arabianbusiness.com/industries/industries-culture-society/463008-uae-kuwait-send-oxygen-to-india-amid-second-coronavirus-wave (Accessed 2 March 2023).

32 Statement made by the External Affairs Minister Dr. S. Jaishankar, in Lok Sabha on 10 December 2021.

2

India and the GCC States: A Growing Engagement

Prasanta Kumar Pradhan

Introduction

The Gulf Cooperation Council (GCC) is a regional organisation consisting of six Gulf Arab States – Bahrain, Kuwait, Oman, Qatar, Saudi Arabia and the UAE. It was established in 1981 in the aftermath of the Islamic revolution in Iran in 1979 and the Iran-Iraq war, which began in 1980. Founded amidst such a turbulent political and security environment in the Gulf region, the GCC aimed to foster unity and cohesion among member states on issues such as trade, culture, education, literature, etc. Though defence and security cooperation was not mentioned in the Charter of the GCC, the issue has emerged as a key component of discussion over the years because of the continuing threat perception for the member States and the need to stay united in the face of such threats. The similar nature of their political systems, economic systems – mainly rentier economies – language, culture, ethnicity and geographical proximity have been the key factors, which have kept them together in an unstable neighbourhood. Through the collective efforts of the member States, the GCC has emerged as a key regional organisation in the Gulf. Over the last four decades, it has played a significant role in regional politics, security and economy in the Gulf.

India has a strong and multi-dimensional relationship with the member States of the GCC. India has also huge political, economic and strategic interests with the GCC countries. India considers the Gulf region as its 'extended neighbourhood' and 'economic hinterland.' Traditionally, strong economic ties have existed between India and the Arab Gulf States. Trade and commerce between the two sides have grown tremendously and the GCC has emerged as a major trading partner for India. The UAE and Saudi Arabia are among the top trading partners of India in the world. A strong economic relationship has remained the backbone of India's ties with the Gulf region for a long period. India relies heavily on the GCC countries for the supply of oil and gas. They have been a reliable source of energy for India for decades. There are around nine million Indian nationals living and working in the GCC States. Their safety and well-being is also a matter of concern for India. Cooperation with the GCC States is crucial for India for security reasons as well. Terrorism and piracy are challenges common to India and the GCC States. India requires the support of the GCC countries to fight terror and to protect the Sea Lines of Communication (SLOCS) from the threats of piracy in the Arabian Sea.

Since Prime Minister Modi came to power, India's engagement with the GCC countries has increased significantly. He has adopted a proactive and pragmatic approach towards the countries of the region and has engaged with them in multiple fields. His multiple visits to the Gulf region and interaction with the leadership have been impressive and have shown results. Moving beyond the traditional areas of cooperation between India and the Gulf region, Prime Minister Modi has visualised and implemented stronger and multifaceted strategic partnerships with the countries of the region.

The GCC Countries have also reciprocated to India's initiatives and have expressed their willingness to engage with India in several fields. High level visits from the Gulf region is a reflective of their changing approach towards India. The Gulf leaders have increasingly realised the benefits of partnership and collaboration with India both in traditional domains as well as in the new and emerging fields. The Gulf leaders find India's approach of non-interference in their regional and internal affairs, coupled with its emphasis on cooperation and collaboration for mutual benefit to be highly appealing.

India's 'Think West' Policy

Prime Minister Modi's approach towards the Gulf countries is driven by India's significant interests and stakes in the region. His approach aims to expand cooperation across various fields which would yield mutual benefits for both. Modi has focused on further strengthening the existing areas of cooperation such as bilateral trade and commerce, energy cooperation and diaspora ties, while at the same time exploring the potential in other areas such as defence, security, food security, renewable energy, climate change, science and technology, etc. To prioritise India's engagement with the West Asian region, India has adopted the 'Think West' policy. While deepening cooperation with the countries of the region, under the Think West policy, India intends to move beyond the traditionally dominant fields of cooperation with the Gulf region.[1] Besides, Modi's approach of prioritising engagement with the neighbouring countries under the 'Neighbourhood first' policy has also found resonance in the India-GCC relationship.

Trade, Investment and Connectivity

The Gulf region holds significant importance as a destination for India's exports. India's trade with the GCC countries includes a diverse range of products such as mineral oils, organic chemicals, cereals, meats, fruits and vegetables, textile products, iron and steel, electrical machinery and equipment, and other mechanical appliances. However, the trade balance heavily favours the GCC countries due to India's substantial import of petroleum crude. Despite the trade imbalance, the economic partnership between India and the GCC countries remains robust.

The total bilateral trade between India and the GCC countries at present stands at over US$ 184.5 billion. The UAE and Saudi Arabia are two important trade partners of India in the region with bilateral trade of US$ 84. 8 billion and US$ 52.7 billion, respectively (Table 2.1). In fact, the UAE is the third largest trading partner of India in the world after the US and China.

Keeping in view the growing trade and commerce between the two, India has always believed that a Free Trade Agreement (FTA) with the GCC will be beneficial for both. In 2004, India and the GCC negotiated for signing an FTA. In the following years, a couple of rounds were held, but the talks could not yield any positive results. In November 2022, the Government announced that India and the GCC have agreed to resume FTA talks.[2] At the bilateral level, India and the UAE have signed a Comprehensive Economic Partnership Agreement (CEPA) in 2022, which will further enhance bilateral trade and business between the two countries.

Table 2.1: India-GCC Bilateral Trade (in US$ million)

Sl. No.	*Country*	*2016-17*	*2017-18*	*2018-19*	*2019-20*	*2020-21*	*2021-22*	*2022-23*
1.	Bahrain	762.40	987.94	1,281.77	980.6	1057.74	1,653.19	1,979.76
2.	Kuwait	5,960.27	8,531.34	8,764.74	10,860.36	6,268.34	12,243.68	13,807.82
3.	Oman	4,018.79	6,703.76	5,005.30	5,931.14	5,443.22	9,988.98	12,388.43
4.	Qatar	8,430.78	9,880.90	12,332.86	10,954.33	9,214.97	15,031.45	18,774.87
5.	Saudi Arabia	25,082.68	27,480.66	34,040.93	33,094.22	22,043.37	42,859.52	52,762.92
6.	UAE	52,685.33	49,885.23	59,912.05	59,110.1	43,302.53	72,878.36	84,840.45
7.	Total	96,940.25	103,469.83	121,337.65	120,930.8	87,330.17	154,655.18	184,554.25

Source: Ministry of Commerce and Industry, Government of India.

The Gulf countries have a large amount of sovereign wealth funds. Prime Minister Modi, during his meeting with the Gulf leaders and the business communities, urged them to invest in India. Modi described India as a 'land of opportunities' and appealed to them to invest in India in different sectors.[3] During his visit to Doha in 2016, while assuring them of the increasingly favourable business environment in India under his government, Modi invited the business community to invest in India.[4] Again, in his virtual address during the Dubai Expo in 2021, Modi invited the investors by reiterating, "India also offers you maximum growth. Growth in scale, growth in ambition, growth in results. Come to India and be a part of our growth story."[5] He also invited the Gulf countries to invest in the 'Make in India' projects, which he believed would bring in substantial investment to the country, which would serve bilateral interests.

Though the GCC countries have surplus capital, India has not been able to attract substantial investment from them. The foreign direct investment (FDI) in India from the GCC countries is much below the potential. However, there has been a substantial increase in the FDI inflows from the Gulf region to India since 2014. According to the Department for Promotion of Industry and Internal Trade, Ministry of Commerce and Industry, Government of India, the cumulative FDI inflow from the Gulf region (GCC countries and Iran) to India from January 2000 to December 2021 was US$ 16.45 billion, which is approximately 2.87 per cent of the total FDI inflow to the country.[6] The total FDI from the Gulf region in 2014 was US$ 326.48 million, which reached its peak at US$ 6.99 billion in 2020.[7] The FDI from the Gulf region has gone to sectors such as computer software, construction, service sector, power and tourism sectors in India.

In September 2023, during the G20 leadership summit in Delhi, a MoU was signed by India, Saudi Arabia, the UAE, France, Germany, Italy, the US and the EU to establish the India–Middle East–Europe Economic Corridor (IMEC).[8] It is a trade and transport corridor which would connect India, the Gulf and Europe. The Eastern corridor of the IMEC will connect India to West Asia through the maritime route and the Northern route will connect West Asia to Europe through rail, road and maritime routes. The UAE and Saudi Arabia are the two most prominent trade partners of India in the Gulf. The IMEC, apart from strengthening India's engagements with the US and Israel, has opened new avenues of cooperation with the Gulf countries.

Energy Cooperation

Energy plays a crucial role in the relationship between India and the GCC countries. India is heavily dependent on the GCC nations, along with Iran and Iraq, for its energy supply. India is a growing economy with an increasing population and industrialisation, which heightens the demand for energy. The Gulf region has been the preferred source of energy due to its geographical proximity and comparatively lower transportation costs. Over the decades, India's dependency on the GCC region for energy has continued to expand and it will continue to, in the near future.

The Gulf region supplies around two-thirds of India's energy requirements. Iraq and Saudi Arabia have remained the top two crude oil suppliers for India. This import of large quantities of petroleum crude underscores the crucial role played by the GCC countries as suppliers of energy resources to India. In 2022-23, Russia surpassed Saudi Arabia to be the second-largest oil supplier as India purchased large volumes of Russian crude at a discounted price since the onset of the Russia-Ukraine War. Table 2.2 below shows India's country-wise oil imports from the Gulf during the last six years.

Table 2.2: India's Crude Oil Imports from the Gulf (in US$ million)

Sl. No.	*Country*	*2017-18*	*2018-19*	*2019-20*	*2020-21*	*2021-22*	*2022-23*
1.	Iraq	17,544.24	22,265.04	22,764.55	12,873.45	26,380.58	33,599.57
2.	Saudi Arabia	15,262.60	21,381.04	20,355.22	10,753.16	19,706.37	29,077.41
3.	Iran	8,978.76	12,110.72	994.81	Nil	Nil	Nil
4.	UAE	6,122.20	9,512.48	10,927.52	7,360.73	10,700.71	16,840.67
5.	Kuwait	5,283.96	5,430.90	4,840.35	3,126.93	6,551.90	8,024.61
6.	Oman	2,413.73	805.61	1,010.43	1,156.36	3,096.58	2,657.57
7.	Qatar	1,264.98	1,215.74	1,365.52	955.73	935.69	1,874.62

Source: Ministry of Commerce and Industry, Government of India.

Besides crude oil, the Gulf region is also important for India for the supply of natural gas as well. Qatar supplies around half of the total LNG imports of India. In 2021-22, Qatar supplied 44 per cent of India's total LNG imports amounting to US$ 5.9 billion.[9] In the same year, the UAE and Oman also supplied LNG to India worth US$ 1.66 billion and US$ 674 million, respectively.[10]

The Gulf region remains highly volatile due to ongoing conflicts, civil unrest and terrorism, which possess the potential to disrupt oil production and supply. In order to ensure energy availability during emergencies, India has taken several steps to establish Strategic Petroleum Reserves (SPR) – to store crude oil in the rock caverns located in various parts of the country. In the initial phase, India has successfully established an SPR with a capacity of five million metric tons (MMT) of crude oil across Visakhapatnam, Mangalore and Padur. The Government has also decided to implement the second phase of the SPR, with two additional locations identified in Odisha and Padur. Cooperation with the Gulf countries plays a critical role in enabling India to attain the desired storage capacity within these reserves. Therefore, India has reached out to key oil suppliers such as Saudi Arabia and the UAE, who have expressed their willingness to support India's SPR initiative. Agreements have already been signed between India and these countries to facilitate collaboration. The leaders of the Gulf nations have also reaffirmed their commitment to supporting India's energy security objectives.

In recent years, India has moved beyond the buyer-seller relationship with the Gulf countries and has engaged in building strategic partnerships and investments in the energy sector. Indian public sector undertakings (PSUs) have started investing in the oil and gas sector in the UAE, Oman and Iraq in oil exploration, production as well as in pipeline projects. Prominent Indian PSUs including ONGC Videsh Limited (OVL), Indian Oil Corporation Ltd (IOCL) and Bharat Petro Resources Ltd (BPRL) are actively engaged in upstream activities in the Lower Zakum oil field located in the UAE. In 2019, Urja Bharat Pte Ltd, a consortium of Indian Oil Corporation and BPRL won a bid to explore and produce oil from the Onshore Block 1 in the UAE.[11] In 2018, Indian Oil Corporation Limited acquired a 17 per cent participating interest in Mukhaizna Oil Field in Oman.[12] Beyond the GCC States, OVL has also stakes in oil fields in Iran and Iraq as well. The involvement of the Indian PSUs in the Gulf energy sector contributes to strengthening India's energy security. Prime Minister Modi's policy entails India's strategic investments in the energy sector in the Gulf, which will foster sustained energy security for India, and strategic partnerships in the energy sector which, ultimately, will contribute to economic growth for both sides.

Renewable Energy

In order to reduce the use of fossil fuels, India is trying to increase the share of renewable energy in its energy basket. During the last decade, India has made a slow but steady progress in this regard by increasing power generation from renewable energy, primarily from solar and wind energy sources. Modi government is committed to attaining a goal of achieving Net Zero Emissions by 2070. In the short term, the country aims to elevate its renewable energy capacity to 500 GW by 2030 while simultaneously reducing cumulative emissions by one billion tonnes within the same timeframe.[13] Prime Minister Modi during his address at the G20 Summit in Bali in 2022 stated that by 2030, half of India's electricity will be generated from renewable sources.[14]

Like India, the GCC countries are also looking to reduce their carbon emissions and have started investing in renewable energy and there is a common interest between India and the GCC countries to cooperate in this sector. Issues such as investment, technology and human resources have been discussed over the years to take the joint efforts forward.

Cooperation on renewable energy is emerging as an important arena of engagement. The UAE has emerged as India's strong partner in the realm of renewable energy cooperation. In January 2023, India and the UAE signed a MoU to promote cooperation in Green Hydrogen development and investment in India. India-UAE cooperation in the energy sector gains further strength as both are members of the India, Israel, the UAE and the US (I2U2) grouping. In July 2022, after the first Leaders' meeting of the I2U2, they agreed to establish a hybrid renewable energy project in Gujarat, India including wind, solar and battery storage systems. The UAE would be a key knowledge and investment partner in this project.[15] During Modi's visit to the UAE in July 2023, both countries issued a joint statement on climate change. Modi and the UAE President Sheikh Mohamed bin Zayed Al Nahyan agreed to invest in renewable energy and Green Hydrogen. They emphasised on the use of technology to reduce emissions and underscored the need for an equitable and sustainable energy transition.[16]

India along with France started the International Solar Alliance (ISA) in 2015. The ISA aims to increase the production and use of solar energy, reduce its production cost and invest in technology, research and development.[17] It also intends to mobilise funds of over US$ 1000 billion for investment by 2030.[18] Prime Minister Modi has been active in promoting the ISA and garnering support from countries all over the world. The GCC countries such as Bahrain, Oman, Saudi Arabia and the UAE have joined the ISA. As the Gulf region receives abundant sunlight throughout the year, they believe this initiative will be helpful to them in future. Besides, they have surplus wealth to invest in the technology and R&D required for producing solar energy.

India has prioritised Green Hydrogen as another important area of renewable energy. On 15 August 2021, Prime Minister Modi announced the launch of India's National Green Hydrogen Mission, to achieve its climate goals and make the country a hub for the production of Green Hydrogen. In January 2023, the Mission secured the cabinet's approval. The National Green Hydrogen Mission document states that the objective of the Mission is to become *Atmanirbhar* (self-reliant) by producing clean energy, reducing dependency on fossil fuel imports, and becoming the world leader in the technology of Green Hydrogen.[19] The Mission targets to produce five MMT of Green Hydrogen per annum by 2030, which will help replace the use of fossil fuels.[20] A number of GCC countries have also set their objective of producing Green Hydrogen and have started working in this regard.[21] Countries like Saudi Arabia and the UAE, in particular, have taken strong futuristic steps to produce Hydrogen. The Emirati cabinet, in July 2023, approved the National Hydrogen Strategy, which aims to promote the production and export of Hydrogen energy.[22] Saudi Arabia's NEOM Green Hydrogen Company (NGHC) is building a large hydrogen production facility at Oxagon in NEOM. It is expected to be operational in 2026 and will have the daily capacity to produce 600 tonnes of Green Hydrogen.[23] Similarly, Oman has also set a target of Net Zero Emissions by 2050 and targets to produce one million tons of Green Hydrogen annually by 2030.[24] There is a convergence of interests between India and the GCC States to cooperate in technology, human resources and investment in the production of Green Hydrogen.

Emphasising Political Dialogue and Strategic Partnerships

To establish a structured and consistent channel of communication, the GCC-India Political Dialogue was established in 2003. This initiative aimed to institutionalise a process for ongoing interaction between India and the GCC. The political dialogue takes place every year on the sidelines of the United Nations General Assembly in New York. This forum has proven to be an effective channel of communication, facilitating a constructive exchange of views and contributing to the strengthening of ties and the promotion of shared interests between the two. Recognising India's importance, the GCC has accorded to it the status of a 'dialogue partner'.

In September 2022, India and GCC signed a MoU on the Mechanism of Consultations between them. In the MoU, both sides agreed to institutionalise an annual dialogue to be held between the two.[25] Following up on the MoU, the first India-GCC Senior Officers Meeting (SOM) was held in Riyadh which discussed a number of important bilateral and regional issues. Importantly, at the meeting, both sides agreed to finalise the India-GCC FTA agreement[26] which would provide a boost to the bilateral trade and commerce.

Besides, as India aspires to assume a leading role on the global stage, the support of GCC countries has become crucial. Consequently, India is actively engaging with the GCC countries to advocate for United Nations (UN) reform and pursue its aspirations of securing permanent membership in the UN Security Council. The GCC countries have expressed their support for India.

Building strategic partnerships with the GCC countries has been an important element of India's approach towards the region. India believes that building strategic partnerships with the GCC countries not only opens multiple fronts of engagement but also deepens cooperation in existing fields. This also provides a boost to the existing trust and confidence between the countries. The signing of strategic partnership agreements has also significantly helped to change the perception of the GCC countries towards India. The economic benefit the GCC countries accrued out of their collaboration with India, the success of cooperation in the field of energy, the emerging defence and security cooperation, and cooperation in emerging fields such as health, renewable energy, climate change, food security etc., have been the important aspects of the strategic partnerships. This is a huge leap forward in the India-GCC relationship, as in the past the general perception of the GCC countries towards India had been dominated by a buyer-seller approach. Building strategic partnerships has taken the India-GCC relationship to a new level of mutual interest and long-term sustainable collaborations in multiple fields.

India has also engaged with the GCC countries in minilateral engagements. The I2U2, has been an active platform to discuss and collaborate on issues such as food security, energy security, water security and climate change; there has been tangible progress in the functioning of the I2U2. Here, India and the UAE get an opportunity not just to collaborate bilaterally but also to take it forward with Israel and the US in the aftermath of the Abraham Accords. Coming on the heels of the signing of the Abraham Accords that normalised the relationship between Israel and the UAE, the I2U2 grouping, therefore, assumes significant political and strategic value. In May 2023, the National Security Advisers of India, Saudi Arabia, the UAE and the US met in Riyadh to discuss, among other issues, the possibility of establishing railway connectivity in West Asia and connecting it to India via the maritime route.[27] Engaging with two key regional players such as the UAE and Saudi Arabia on connectivity and infrastructure would further deepen India's existing strategic partnership with them.

Defence and Security Cooperation

The growing cooperation in defence and security has emerged as a key pillar of cooperation between India and the GCC countries. Prime Minister Modi's proactive approach towards the GCC countries aims to bolster India's defence and security ties by enhancing cooperation beyond the traditionally dominant realms of trade, energy and diaspora. Modi has recognised the shared security challenges of terrorism and piracy faced by India and the GCC countries and is engaging with them at different levels to deter these threats.

The defence cooperation between India and the GCC countries has witnessed significant progress in recent years. The turbulences in the West Asian region since the beginning of the Arab unrest, spread of terrorism and extremism, civil wars, increasing activities of non-state actors, need to maintain maritime security are some of the factors that propelled a stronger India-GCC defence and security cooperation.[28] There is a growing convergence between India and the GCC countries in further collaborating on defence and security issues. Joint military exercises and training programmes have facilitated interoperability and sharing of experiences and skills between the armed forces. Traditionally, the Indian Navy has been at the forefront of military-to-military engagement with the GCC countries, but of late, land forces, air forces and the Coast Guard have also been involved in joint exercises and training programmes.

India has signed defence cooperation agreements with Oman, Qatar, Saudi Arabia and the UAE. Broadly, the agreements elaborate on different aspects of defence cooperation such as joint exercises, training, sharing technology, joint production, etc. While joint training programmes and military-to-military contacts are taking place regularly, issues such as joint production of weapons and technology-sharing seem to be lagging as these require huge investments as well as technology.

Security cooperation has witnessed substantial progress between the two. India and the GCC have recognised the importance of addressing transnational security threats, including terrorism, extremism and maritime piracy. Security collaboration in the form of intelligence sharing and exchange of information has deepened which has strengthened joint efforts to deal with such challenges.

Both India and the GCC countries have been victims of terrorist attacks in the past and the threat of terror attacks continues to be present. Terrorist organisations such as ISIS and Al Qaeda who have exploited the regional instability in West Asia, pose a significant threat to India as well as the GCC countries. The rise of ISIS in the aftermath of the Arab unrest emerged as a major security threat for all. Therefore, for India, cooperation against such transnational challenges is important for the GCC countries.

In recent years, India and the GCC countries have cooperated to successfully deport terrorists and criminals who have committed crimes in the country. Cooperation with Saudi Arabia and the UAE has been particularly successful. For instance, in 2019, the UAE deported a Jaish-e-Mohammed terrorist Nisar Ahmed Tantray, a key conspirator in the 2017 attack on the Central Reserve Police Force (CRPF) camp in Pulwama, wanted by the Indian authorities.[29] Similarly, two terror accused were deported from Saudi Arabia and were arrested upon their arrival in India.[30]

Additionally, fighting piracy and maintaining the safety of the Sea Lines of Communications (SLOCs) is important for India and the GCC countries. Piracy in the Arabian Sea and the Gulf of Aden off the Somalian coast poses a grave challenge to maritime security. In the past, India and the GCC States have suffered at the hands of pirates operating in this region. High ransom amounts have been paid to them on a number of occasions. India and the GCC States heavily rely on the sea route for their bilateral trade; around 95 per cent of India's total trade by volume and 68 per cent by value is undertaken through the maritime route.[31] Therefore, maritime safety and that of the SLOCs is of utmost importance for the economies of GCC countries, which heavily depend on the export of oil and gas. India has deployed a naval ship in the Gulf of Aden since 2008 and has successfully escorted a number of merchant ships thwarting pirate attacks.[32] Thus, India's anti-piracy cooperation with the GCC countries ensures maritime security in the western Indian Ocean and protects its trade routes in the region. This also contributes to securing the supply of energy and other goods and enhances India's role and image as a responsible maritime player in the region. In 2022, India joined the Bahrain-based Combined Military Forces (CMF) as an Associate Partner.[33] In July 2023, *INS Sunayna* participated in the 'Op Southern Readiness 2023' in Seychelles conducted by the CMF[34] Earlier, *INS Sunayna* had also participated in the 'Operation Southern Readiness' at Seychelles in September 2022.[35] India's involvement in the CMF will enhance its footprint in the western Indian Ocean, facilitating collaboration with diverse navies to combat piracy, help secure the SLOCs and bolster regional security in its extended neighbourhood.

Engaging with the GCC Countries on G20 Issues

India assumed the presidency of the G20 for 2023 and adopted the theme *Vasudhaiva Kutumbakam* (One Earth - One Family - One Future). Under its presidency, India engaged with G20 member countries on climate change, renewable energy, reform of multilateral institutions and sustainable development goals, among others. Among other countries, India invited two GCC member States – Oman and the UAE – as guest countries for the meetings.

Officials from both these countries participated in the G20 meetings and shared their perspectives. For instance, Sayyid Saeed bin Sultan Al Busaidi, Undersecretary of the Ministry of Culture, Sports and Youth for Culture of Oman, participated in the G20 Culture Working Group (CWG) in August 2023.[36] Oman also participated in the Anti-Corruption Working Group (ACWG) in Kolkata in August

2023. The Omani Minister of Commerce, Industry and Investment Promotion, Qais Mohammed Al Yousef, participated in the G20 Trade and Investment Ministers' meetings in Jaipur in August 2023 where he emphasised collective efforts for sustainable growth and reinforcing global supply chains.[37] The Sultanate views its participation in the G20 meetings as a valuable opportunity to foster collaboration with other nations across various domains, which aligns suitably with the objectives of the Oman Vision 2040.[38]

In the run-up to the G20, the UAE announced that supporting India's bid for the G20 presidency had been a priority for the country.[39] The UAE has participated in a number of G20 meetings held in India. Sheikh Abdullah bin Zayed Al Nahyan, Minister of Foreign Affairs, participated in the G20 Foreign Ministers' Meeting in August 2023. In June 2023, the UAE's Minister of State to the Cabinet, Ahmed Al Sayegh, participated in the G20 Development Ministers' Meeting in Varanasi. Sayegh reaffirmed his country's commitment towards the G20 agenda and called on all the participants to benefit from the COP28, hosted by the UAE.[40] The UAE also participated in the G20 Digital Economy Ministerial Meeting in India.

Participation of these countries in the G20 meetings has brought to the fore the similarities in their approach and convergence of interests. It opens the door for further cooperation in these fields at the bilateral level. Climate change, tourism, digital economy, global supply chains, etc. are some of the issues over which India has engaged with the UAE, Oman and other GCC countries.

Reaching Out to the Indian Community in the Gulf

About nine million Indians are living and working in the GCC countries. The Indian expatriate community forms a natural link between India and the Gulf region. Indians in the Gulf are known to be disciplined, skilful and law-abiding. Their contribution to the development and progress of the Gulf countries has been acknowledged by their rulers. For Modi, the Indian diaspora are the true ambassadors of India around the world.[41] The diaspora originates from different parts of India and carries India's rich culture and cherished values. Prime Minister Modi has acknowledged the 'hard work and commitment' of the Indian diaspora and its contribution to the strengthening of bilateral relations.[42] Indian community in the Gulf has achieved remarkable success across a wide range of fields. Their contribution to the economic development and progress of these countries has fostered a positive perception of India which helps to strengthen bilateral relations. Therefore, engagement with the expatriate community in the Gulf has been a key priority in Modi's foreign policy towards the region.

This has been reflected in the interactions Prime Minister Modi has had with the Indian expatriate communities during his visits to the Gulf region. Modi has often interacted with a wide range of the expatriate community – from blue-collar workers to business leaders – and has offered support. During his visit to the UAE in 2015, Modi addressed the Indian diaspora and announced the establishment of an Indian Community Welfare Fund (ICWF) in the UAE, to help the Indian expatriate community in times of distress. He also announced an online platform 'MADAD', to address the problems of the Indian community and to connect the Indian diaspora around the world.[43] During his visit to Oman in 2018, Modi met members of the Indian community and described them as a 'mini-India' in Oman.[44] In Bahrain, Modi appreciated the honesty and integrity of the Indian expatriate community and their contribution to the economic and social life of Bahrain during his visit to the country in August 2019.[45] Besides, Modi appealed to the Indian business community in the Gulf to invest in India and expand their business in India as well.

Often, the Hindu community in the Gulf countries faces challenges in practising their faith due to the limited number of temples in the region. India has taken up the issue with some of the rulers and in 2015, during Modi's visit, the UAE government allocated land for Abu Dhabi's first Hindu temple. During his visit to Bahrain in 2019, Modi launched the US$ 4.2 million redevelopment project of the Srinathji Temple in Manama – the oldest in the Gulf region, which is around 200 years old.[46]

India receives substantial remittances and foreign exchange from the Indian diaspora and is the largest remittance-receiving country in the world; in 2021-22, India received remittances amounting to US$ 89.12 billion.[47] A significant amount of this came from the Gulf region. Due to the fact that a significant number of Indian expatriates have their families residing in India, they regularly send money to support them. Besides, India has also introduced its indigenous RuPay card in the Gulf. In his address to the Indian community in Manama in 2019, Modi stated that a MoU in this regard had been signed with the Bahraini authorities and that Indians in the Gulf would be able to send money home using the RuPay card.[48] In August 2029, the RuPay card was launched in the UAE.[49] In the same year, India signed a MoU with Saudi Arabia to launch it in the kingdom. Oman is the latest country in the region to accept the RuPay card in October 2022, when a MoU was signed between the two countries.[50]

Cooperation during the COVID-19 Pandemic

The COVID-19 pandemic brought on unsurmountable challenges and difficulties for the people and the governments. India and the GCC States cooperated with each other during the pandemic. India sent medicines, doctors and healthcare professionals as well as the required equipment to the GCC countries to help them fight the pandemic. India bolstered its reputation as a steadfast and dependable friend by promptly offering medical assistance and expertise to the GCC countries during times of crisis.[51] In 2022, when India was under the severe grip of the contagious delta variant, all the GCC countries came forward and supplied liquid oxygen immediately.

The close cooperation between India and the GCC countries during the pandemic has further enhanced their level of trust. Beginning with despatching medicines, sending experts and vaccines to seeking their cooperation to repatriate Indian nationals from the Gulf countries, the India-GCC cooperation during the pandemic proved effective and trustworthy. The three years of the pandemic proved that the fundamentals of cooperation, understanding and trust between India and the GCC countries remain strong; all the GCC leaders expressed enormous faith in the policies and approach taken by Prime Minister Modi to deal with the pandemic.[52] The pandemic also opened the door for further cooperation in the health sector – which had been hitherto overlooked – between India and the GCC countries.

India started the largest repatriation exercise, known as the *Vande Bharat Mission*, during the pandemic to bring its nationals back who were struck abroad. India repatriated its nationals from all the six GCC States by air bubble agreements and with positive cooperation from the local rulers. The highest number of stranded Indians were repatriated from the UAE followed by Saudi Arabia, the USA and Qatar.[53] India's cooperation with the GCC States to fight the pandemic, appealing to the host governments to look after the well-being of the Indian community during the pandemic and the successful repatriation of Indians who were desperate to come back home are among the successes of Modi's engagement with the GCC States during the difficult times.

Conclusion

India's engagement with the GCC countries has significantly intensified since Modi assumed office in 2014. In fact, India's deepening engagement with the Gulf and West Asian countries has been one of the most important successes of India's foreign policy under Prime Minister Modi. India's 'Neighbourhood first' approach and the 'Think West' policy to emphasise engagement with the West Asian countries have given a new direction to India's relationship with the GCC States and have resulted in a deeper engagement on a wide range of issues. Apart from trade, energy and diaspora ties, the recent emphasis on strengthening defence and security cooperation with the Gulf including new issues such as food security, renewable energy, cyber security, climate change, space cooperation, science and technology etc., have added further meaning and purpose to the existing relationship. In the last ten years, Modi's pragmatic engagement has resulted in building new strategic partnerships and opening new fronts of engagement with the GCC States. The GCC countries' perception of India as an emerging and reliable partner also demonstrates their confidence in fostering deeper collaboration. This evolving partnership not only reflects their converging interests but also underscores their commitment to addressing shared challenges and harnessing the potential for mutual growth and cooperation.

NOTES

1 Statement by External Affairs Minister S. Jaishankar in Lok Sabha on 8 December 2023.
2 "India-Gulf Cooperation Council (GCC) decide to pursue resumption of Free Trade Agreement (FTA) Negotiations", Press Information Bureau, 25 November 2022, at https://pib.gov.in/PressReleasePage.aspx?PRID=1878714 (Accessed 12 July 2023).
3 "India a land of opportunities, open to innovation and investment: PM Modi at Dubai Expo address", *First Post,* 2 October 2021, at https://www.firstpost.com/india/india-a-land-of-opportunities-open-to-innovation-and-investment-pm-modi-at-dubai-expo-address-10017751.html (Accessed 22 February 2023).
4 "India is a land of Opportunity, PM Modi tells business leaders in Qatar", NDTV, 5 June 2016, at https://www.ndtv.com/india-news/pm-modi-meets-business-leaders-in-qatar-1415643 (Accessed 12 January 2023).
5 "India a land of opportunities, open to innovation and investment: PM Modi at Dubai Expo address", *First Post,* 1 October 2021, at https://www.firstpost.com/india/india-a-land-of-opportunities-open-to-innovation-and-investment-pm-modi-at-dubai-expo-address-10017751.html (Accessed 12 January 2023).
6 Department for Promotion of Industry and Internal Trade, Ministry of Commerce and Industry, Government of India.
7 Ibid.
8 "Partnership for Global Infrastructure and Investment (PGII) & India-Middle East-Europe Economic Corridor (IMEC)", Press Information Bureau, 9 September 2023, at https://pib.gov.in/PressReleaseIframePage.aspx?PRID=1955921#:~: text= In%20 his%20remarks %2C% 20Prime%20Minister, %2C%20Italy%2C %20France%20 and%20Germany (Accessed 12 December 2023).
9 Export-Import data bank, Ministry of Commerce and Industry, Government of India.
10 Ibid.
11 "Indian Oil, BPCL arm bag entire stake in Abu Dhabi block", *Hindu Business Line,* 25 March 2019, at https://www.thehindubusinessline.com/companies/indianoil-bpcl-arm-bag-entire-stake-in-abu-dhabi-block/article26635965.ece (Accessed 18 December 2022).
12 "Indian Oil acquires 17% participating interest in Mukhaizna oil field in Oman from Shell", Indian Oil, 6 April 2018, at https://iocl.com/NewsDetails/49385 (Accessed 18 December 2022).
13 "Renewable Energy in India", Press Information Bureau, 9 September 2022, at https://pib.gov.in/FeaturesDeatils.aspx?NoteId=151141&ModuleId%20=%202 (Accessed 18 January 2023).
14 See Prime Minister Shri Narendra Modi's address at the G-20 Summit in Bali, Ministry of External Affairs, Government of India, 15 November 2022, at https://mea.gov.in/Speeches-Statements.htm?dtl/35884/english+translation+of+prime+minister+ shri+ narendra+ modis+address+at+the+g20+summit+in+bali+session+i+food+and+energy+security (Accessed 18 January 2023).
15 "Joint Statement of the Leaders of India, Israel, United Arab Emirates, and the United States (I2U2)", The White House, 14 July 2022, at https://www.whitehouse.gov/briefing-room/statements-releases/2022/07/14/joint-statement-of-the-leaders-of-india-israel-united-arab-emirates-and-the-united-states-i2u2/ (Accessed 8 March 2023).
16 "India-UAE: Joint Statement on Climate Change", Ministry of External Affairs,

Government of India, 15 July 2023, at https://mea.gov.in/bilateral-documents.htm?dtl/36812/indiauae+joint+statement+on+climate+change (Accessed 5 August 2023).

17 "International Solar Alliance", Ministry of New and Renewable Energy, Government of India at https://mnre.gov.in/isa/ (Accessed 5 August 2023).

18 Ibid.

19 "National Green Hydrogen Mission", Ministry of New and Renewable Energy, Government of India, January 2023, at https://mnre.gov.in/img/documents/uploads/file_f-1673581748609.pdf (Accessed 5 August 2023).

20 Ibid.

21 "The Hydrogen Ambitions of the Gulf States", SWP, 21 July 2022, at https://www.swp-berlin.org/10.18449/2022C44/ (Accessed 2 August 2023).

22 "UAE Cabinet approves national energy and hydrogen strategies, establishes UAE Ministry of Investment", Emirates News Agency, 3 July 2023, at https://wam.ae/en/details/1395303173983 (Accessed 2 August 2023).

23 "NEOM accelerates progress towards green hydrogen future", NEOM, 24 May 2023, at https://www.neom.com/en-us/newsroom/neom-accelerates-green-hydrogen-future (Accessed 4 August 2023).

24 "Oman announces investment opportunities in green hydrogen", Ministry of Foreign Affairs, Oman, 23 October 2022, at https://fm.gov.om/oman-announces-investment-opportunities-in-green-hydrogen/ (Accessed 4 August 2023).

25 "EAM concludes visit to Saudi Arabia September", Embassy of India, Riyadh, 12 September 2022, https://www.eoiriyadh.gov.in/news_letter_detail/?id=35#:~:text=EAM%20and% 20GCC %20Secretary%20General,on%20different%20areas%20of%20cooperation (Accessed 12 January 2024).

26 "First India-GCC Senior Officers Meeting (SOM)", Ministry of External Affairs, Government of India, 20 March 2023, at https://www.mea.gov.in/press-releases.htm?dtl/36380/First_IndiaGCC_Senior_Officers_Meeting_SOM (Accessed 12 January 2024).

27 "Doval in Saudi to discuss US rail link plan for West Asia", *Indian Express*, 8 May 2023, at https://indianexpress.com/article/india/doval-in-saudi-to-discuss-us-rail-link-plan-for-west-asia-8596962/ (Accessed 12 July 2023).

28 Prasanta Kumar Pradhan, "India-UAE defence and security cooperation", *Strategic Analysis*, 44 (2), 2020, p. 125.

29 "UAE deports Jaish terrorist Nisar Tantray wanted for 2017 CRPF camp attack in Kashmir: NIA", *Hindustan Times*, 3 April 2019, at https://www.hindustantimes.com/india-news/nisar-tantray-jem-terrorist-wanted-for-2017-lethpora-attack-arrested-by-nia/story-Ti4oJbrDuZTmKlTg9aDK9L.html (Accessed 12 January 2024).

30 "Terror case accused deported from Saudi arrested from airport", *Times of India*, 22 September 2020, at https://www.hindustantimes.com/india-news/nisar-tantray-jem-terrorist-wanted-for-2017-lethpora-attack-arrested-by-nia/story-Ti4oJbrDuZTmKlTg9a DK9L.html (Accessed 12 January 2024).

31 Ministry of Ports, Shipping and Waterways, Government of India, *Annual Report 2022-23*, p. 4.

32 "Anti-Piracy Operations, Gulf of Aden Deployment", Indian Navy at https://www.indiannavy.nic.in/content/anti-piracy-operations-gulf-aden-deployment/page/0/1 (Accessed 22 July 2023).

33 "Press Statement by Raksha Mantri Shri Rajnath Singh after India-US 2+2 Ministerial Dialogue", Press Information Bureau, Government of India, 12 April 2022, at https://pib.gov.in/PressReleaseIframePage.aspx?PRID=1815838 (Accessed 22 July 2023).

34 "INS Sunayna Participates in CMF Ex 'Op Southern Readiness - 2023'", Indian Navy at https://indiannavy.nic.in/content/ins-sunayna-participates-cmf-ex-op-southern-readiness-2023#:~:text=Southern%20Readiness%202023'-,INS%20 Sunayna%20 Participates%2 0in%20CMF% 20Ex%20'Op%20Southern%20 Readiness%20%2D%202023, Combined %20 Maritime%20Forces(CMF) (Accessed 25 August 2023).

35 "INS Sunayna Participates in Combined Maritime Forces (CMF) Exercise at Seychelles" Indian Navy, at https://indiannavy.nic.in/content/ins-sunayna-participates-combined-maritime-forces-cmf-exercise-seychelles (Accessed 25 August 2023).

36 "Oman participates in meeting of G20 Culture Working Group in India", *Times of Oman*, 27 August 2023, at https://timesofoman.com/article/135307-oman-participates-in-meeting-of-g20-culture-working-group-in-india#:~:text=Muscat%3 A%20The%20 Sultanate%20of%20Oman,between%20August%2024%20and%2027 (Accessed 28 August 2023).

37 "Oman participates in G20 Trade and Investment Ministers Meeting in India", *The Arabian Daily*, 27 August 2023, at https://arabiandaily.com/oman-participates-in-g20-trade-and-investment-ministers-meeting-in-india/ (Accessed 28 August 2023).

38 "Media briefing highlights Oman's participation in G20 meetings in India", *Oman Observer*, 14 June 2023, at https://www.omanobserver.om/article/1138755/oman/media-briefing-highlights-omans-participation-in-g20-meetings-in-india (Accessed 28 August 2023).

39 "Minister of Foreign Affairs and International Cooperation of UAE writes: Supporting India's G20 presidency is a priority for the UAE", *Indian Express*, 2 December 2022, at https://indianexpress.com/article/opinion/columns/minister-of-foreign-affairs-and-international-cooperation-of-uae-writes-supporting-indias-g20-presidency-is-a-priority-for-the-uae-8301279/ (Accessed on 22 July 2023).

40 "UAE participates in G20 Development Ministers' meeting", Emirates News Agency, 12 June 2023, at https://www.wam.ae/en/details/1395303168209 #:~: text=VARANASI %2C%20 India%2C%2012th%20June%2C,India%20on%2012% 20June%202023 (Accessed 22 July 2023).

41 "Indian diaspora are our 'Rashtradoots', says PM Modi at Pravasi Bharatiya Divas event", *The Times of India*, 9 January 2023, at https://timesofindia.indiatimes.com/india/indian-diaspora-are-our-ambassadors-says-pm-modi-at-pravasi-bharatiya-divas-event/articleshow/96849722.cms (Accessed 12 June 2023).

42 "Hard work, commitment of diaspora helped to strengthen India-Saudi bilateral ties: PM Modi", *The Times of India*, 29 October 2019, at https://timesofindia.indiatimes.com/nri/middle-east-news/hard-work-commitment-of-diaspora-helped-to-strenghten-india-saudi-bilateral-ties-pm-modi/articleshow/71803941.cms (Accessed 12 June 2023).

43 "PM Narendra Modi reaches out to Indian diaspora in Dubai; announces 'MADAD' platform, e-migrant portal", *Economic Times*, 18 August 2015, at https://economictimes. indiatimes.com/news/politics-and-nation/pm-narendra-modi-reaches-out-to-indian-diaspora-in-dubai-announces-madad-platform-e-migrant-portal/articleshow/48518808.cms?from=mdr (Accessed 12 January 2023).

44 "Seeing a mini-India in Oman, says PM Modi in address to Indian community", *Hindustan Times*, 11 February 2018, at https://www.hindustantimes.com/india-news/modi-in-uae-live-pm-pays-tribute-at-war-memorial-wahat-al-karama-in-abu-dhabi/story-OaI0jglXEzwIxfTZ0FRwAL.html (Accessed 12 January 2023).

45 "PM addresses Indian Community in Bahrain", Press Information Bureau, Government of India, 24 August 2019, at https://pib.gov.in/PressReleseDetailm.aspx?PRID=1582948 (Accessed 2 March 2023).

46 "PM Modi launches $4.2 million redevelopment project of temple in Bahrain", *Indian Express*, 25 August 2019, at https://indianexpress.com/article/india/pm-modi-launches-4-2-mn-redevelopment-project-of-temple-in-bahrain-5935151/ (Accessed 21 March 2023).

47 "India received highest ever foreign inward remittances in a single year of $89,127 million in FY 2021-22", Press Information Bureau, Government of India, 7 February 2023, at https://pib.gov.in/PressReleasePage.aspx?PRID=1897036#:~:text=I ndia%20 received%20 highest%20ever%20foreign,million%20in%20FY%202021%2D22 (Accessed 11 May 2023).

48 "PM addresses Indian Community in Bahrain", Press Information Bureau, Government of India, 24 August 2019, at https://pib.gov.in/PressReleseDetailm.aspx?PRID=1582948 (Accessed 2 March 2023).

49 "PM Modi launches RuPay card in UAE", *Economic Times*, 24 August 2023, at https://economictimes.indiatimes.com/news/politics-and-nation/pm-modi-launches-rupay-card-in-uae/articleshow/70816228.cms?from=mdr (Accessed 11 May 2023).

50 "Milestone MOU signed for acceptance of RuPay card and UPI QR Code based mobile payments in Oman", *Times of Oman*, 4 October 2022, at https://timesofoman.com/article/122011-milestone-mou-signed-for-acceptance-of-rupay-card-and-upi-qr-code-based-mobile-payments-in-oman (Accessed 11 May 2023).

51 Prasanta Kumar Pradhan, "India and GCC Countries Amid COVID-19 Pandemic", MP-IDSA Comment, 13 May 2020, at https://www.idsa.in/idsacomments/india-and-gcc-covid-19-pandemic-ppradhan (Accessed 11 December 2023).

52 See Prasanta Kumar Pradhan, "Indians in the Gulf during the Pandemic: Analysing Responses from India and the GCC Countries", in Sujan Chinoy and Prasanta Kumar Pradhan (eds.), *India's Approach to West Asia: Trends, Challenges and Possibilities*, Pentagon Press, New Delhi, 2024, pp. 154-165.

53 "Statement by External Affairs Minister in Lok Sabha on Recent Developments Pertaining to the welfare abroad of Indians, NRIs and PIOs", Ministry of External Affairs, Government of India, 15 March 2021, at https://meaindia.nic.in/cdgeneva/?12517?000 (Accessed 22 October 2023).

3

India-Iran Connectivity Partnership: Opportunities and Challenges

Deepika Saraswat

Since the New Delhi Declaration, signed in 2003 by the then Prime Minister of India Atal Bihari Vajpayee and Iranian President Mohammed Khatami, India-Iran relationship has been marked by a regional and geo-economic dimension. At the turn of the century, geopolitical developments such as the emergence of independent countries in Central Asia, and the US invasion of Afghanistan overthrowing Taliban rule in the country, led New Delhi to broaden its strategic vision through the concept of the extended neighbourhood. India and Iran have continued to frame their partnership within a regional context that can best be described as Southwest-Central Asia.[1] The New Delhi Declaration expressed hope that the initial trilateral agreement signed between the Governments of India, Iran and Afghanistan to develop the Chabahar route through Melak, Zaranj and Delaram in Afghanistan, will advance regional trade and transit to Afghanistan and Central Asia, contributing towards enhanced regional economic prosperity.[2] By promoting regional connectivity with and via Afghanistan, Iran and India hoped to support independent state-building in the country as opposed to an isolated, ineffective State, which becomes a source of regional instability or falls under the geopolitical orbit of Pakistan or any other state. For both Iran and India, therefore, the issue of regional connectivity has been inextricably linked to regional peace, security and stability, especially in the context of the prolonged conflict in Afghanistan.

India-Iran cooperation in regional connectivity has had to contend with 'the US factor', in a context where Iran-US relations have remained hostile, while India-US ties strengthened especially after the two countries signed a civil nuclear cooperation agreement in 2005. This chapter aims to analyse the India-Iran connectivity partnership, especially since the signing of the Chabahar Agreement in 2016, during Prime Minister Narendra Modi's visit to Iran. While doing so, the chapter situates the India-Iran connectivity partnership within the broader Eurasian outreach of the two countries. At a time, when various connectivity and regional economic integration projects by a multitude of great powers have created a contentious connectivity landscape in Eurasia, Iran is keen to advance its gateway status. While contextualising Iran's rising gateway status, the chapter delves into opportunities and challenges facing India's Eurasian outreach via Iran.

An Overview of Iran's 'gateway' Status

Over the last two decades Chabahar, Iran's only deep oceanic port, and Pakistan's Gwadar – located only 72 km apart on the Makran coast along the Gulf of Oman – have made competing claims as potential 'gateways' connecting Eurasian hinterland to the Indian Ocean. For fin-de-siècle geopolitical thinkers, who were formulating their theses in the context of the inter-imperial rivalry of the late nineteenth century, the Eurasian littoral was considered to be of geostrategic importance in the struggle for primacy between continental and maritime powers. First, the invention of the steam engine fuelled the Industrial Revolution in Europe, then the rise of the steam-driven locomotive enabled the railway revolution of the nineteenth century, leading continental powers such as Germany and Russia to advance terrestrial alternatives to the global maritime economy.[3] Unlike naval powers, who sought to maximise their economic efficiency through maritime trade, land powers, wary of their dependence on the security of freedom of navigation, feared risking their economic survival on the good graces of the naval hegemon.[4] British Geographer Halford Mackinder was alarmed by rapid-pace development of the network of trans-continental railways by Russia in the aftermath of its defeat in the Crimean War of 1856. During the War, Russia had struggled with weak transport links compared to Britain and France, who were able to transport supplies and reinforcements faster through a maritime corridor from Gibraltar to Crimea.[5] Mackinder's 'Heartland thesis' warned about a Eurasian interior unified by a single power and becoming 'inaccessible to oceanic commerce'. He argued that efficient overland connectivity would extend continental hegemony over the Eurasian littoral, potentially challenging the dominance of the oceanic empires.[6]

On the historical geo-economic character of Makran, Philip Reid writes that despite its location in the open sea, its rugged and barren topography, absence of navigable river connecting with the interior, and sparse population, stifled the growth of ocean-facing emporia. On the other hand, the nearby port of Karachi (called Barbaricum) located on the mouth of the Indus River, from as far back as antiquity when it was under the control of Indo-Scythian tribes or the Saka kingdoms, channelled trade from Bactria, the neighbouring parts of Central Asia, China to the Roman Empire.[7] From antiquity to the early modern period, India's terrestrial connection to the overland trans-Eurasian trade routes in Central Asia and Iran was by way of the North-west Frontier.[8] This overland route, connecting the Indian subcontinent with the wider Silk Road network in Eurasia, lost its salience first as a result of the emergence of long-distance maritime commerce from the late 17th century, and then in the wake of the Great Game in the 19th century between the Tsarist Russian Empire and the British Empire in India. The Anglo-Russian Great Game turned Afghanistan and Iran into contested buffer zones between the two imperial powers. During the course of the 19th century, Iran suffered territorial losses in its peripheries, to Russia in the South Caucasus and Britain in Afghanistan and Baluchistan. It was barely able to maintain its nominal sovereignty. The British feared Russian advances into Central Asia and towards Iran in the Persian Gulf as ultimately aimed at the British Empire in the Indian subcontinent. As a result, the question of railways in Iran, much like elsewhere in Asia, became a matter of strategic rivalry between the two imperialist powers.[9]

Under an agreement with Iran's Qajar ruler Nasir al-din Shah in 1889, Russia had secured a five-year exclusive option of building railways in Persia. Moscow was able to exercise a veto on railways in Iran until 1909 when Russian protégé Muhammad Ali Shah was exiled in the aftermath of the constitutional revolution in Iran.[10] For Russia, its commercial interests in northern Iran benefited from the geographical isolation of the region from the Persian Gulf.[11] Russia, therefore, saw any railway connecting the Eurasian hinterland and the Gulf coast as strategic exposure to Britain, which had naval supremacy in the Persian Gulf. Britain, for its part, was concerned that a railway extending from Russia to the Indian Ocean littoral or for that matter Germany's Berlin-Baghdad Railway would facilitate continental hegemony over the Eurasian littoral.[12] The Russian and British strategic concerns delayed any serious construction of railroads in Iran except for some short sections such as between Jolfa and Tabriz in north Iran, completed in 1916 and connected with the Russian railway system. The Baluchistan Railway, constructed by the British, connected Quetta with the Iranian city of Duzdab (today Zahedan).[13] Naturally, these lines were constructed with British and Russian commercial and strategic interests in mind. The 1907 Anglo-Russian entente that delineated Russian and British zones of influence in northern and southern Iran respectively and a neutral middle region, enabled Anglo-Russian cooperation on Trans-Persian railway from the Russian to the Indian frontiers.[14] The two powers had shared interests in outflanking Germany's Berlin-Baghdad railway by developing the trans-Persian railway as a link between Europe and India.[15] As they engaged in protracted negotiations over the prospective route and financing, with the onset of the First World War, the construction never took off.

It was only after Reza Khan's coup d'état in 1921 and the foundation of the Pahlavi dynasty in 1925, that the Trans-Iranian Railway, linking the Caspian Sea and Persian Gulf coasts was seen as an important instrument for modernising the country. Given the fraught history of the development of the railway network in the country, the two terminals of the Trans-Iranian route – the Caspian harbour city of Bandar-e Shah (today Bandar-e Torkaman) and Bandar-e Shahpur (today Bandar-e Emam Khomeini) on the Persian

Gulf – were selected for their location being as far away as possible from Russian and British territories respectively.[16] During the course of the Second World War, the Allied forces invaded Iran in August 1941 to ensure the use of Iranian transportation facilities for the supply line of Allied war material to Russia. The so-called 'Persian Corridor' stretched from the Iranian port of Khorramshahr and the nearby Iraqi port of Basra to the Caucasus and the Caspian Sea ports in the Soviet zone.[17] It underscored Iran's unique geographical advantage in north-south transit and connectivity.

Following the end of the War, when the Soviet Union delayed the withdrawal of its troops from northern Iran and supported the autonomy movement led by pro-Soviet forces in Iran's Azerbaijan province, Iran sought American support for its territorial integrity.[18] Diplomatic support and pressure from the US in the United Nations Security Council and outside was instrumental in pushing back against Soviet demands for oil concession in Iran's Northern provinces, and eventually forcing Soviet withdrawal in January 1946.[19] The 'Iran Crisis' of 1945-46 therefore set the stage for Iran's role in the northern tier of the United States' Soviet containment strategy and as the pillar of the US position in the Persian Gulf. Around the time when Iran became the pillar of containment of the Soviet Union, the partition of India and Pakistan's occupation of parts of Kashmir, severed overland connectivity between the Indo-Gangetic plains and Central Asia, two geopolitical developments effectively 'spelling a death knell for India's northern outreach.'[20]

Though neither India nor Pakistan are immediate neighbours of the Central Asian Region, Pakistan has pursued a zero-sum approach to regional connectivity by excluding India. Islamabad not only denies India its natural overland access to Eurasia, but also its initiatives at inter-regional connectivity between Central and South Asia are pitted against similar efforts by India via Iran. P. Stobdan notes that from a geo-economic point of view, the issue is not limited to India's physical access to Eurasia per se, "it is about orienting and benefiting from [the] economic integration of India's immediate borderland with that of [the] Eurasian growth line."[21] It was only in the post-Cold War geopolitical context, when Iran no longer shared a direct border with Russia – which had shaped its historical threat perception from the north – and the emergence of land-locked states in Central Asia, that India found a strategic opportunity to seek a land-sea alternative connectivity to Eurasia via Iran. So long as Pakistan continues to deny India its centuries-old overland access which played a role in forging the historical 'civilizational connect routinely recounted in our bilateral ties with Uzbekistan and Iran, the latter will remain the veritable 'gateway' for India and Central Asia.[22]

India and Iran's Foray into a Contested Eurasian Connectivity Landscape

It was only towards the late 1990s that India, Iran and Russia found convergence in developing trans-continental connectivity along a north-south axis via Iran. Following the emergence of independent States in Central Asia and the Caucasus, the United States and the European Union pursued a zero-sum approach to connectivity in Asia. The European Union's flagship east-west connectivity project of the Transport Corridor Europe-Caucasus-Asia (TRACECA), linking the newly independent Republics in Central Asia with Europe along the Caspian-Caucasus-Black Sea route, bypassed both Russia and Iran. It was aimed at consolidating the independence of these fledgling Republics in Russia's immediate backyard. Though Iran was admitted as a TRACECA member in 2009, it never received any technical assistance or investment because of international and EU sanctions on the country that remained in place until the implementation of the nuclear agreement between Iran and six major world powers in January 2016. Given that the underlying logic of trans-regional connectivity between Europe and post-Soviet States in Asia was to promote Western orientation in their economy and thus foreign policy, the US was cautious about giving Tehran any influence over its strategy in Eurasia.

Russia-Iran-India Convergence on North-south Connectivity

At the turn of the century, Moscow increasingly realised that the Yeltsin-era attempts at liberalising Russia's economy and seeking integration into the West had not borne fruit. Subsequently, Moscow made renewed efforts to strengthen ties with its traditional partners in the East including India. India-Central Asia ties in the decade since the collapse of the Soviet Union had suffered considerably. It therefore signed on to the idea of north-south connectivity with Russia and Central Asia via Iran.[23] Further, multilateral efforts led by two leading non-Western powers – Russia and India – to implement a trans-continental land-sea corridor linking them with each other, also fitted well within their overarching vision of a multipolar world in the twenty-first century. For its part, Tehran looked towards cooperation with neighbours, nearby Muslim States, and with possible major alternative centres of power (Russia, and India) to counter Washington's efforts to isolate Iran. Furthermore, it actively sought to use its advantageous location to participate in international trade and attract international investment to support its development efforts. Given Iran's strategic location straddling the Persian Gulf in the south and the Caspian Sea in the north, it was envisaged as an optimal gateway between Russia and India. In the New Delhi Declaration, India and Iran recognised that their growing strategic convergence in Afghanistan and the wider region needs to be underpinned with a strong economic relationship including greater trade and investment flows.[24] The two countries agreed to broad base their cooperation in the oil and gas sector, boost non-oil trade, and jointly develop the Chabahar port complex and free trade zone. Chabahar was also expected to boost economic activity in Iran's underdeveloped Sistan and Balochistan province.

For developing countries in Asia, such as Iran and India, the push for a coordinated approach to regional connectivity, instead of being driven by the intensity of interdependent relations came from these States trying to address the artificially low level of such interdependence, giving regional connectivity initiatives the character of 'development integration'.[25] Also, given the limited demand, and paucity of investment, enhancing the connectivity of national transport systems, including railways, has been seen as the most viable solution for the development of regional as well as trans-regional transport.[26] However, a variety of factors, including the imposition of international sanctions on Iran since 2006, American presence and instability in Afghanistan, the inability of the member states to mobilise sufficient financing for constructing the 'missing links', and their disparate connectivity priorities, have resulted in the International North–South

Transport Corridor (INSTC) and Chabahar progressing at a snail's pace over the last two decades.

In 2011, the United States launched its New Silk Road Strategy, with the declared aim of supporting continental corridors through Afghanistan and Central Asia, a region it dubbed as 'Greater Central Asia'. It envisaged Afghanistan as the pivot and the missing link in the Eurasia-wide continental corridors for the transport of goods and energy between Europe, the Indian subcontinent and Southeast Asia.[27] Washington, in taking the leadership role in creating transportation corridors connecting Greater Central Asia with the Indian subcontinent through Afghanistan, hoped that transit revenues would help efforts to sustain the US-backed government in Kabul.[28] Given Pakistan's reluctance to provide overland transit to India, and the US approach of bypassing Iran in Eurasian connectivity, Washington's Silk Road strategy did not take off, thus ceding the initiative to China's Belt and Road Initiative, and to some extent to Russia.

In 2014, Russia's annexation of Crimea, and the subsequent Western sanctions induced Moscow to strengthen its pivot to Asia, and at the same time alerted the Central Asian States to the imperative of diversifying their partnerships, including with India. Amid a rapid deterioration in ties with the West, Russia began considering the expansion of the functions and membership of the Shanghai Cooperation Organisation (SCO) to make the grouping a more effective and non-Western counterweight to Western structures. Until 2015, Russia had taken an ambivalent approach to economic cooperation within the SCO, preferring to deepen multilateral economic cooperation within the Russian-led Eurasian Economic Union (EAEU).[29] However, after concluding that deterioration in relations with the West over the Ukrainian crisis was irreversible, Moscow substituted the concept of 'Greater Europe' made up of the European Union and the Russian-led EAEU with 'Greater Eurasia', centred on linking the EAEU with China's Silk Road Economic Belt.[30] Notably, China and Russia's cooperative approach towards developing Eurasia-wide transport networks, such as the 'Northern corridor' connecting East Asia with Europe via an upgraded Trans-Siberian Railway and the Baikal-Amur Railway, is part of broader Chinese efforts at developing "reliable connectivity in a multipolar format."[31]

At a time of growing rivalry with the United States, China is asserting greater control over transport corridors to ensure reliable access to resources and markets, which is necessary for sustaining China's economic growth. Though both Russia and the Central Asian States saw China's economic activities as playing a stabilising role and advancing Eurasian integration, they have continued to see engagement with India and its SCO membership, which was approved at the 2015 Ufa Summit, as important to diversify their external economic relations.[32] As India's economy continued registering high growth (7.6 per cent for the 2015-16 fiscal year and an average of 7.5 per cent in the 2014-19 period), it came to be seen as an attractive large-size economic partner.

Notwithstanding, the view in Moscow and certain Central Asian capitals that India could play a balancing role in the region, India's accession to the SCO came in the context of a very competitive geo-economic and geopolitical landscape in Central and South Asia. Philip Reid, using the language of inter-imperialist geopolitical rivalry of the late nineteenth and early twentieth century, observes that the "scramble for connectivity leadership in Central and South Asia" that began in the years following the collapse of the Soviet Union intensified with the launch of China's Silk Road Economic Belt in 2013.[33] While Russia had been consolidating the Eurasian Economic Union and the Collective Security Treaty Organisation (CSTO), China's BRI was advancing new continental transport corridors to Europe across Central Asia and Russia. India is the only SCO country that has not signed up to the Chinese Belt and Road Initiative (BRI). At the SCO Summit of Heads of State in Qingdao, Prime Minister Modi noted that "connectivity with our neighbourhood and in the SCO region is our priority."[34] He maintained that mega connectivity projects must respect the sovereignty and territorial integrity of the countries, as he assured India's full support to initiatives which are "inclusive, sustainable and transparent, and which [respect] member states' sovereignty and territorial integrity. India's articulation of 'inclusive connectivity', has to be seen together with other narratives such as 'debt-trap diplomacy', which seeks to delegitimise China's infrastructure investment activities based on State capitalism as economic statecraft aimed at cultivating powerful followers for a

Chinese order-remaking project, while foregrounding public-debt implications of the BRI projects in the recipient countries.[35] Even as Russia, Central Asian States and Iran are keen to avoid a zero-sum competition among various connectivity projects, they have continued to look at India as a useful balancer in Eurasia.

Amid a variety of connectivity initiatives in Eurasia, the Makran Coast, the southern coastal region of Baluchistan divided between Iran and Pakistan, has gained a strategic profile as the littoral interface or 'gateway' between Central Asia and the Indian Ocean, the two regions that have historically played the role of east-west thoroughfares.[36] China's plans to build overland transport corridors connecting its landlocked provinces to the Indian Ocean, such as the China-Pakistan Economic Corridor (CEPC) and the China-Myanmar Economic Corridor (CMEC), notwithstanding their framing in the language of economic diplomacy, have serious implications for the centuries-old geo-strategic character of the Indian Ocean. David Brewster argues that historically, two geographical constraints of the Indian Ocean, namely the absence of connection between the Indian Ocean littoral and interior of the Eurasian continent through navigable rivers, and that the access to the Ocean is through a few maritime entrance points, have contributed to the domination of this Ocean by a succession of extra-regional maritime powers.[37] By corollary, these geographic factors have had the effect of virtually excluding Eurasian land powers such as China and Russia from projecting their naval power in the Indian Ocean.[38] Therefore, just as the Chinese efforts to establish maritime infrastructure across the Indian Ocean littoral, which have been dubbed by analysts as the 'string of pearls' strategy, Beijing's investment in overland transport corridors reaching up to 'gateway' ports such as Gwadar, have implications beyond their declared aims of addressing China's internal development priorities and mitigate strategic vulnerabilities on 'choke points'. In geo-economic terms, overland pathways are advancing China-led economic and strategic integration of much of the Eurasian littoral, and in doing so fundamentally transform the traditional character of the Indian Ocean as a semi-closed strategic space capable of domination by a single naval power.[39] Notwithstanding the discourse surrounding Gwadar and Chabahar as 'gateways' to the Chinese interior, and to Afghanistan and Central Asia respectively, such investments seem to be driven less by commercial logic and more by geostrategic priorities of China and India as they engage in a strategic rivalry in the Indian Ocean and Eurasia.

India-Iran-Afghanistan: Chabahar

Maysam Bizaer notes that Iran was one of the largest donors at the 2002 Tokyo International Conference on Reconstruction Assistance to Afghanistan. It dedicated a bulk of this assistance to building schools, power plants, new border crossings and roads in western Afghanistan, which shares strong historical and cultural ties with Iran.[40] Iran's interest in western Afghanistan has to do with the security of their more than 900 km long shared border, creating job opportunities that can help in stemming the flow of refugees into Iran and also seeking economic benefits for Iran at a time when it has been reeling under US sanctions. In 2005, Iran opened the 122 km Dogharun-Herat Highway, which over the years has become one of the major import-export gateways to Afghanistan. The Dogharoon Special Economic Zone located at the zero point of the border with Afghanistan emerged as a key hub for trade with Afghanistan and to Central Asian countries.[41] In 2017, Iran replaced Pakistan as Afghanistan's largest trading partner followed by China and Pakistan, a position that Iran has continued to hold even after the return of Taliban to power.[42] India's construction of the 215 km long highway from the Zaranj-Delaram highway stretching from the Iran-Afghanistan border to Delaram in Nimruz province of Afghanistan, also facilitated the growth of this trade. The strategic highway, completed in 2009 at the cost of Rs 600 crores, feeds into the 2,200 km two-lane metalled road called 'garland road' connecting major cities of Afghanistan.

In 2007, Tehran had committed US$ 75 million for constructing a railway line from Khaf in north-eastern Iran to Herat in western Afghanistan. The Khaf-Herat railway project was part of the trilateral agreement between Iran, Afghanistan and India to develop the Chabahar route, and the larger East-West Railway Corridor extending to China and Europe.[43] In December 2020, Tehran inaugurated a 140 km section from Khaf to Ghoryan in western Afghanistan, while the last section from Ghoryan to Herat, financed by Italy, was 80 per cent complete. Though New Delhi struggled to make good on its plan to develop the Chabahar port due to sanctions, it upgraded the road from Chabahar to Zaranj on Iran's border with Afghanistan. India invested in infrastructure in Iran and Afghanistan aiming to establish transit and connectivity with Central Asian countries.[44]

The signing of the Joint Comprehensive Plan of Action (JCPOA) and lifting of international sanctions on Iran in January 2016 created new momentum for India's hitherto delayed northern outreach. Prime Minister Modi visited Tehran in May 2016, where the India-Iran-Afghanistan Trilateral Agreement on the establishment of an International Transit and Transport Corridor, called the Chabahar Agreement, was signed. Under Phase-I of the Agreement, New Delhi committed to equip and operate two berths in Chabahar Port with a capital investment of US$ 85.21 million, and an annual revenue expenditure of US$ 22.95 million on a 10-year lease.[45] India and Iran agreed to jointly construct the Chabahar-Zahedan railway line, as part of a transit and transportation corridor under the Chabahar Agreement. Indian Railway Construction Limited (IRCON) signed a MoU with Iran's Construction and Development of Transportation Infrastructures Company (CDTIC) to provide requisite services for the construction of the railway line.

In December 2018, just before the snapback of the US sanctions following the Trump administration's withdrawal from the nuclear agreement, India took over the operations of a part of the Shahid Beheshti port.[46] Subsequently, New Delhi was able to negotiate with Washington a limited sanctions exemption for the construction of Chabahar Port and the associated railway line. As President Trump's South Asia strategy, announced in August 2017, exhorted India to play a bigger role in Afghanistan, especially in the field of economic assistance and development, the US Treasury's exemption of Indian investment in Chabahar was a necessary compromise even from Washington's point of view.[47] However, Washington maintained that it would extend the exemption so long as Iran's Revolutionary Guards Corps (IRGC), which had been put on the US State Department's list of foreign terrorist organisations in April 2019, does not participate in the port project.[48] With Tehran's insistence that Khatam-al Anbiya

Construction Headquarters, the engineering arm of the IRGC, be entrusted with the civil work for the Chabahar-Zahedan railway line, New Delhi became circumspect about its role in the construction of the strategic railway line.[49] Subsequently, citing delays from the Indian side, Iran decided to go alone on the railway line. Soon after, Iran's Port and Maritime Organisation (PMO) requested India to help it procure the equipment to run the railway line and activate the US$ 150 million credit line to pay for equipment procurement.[50] India had promised the credit line during President Rouhani's visit to India in 2018. India has stakes in developing port-hinterland connectivity from Chabahar, especially given that New Delhi is keen to integrate Chabahar with the eastern branch of the INSTC towards Central Asia. In March 2021, at an event marking 'Chabahar Day', External Affairs Minister S. Jaishankar proposed the inclusion of the port in the INSTC. While welcoming Uzbekistan's interest and Afghanistan joining the 12-member multimodal corridor project, the Minister noted that an 'eastern corridor through Afghanistan' would maximise the potential of the project.[51]

While Iran has followed a policy of pragmatic engagement with the Taliban after it overthrew the West-backed government in August 2021, India took a wait-and-watch approach before it reopened its Embassy, with a skeletal technical staff, in June 2022. New Delhi maintained that the purpose of the 'technical team' in Kabul was to "closely monitor and coordinate" the delivery of humanitarian assistance to the country.[52] Subsequently, in partnership with the United Nations World Food Programme, India delivered 40,000 MT of wheat through the overland route via Pakistan, and another 20,000 MT of wheat through the Chabahar port.[53] Given Pakistan's role in nurturing, and supporting the Taliban, Taliban-ruled Afghanistan is being integrated into the CPEC. At a China-Pakistan-Afghanistan ministerial dialogue in Islamabad in June 2023, Beijing and Islamabad announced the extension of the CPEC into Afghanistan.[54] India for its part, has redoubled its efforts to develop Chabahar as a gateway for Indian trade with Russia and the Commonwealth of Independent States (CIS) countries.[55] After the approval of Iran's full membership of the SCO, and the imperative for Central Asian States to diversify their transit and transport routes to Europe in the wake of the Russia-

Ukraine war and European sanctions on Russia, Iran is keen to project Chabahar as a trans-shipment hub for SCO member countries.[56]

Opportunities: The New Momentum on the INSTC

The INSTC has been long hailed by its three key proponents, namely India, Iran and Russia, as a faster, cheaper alternative to the Suez Canal route. However, the corridor has not received the same level of attention and commitment even from these three countries.

The new momentum on the INSTC is owed to Russia's 'turn to the East', which was aimed at correcting its commercial over-reliance on Europe and provide economic dynamism to its Far Eastern provinces. However, it became more of a survival strategy following its February 2022 'special operation' in Ukraine, which resulted in the European countries imposing comprehensive sanctions on Russia, and closing their border with Russia. In recent years Iran and Russia have developed increasing geopolitical and geo-economic convergence based on their shared security objectives in limiting Western influence in the region, preference for regional dialogue and cooperation on issues ranging from the Caspian Sea to Afghanistan and terrorism, and on north-south connectivity via Iran. Iran has undertaken an ambitious programme of expanding its Caspian Sea shipping, mainly to facilitate its own growing trade with the Eurasian Economic Union, with which it signed an interim free trade agreement in March 2018. The augmented shipping facilities at the Caspian ports of Russia and Iran have helped operationalise the INSTC, especially as the 164-kilometre Rasht-Astara railway line crucial to interlink the railway networks of Russia, Azerbaijan and Iran, remains the missing link of the multimodal INSTC. In June 2022, the State-run Islamic Republic of Iran Shipping Lines (IRISL) ran a pilot test on the INSTC.[57] It coordinated transport of containers of wood laminate sheets, weighing 41 tons by road from St Petersburg to the jointly owned Iranian-Russian terminal in the Caspian seaport city of Astrakhan to Iran's Caspian port of Anzali, and from there by road to Iran's Bandar Abbas port in the Persian Gulf and then on to the Nhava Sheva port on India's western coast.

Iran's Vision of the INSTC

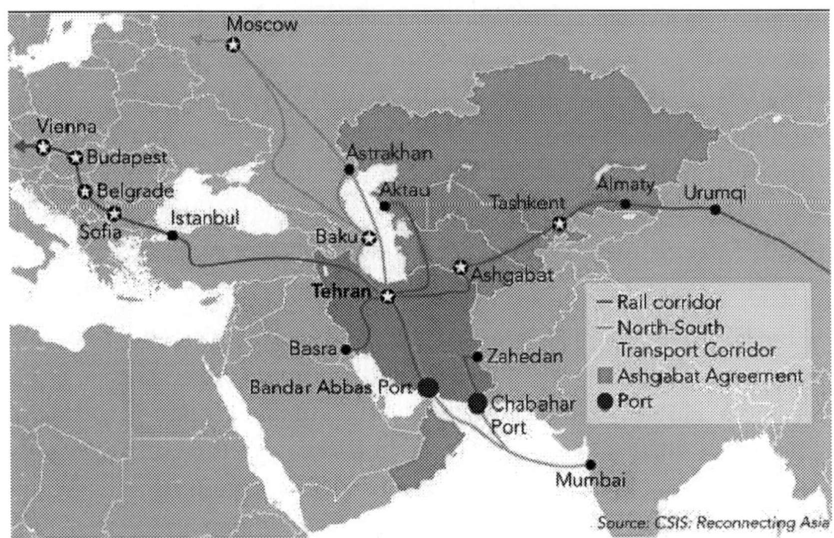

Source: CSIS: Reconnecting Asia.

It is noteworthy, that during Iranian President Ebrahim Raisi's visit to Moscow in January 2022, Russia finalised the previously agreed US$ 5 billion credit line for the completion of several projects in Iran, including the financing of the Rasht-Astara railway line and electrification of railway line between Garmsar in the south-west of Tehran to Incheh-Borun on Iran–Turkmenistan border, which is part of the eastern branch of the INSTC.[58] This recent mobilisation of financial resources and political will by Russia, Iran and India for expediting the INSTC, indicates an optimistic future for this long-awaited corridor. In addition, it is hoped that Iran's membership in the SCO will contribute to the attractiveness of the INSTC, especially to the Central Asian States.

Iran's interpretation of the INSTC entails a connection between Chabahar to Sarakhs on the Turkmen border. Following the war in Ukraine, there has been momentum on this eastern branch of the corridor. In August 2022, while hosting an international conference of transport ministers from landlocked countries, Turkmen Deputy Prime Minister and Foreign Minister Rashid Meredov noted that Turkmenistan had begun the process of joining the INSTC agreement.[59] Under the agreement, the Caspian Sea port of

Turkmenbashi will become an INSTC node.[60] In June 2022, the North–South railway corridor also became operational when the first freight train from Kazakhstan, carrying sulphur destined for Europe, arrived at Incheh Borun at the Iran–Turkmenistan border. In Tehran, President Ebrahim Raisi, along with the Kazakh President Kassym-Jomart Tokayev launched the Kazakhstan–Turkmenistan–Iran (KTI) transit corridor, to Europe via Turkey.[61] These developments indicate that Iran's outreach to the Central Asian States to use Iranian soil for both East-West and North-South transit has supplemented India's efforts in operationalising the INSTC and Chabahar.

Challenges: Connectivity and Competition

In the geo-economic competition between Iran and Turkey in the Caucasus and the Central Asian region, socio-cultural considerations – that is, Iran being a predominantly Persian country among the majority of Turkic States – act as strategic constraints for Iran's overtures to the region. Turkey has tried to leverage ethnic-linguistic commonalities for fostering regional economic cooperation within the framework of the Organisation of Turkic States. It continues to receive support from Europe, and is courting China to develop East-West connectivity from Central Asia to Europe through the Trans-Caspian International Transport Route (TITR), called the Middle Corridor. It charts a middle passage bypassing Russia in the north and Iran in the south.[62]

In a similar vein, Uzbekistan, which has the distinction of sharing borders with all other Central Asian States, and also Afghanistan, has supported infrastructure and connectivity projects leading south via Afghanistan rather than Iran. Over the last decade, Afghanistan and Uzbekistan – both landlocked States – have depended on each other for trade, transport and connectivity to Central Asia and South Asia respectively. In the last couple of years, Uzbekistan sought to engage the European Union and the United States, by interlinking regional connectivity projects with the political survival of the US-backed government in Kabul.[63] Tashkent's view that economic integration of Afghanistan with the region is not only essential for stability in the war-torn country but also the best bet for regional stability, explains its early outreach and willingness to work with the Taliban in taking forward regional connectivity projects. At the 'Central and South Asia Connectivity: Challenges and Opportunity', organised by Tashkent in July 2021, Uzbekistan joined the United States, Afghanistan, and Pakistan in a quadrilateral diplomatic platform, focused on enhancing regional connectivity. Taliban's takeover of Afghanistan merely a month later raised a question mark on Western involvement, but Uzbekistan hosted the 2022 version of the connectivity conference focussing on economic recovery and mitigating the humanitarian crisis in Afghanistan.[64] At the end of the conference, Tashkent facilitated direct talks between the visiting Taliban and US delegations on unfreezing some of the Afghan assets for humanitarian aid. Uzbekistan has also led efforts to secure European investment in the Trans-Afghan railway.[65]

For transit countries to maximise their potential benefits, they actively seek integration of international transport corridors with regional and national logistics infrastructure. It is in this context that Iran has been keen to foster complementarity between the INSTC and other East–West latitudinal corridors. However, such integration efforts will require Iran to navigate the competitive East-West connectivity dynamics. After the Northern Corridor connecting Northeast Asia with Europe via Russia came to an abrupt halt, Kazakhstan and Uzbekistan have sought to work with the European Union to increase the capacity of the Middle Corridor. In a move that will give Uzbekistan more heft in Europe-Central Asia connectivity, during the SCO summit in Samarkand in September 2022, an agreement was reached on the long-delayed China-Kyrgyzstan-Uzbekistan (CKU) Railway Corridor.[66] The CKU route as the southern part of China-Europe freight train, will link to Central and Eastern Europe via Iran and Turkey. Among the existing routes, the route linking China's rail freight transport networks and the EU through Kazakhstan's Caspian Sea ports of Aktau and Kuryk to Baku port in Azerbaijan and then via Baku–Tbilisi–Kars Railway is considered the second-best option after the Northern Corridor. However, with increasing volume, Caspian shipping will need expansion. Uzbekistan recently used the Turkmenistan route of the Middle Corridor when a cargo train carrying 91 containers of copper concentrate crossed a distance of 4000 km across Turkmenistan, Azerbaijan, Georgia, and

Bulgaria.[67] The European Bank for Reconstruction and Development (EBRD), which has been mandated by the European Commission to conduct a study on sustainable transport connections between Central Asia and Europe, has estimated that the Middle Corridor infrastructure upgrade will require an estimated € 3.5 billion.[68]

The EU's interest in developing the Middle Corridor as the alternative to the Russian Corridor underscores how Iran, despite its geographical advantage, is often left out. Given the fact that the key participants in the Middle Corridor initiative Kazakhstan, Uzbekistan, Azerbaijan, Turkey and Kyrgyzstan are members of the Organisation of Turkic States, while Turkmenistan is an observer, the grouping has adopted a transportation cooperation agenda.[69] The activities of the Turkic grouping, especially support for controversial projects such as the Zangezur Corridor will inevitably run into problems with Iran, which opposes the Corridor on the ground that it will undermine its own narrow border with Armenia. These contestations in the Caucasus create rival visions of north-south connectivity as countries see infrastructure projects through a geopolitical prism of leverage and avoiding dependencies. Armenia has been determined to construct its north-south road corridor with the aim of connecting the southern and northern borders of the country through the 556 km-long Meghri-Yerevan-Bavra highway. Armenia had signed contracts with the Asian Development Bank, the European Bank for Reconstruction and Development and the Almaty-based Eurasian Development Bank to secure funding for the strategic road project connecting Armenia to the Georgian border in the north and up to Iran in the south. This can be a key link in the Black Sea-Persian Gulf corridor if Georgia, a Western ally, is willing to cooperate.[70] Yerevan hopes that this highway can be a key link in realising the Black Sea-Persian Gulf Transport corridor, and the INSTC. Crucially, India and Iran have found converging interests in supporting Armenia at a time when Baku, with backing from Turkiye, is making a claim over its southern province of Syunik and its traditional security partner Russia has taken a more balanced approach between Baku and Yerevan. Apart from cooperation in the military-technical sector, trade and transit sector cooperation was the focus of the first India-Iran-Armenia trilateral consultation in Yerevan in April 2023.[71]

Conclusion

In the last seven years since the signing of the historic Chabahar Agreement, India and Iran have made slow but steady progress towards creating stable north-south connectivity. While the return of the US sanctions on Iran in 2018 and the Taliban takeover of Afghanistan in 2021 posed serious challenges in implementation of the Chabahar port and related railway projects, other geopolitical factors such as the US withdrawal from Afghanistan, Iran's accession to the SCO and the war in Ukraine have convinced Iran and India to continue their connectivity partnership. For India to play its balancing role in Eurasia, which is desired by Russia, Iran and most Central Asian States, the importance of reliable transport corridors cannot be overestimated. Similarly, in the aftermath of the US withdrawal from the JCPOA and the dismal status of the talks for restoring US and Iran's compliance to the same, Iran has strengthened its 'Asia orientation' in both foreign policy and geo-economics. Tehran's 'Look to the East' policy seeks to diversify economic connectivity with neighbouring Asian countries and strengthen its geo-economic position within the global economy and thus goes beyond a tactical shift to overcome Western economic sanctions. In this context, Iran's cooperation with India, together with deepening partnerships with China and Russia, will continue in the near future. New Delhi for its part, in keeping with the trend over the last two decades, will have to balance its continental interests, with Iran being a crucial partner in continental Asia, and its priorities in the Indo-Pacific, where it has a burgeoning partnership with Washington.[72]

NOTES

1 Deepika Saraswat, "The US challenge to India's ties with Iran", *The Round Table: The Commonwealth Journal of International Affairs*, 111 (6), December 2022, pp. 735-736.

2 "The New Delhi Declaration", Ministry of External Affairs, Government of India, 25 January 2003, at https://mea.gov.in/outoging-visit-detail.htm?20182/The+Republic+ of+ India+and+the+Islamic+Republic+of+Iran+quotThe+New+Delhi+Declarationquot (Accessed 22 December 2022).

3 Philip Reid, *Makran Gateways: A Strategic Reference for Gwadar and Chabahar*, MP-IDSA Occasional Paper No. 53, 2019, at https://idsa.in/occasionalpapers/makran-gatways-op-53 (Accessed 19 December 2022).

4 Glenn Diesen, "New Trajectories of Transportation Corridors in Eurasia", Valdai Club, 11 October 2022, at https://valdaiclub.com/a/highlights/new-trajectories-of-

transportation-corridors/ (Accessed 19 December 2022).
5 Ibid.
6 Philip Reid, *Mahan and Mackinder: Addressing the False Dichotomy in the Eurasian Pivot Theory*, MP-IDSA Occasional Paper No. 59, December 2022, at https://www.idsa.in/system/files/opaper/op-59-mahan-and-mackinder_0.pdf (18.
7 P. Stobdan, *Central Asia: India's Northern Exposure*, MP-IDSA Monograph Series No. 44, 2015, at https://www.idsa.in/monograph/CentralAsiaIndiasNorthern Exposure_ pstobdan_ 44 (22 December 2022); Ravi K. Mishra, "The 'Silk Road': Historical Perspectives and Modern Constructions", *Indian Historical Review*, 47 (1), 2020, pp. 21–39.
8 Philip Reid, no. 3, p. 5.
9 John Hayhurst, "Technologies of Power: Railway Records and what they can tell us", Qatar Digital Library, 3 May 2022, at https://www.qdl.qa/en/technologies-power-railway-records-and-what-they-can-tell-us (Accessed 15 December 2022).
10 D.W. Spring, "The Trans-Persian Railway Project and Anglo-Russian Relations, 1909-14", *Middle Eastern Studies*, 49 (2), 2013, p. 61.
11 Ibid., p. 60
12 Philip Reid, No. 3.
13 Szczepan Lemañczyk, "The Trans-Iranian Railway – History, Context and Consequences", *Middle Eastern Studies*, 49 (2), March 2013, p. 238.
14 Abbas Amanat, *Iran: A Modern History*, Yale University Press, New Haven and London, 2017, p. 338.
15 D.W. Spring, "The Trans-Persian Railway Project and Anglo-Russian Relations, 1909-14", *The Slavonic and East European Review*, 54 (1), January 1976.
16 Szczepan Lemañczyk, no.13, p. 239.
17 Philip Reid, no. 3.
18 Gary R. Hess, "The Iranian Crisis of 1945-46 and the Cold War", *Political Science Quarterly*, 89 (1), 1974, pp. 117-146.
19 Ahed George Samaan, "The policy of containment and the Middle East, 1946-1958", 1972, at https://doi.org/10.15760/etd.967 (Accessed 28 November 2022).
20 P. Stobdan, no. 7, p. 5.
21 Ibid., p.16.
22 Philip Reid, no. 3, p. 6.
23 Mher D. Sahakyan. "Rebuilding Interconnections: Russia, India and the International North-South Transport Corridor", *Asia Global Online*, 2020, at https://hal.archives-ouvertes.fr/hal-02980041/document (Accessed 23 December 2022).
24 "The New Delhi Declaration", no. 2.
25 Edmund Herzig, "Regionalism, Iran and Central Asia", *International Affairs*, 80 (3), 2004, pp. 503-17.
26 Alexander Karavayev and Mandana Tishehyar, "International North–South Transport Corridor and Transregional Integration Scenarios", Valdai Club, 26 June 2019, at https://valdaiclub.com/a/reports/north-south-transport-corridor (Accessed 11 December 2022).
27 Conference Report, "Central Asia, Afghanistan and the New Silk Road: Political, Economic and Security Challenges", *The Jamestown Foundation*, 14 November 2011, https://jamestown.org/wp-content/uploads/2011/11/Afghan_Silk_Road_conf_report _-_ FULL.pdf?x87069 (Accessed 11 December 2022).
28 Ibid.
29 Alexander Lukin, "Russian–Chinese Cooperation in Central Asia and the Idea of Greater Eurasia", *India Quarterly*, 75 (1), 2019, pp. 1-14.

30 Richard Sakwa, "Eurasian Integration: A Project for the 21st Century?", in D. Lane and V. Samokhvalov, (eds.), *The Eurasian Project and Europe,* Palgrave Macmillan, London, 2015, at https://doi.org/10.1057/9781137472960_4

31 Glenn Diesen, no. 4.

32 Alexander Lukin, no. 29.

33 Philip Reid, no. 3.

34 Elizabeth Roche, "Narendra Modi pushes for stronger economic ties at SCO summit", *Mint,* 10 June 2018, at https://www.livemint.com/Politics/lBDkvSPdjPBy4TGka4gKNJ/Narendra-Modi-says-connectivity-with-neighbourhood-and-in-SC.html (Accessed 11 December 2022).

35 Lai-Ha Chan, "Can China remake regional order? Contestation with India over the Belt and Road Initiative", *Global Change, Peace & Security,* 32 (2), 2020, pp. 199-217.

36 Philip Reid, no. 3, p.14.

37 David Brewster, "Silk Roads and Strings of Pearls: The Strategic Geography of China's New Pathways in the Indian Ocean", *Geopolitics,* 22 (2), 2017, pp. 269-291.

38 Ibid.

39 Ibid.

40 Maysam Bizaer, "Iran's railway ambitions go beyond Afghanistan", Atlantic Council, 4 January 2021 at https://www.atlanticcouncil.org/blogs/iransource/irans-railway-ambitions-go-beyond-afghanistan/ (Accessed 18 December, 2022).

41 "Dogharoon Special Economic Zone", at https://dogharoon.ir/home-2/ (Accessed 13 July 2023).

42 "Is Afghanistan's Main Trade Partner, Official Says", *Tasnim News,* 18 March 2023, at https://www.tasnimnews.com/en/news/2023/03/18/2869466/iran-is-afghanistan-s-main-trade-partner-official-says (Accessed 10 July 2023).

43 Maysam Bizaer, no. 40.

44 P. Stobdan, no. 7.

45 "India to fully operationalise Chabahar port soon; Iranian bank branch to open in Mumbai: Nitin Gadkari", *The Economic Times,* 8 January 2019, at https://economictimes.indiatimes. com/news/economy/foreign-trade/india-to-fully-operationalise-chabahar-port-soon-iranian-bank-branch-to-open-in-mumbai-nitin-gadkari/articleshow/67435229.cms? from=mdr (Accessed 19 December 2022).

46 "India takes over operations of part of Chabahar Port in Iran", Press Information Bureau, 7 January 2019, at https://pib.gov.in/Pressreleaseshare.aspx?PRID=1558896 (Accessed 18 December 2022).

47 Deepika Saraswat, "How India Got US Waiver on Iran Oil, Chabahar – And Its Importance", *The Quint,* 17 November 2018, at https://www.thequint.com/opinion/us-waiver-iran-oil-chabahar-port-india-advantage#read-more (Accessed 25 July 2023).

48 Lalit K. Jha, "US grants India 'narrow exemption' from sanctions to continue Chabahar port development in Iran", *The Print,* 19 December 2019, at https://theprint.in/diplomacy/us-grants-india-narrow-exemption-from-sanctions-to-continue-chabahar-port-development-in-iran/337733/ (Accessed 15 December, 2022).

49 Geeta Mohan, "Real reason why India sits out of Iran's Chabahar-Zahedan rail link project", *India Today,* 21 July 2021, at https://www.indiatoday.in/india/story/iran-chabahar-zahedan-rail-link-project-india-1702928-2020-07-21 (Accessed 11 December 2022).

50 Suhasini Haidar, "Months after starting Chabahar rail project without India, Iran

seeks equipment", *The Hindu*, 7 November 2021, at https://www.thehindu.com/news/national/months-after-starting-chabahar-rail-project-without-india-iran-requests-help-with-equipment/article33048813.ece (Accessed 11 December 2022).

51 Dipanjan Roy Chaudhury, "India proposes inclusion of Iran's Chabahar Port in International North South Transport Corridor", *The Economic Times*, at https://economictimes.indiatimes.com/news/politics-and-nation/india-proposes-inclusion-of-irans-chabahar-port-in-international-north-south-transport-corridor/articleshow/81336893.cms?from=mdr (Accessed 15 December 2022).

52 Naynima Basu, "India reopens embassy in Kabul, sends 'technical team' with relief material for Afghanistan", *The Print*, 23 June 2022, at https://theprint.in/diplomacy/india-reopens-embassy-in-kabul-sends-technical-team-with-relief-material-for-afghanistan/10094 (Accessed 11 July, 2023).

53 Madhu Kapparath, "India sends food aid to Afghanistan on humanitarian grounds, upon Taliban's request", *Forbes India*, 12 June 2023, at https://www.forbesindia.com/article/news/india-sends-food-aid-to-afghanistan-on-humanitarian-grounds-upon-talibans-request/85659/1/ (Accessed 17 December, 2022).

54 "At Islamabad meeting, China & Pakistan agree to extend Belt and Road initiative to Afghanistan", *The Indian Express*, 8 May 2023, at https://indianexpress.com/article/world/chinas-belt-and-road-initiative-to-enter-afghanistan-8596584/ (Accessed 18 December 2022).

55 Suhasini Haidar, "Explained: Reinvigorating the Chabahar port", *The Hindu*, 23 August 2022, at https://www.thehindu.com/news/international/explained-reinvigorating-the-chabahar-port/article65802514.ece (Accessed 22 December 2022).

56 Deepika Saraswat, "Iran's Central Asia Policy Gains Momentum amid Russia–Ukraine War", MP-IDSA Issue Brief, 19 July 2022, at https://www.idsa.in/issuebrief/iran-central-asia-policy-gains-momentum-dsaraswat-190722 (Accessed 19 December 2022).

57 "Iran kicks off pilot transit via North-South Corridor", *IRNA*, 11 June 2022, at https://en.irna.ir/news/84784416/Iran-kicks-off-pilot-transit-via-North-South-Corridor (Accessed 19 December, 2022).

58 Vali Kaleji, "Will Russia Complete Iran's Rasht–Astara Railway?", The Jamestown Foundation, 16 May 2022, at https://jamestown.org/program/will-russia-complete-irans-rasht-astara-railway/ (Accessed 20 December 2022).

59 "Turkmenistan will join the transport corridor 'North–South'", *Turkmenportal*, 8 August 2022, at https://turkmenportal.com/en/blog/50762/turkmenistan-will-join-the-transport-corridor-north—south (Accessed 18 December 2022).

60 "Turkmenistan to Officially Join the International North-South Transport Corridor", Silk Road Briefing, 29 August 2022, at https://www.silkroadbriefing.com/news/2022/08/23/turkmenistan-to-officially-join-the-international-north-south-transport-corridor/ (Accessed 12 December 2022).

61 "1st Kazakhstan-Turkey Transit Train Arrives in Iran", *Tehran Times*, 19 June 2022 at https://www.tehrantimes.com/news/473795/1st-Kazakhstan-Turkey-transit-train-arrives-in-Iran (Accessed 13 December 2022).

62 James Jay Carafano, "Central Asia's Middle Corridor gains traction at Russia's expense", GIS Report Online, 29 August 2022, at https://www.gisreportsonline.com/r/middle-corridor/ (Accessed 11 December, 2022).

63 Timor Sharan, "Andrew Watkins, Stabilization and Connectivity Uzbekistan's dual-track strategy towards Afghanistan", *Friedrich-Ebert-Stiftung*, 2021, at https://library.fes.de/pdf-files/bueros/kabul/17313.pdf (Accessed 15 December 2022).

64 Ayaz Gul, "Uzbekistan to Host US-Taliban Talks on Economic Challenges Facing Afghans", *Voice of America*, 25 July 2022, at https://www.voanews.com/a/uzbekistan-to-host-us-taliban-talks-on-economic-challenges-facing-afghans/6673250.html (Accessed 12 December 2022).

65 "Trans-Afghan rail corridor needs EU as much as Taliban", Rail Freight, 3 November 2022, at https://www.railfreight.com/corridors/2022/11/03/trans-afghan-corridor-needs-eu-as-much-as-taliban/?gdpr=deny (Accessed 18 December, 2022).

66 Li Xuanmin, "China-Kyrgyzstan-Uzbekistan railway to open 'southern Eurasia corridor, facilitates BRI cooperation with Central Asia: analysts", *Global Times*, 15 September 2022, at https://www.globaltimes.cn/page/202209/1275365.shtml (Accessed 12 December 2022).

67 "Turkmenbashi port transported copper concentrate from Uzbekistan to Europe", *Orient*, 28 December 2022 at https://orient.tm/en/old/post/44075/turkmenbashi-port-transported-copper-concentrate-uzbekistan-europe (Accession date 30 December, 2022).

68 Antov Usov, "EBRD researches sustainable transport connections between Central Asia and Europe", European Bank for Reconstruction and Development, 7 November 2022, at https://www.ebrd.com/news/2022/ebrd-researches-sustainable-transport-connections-between-central-asia-and-europe-.html (Accessed 18 December 2022).

69 Muhammad Rafiq, "China-Kyrgyzstan-Uzbekistan Railway Corridor to Boost Regional Cooperation", *The Astana Times*, 9 September 2022, at https://astanatimes.com/2022/09/china-kyrgyzstan-uzbekistan-railway-corridor-to-boost-regional-cooperation/ (Accessed 11 July 2023).

70 "North-South Road Corridor Investment Program", at https://armroad.am/en/projects/north-south-road-corridor-investment-program (Accessed 11 July 2023).

71 "Armenia hosts first trilateral meeting with Iranian and Indian officials", *Tehran Times*, 23 April 2023, at https://www.tehrantimes.com/news/483916/Armenia-hosts-first-trilateral-meeting-with-Iranian-and-Indian (Accessed 11 July, 2023).

72 Deepika Saraswat, no. 1.

4

India-Israel Ties Under Prime Minister Narendra Modi

Jatin Kumar

Israel holds an important place in India's West Asia Policy. While India recognised Israel in 1950, it established formal diplomatic ties with the latter under the leadership of P.V. Narasimha Rao, on 29 January 1992. This was facilitated by a change in the international order at the end of the Cold War, wherein the US emerged as a major power.[1] Though India took 42 years to establish bilateral relations with Israel, it successfully maintained the image of a time-tested friend for India in difficult times since 1950.

In the early decades of India's independence, its policy towards Israel was dominated by the presence of a significant Muslim population in India and its energy concerns which were largely dependent on Arab countries. While these factors prevented the successful maturing of relations between the two countries, Israel helped India in its wars with countries such as China in 1962 and Pakistan in 1965, 1971 and 1999.[2]

Despite the advancements in India and Israel's relations after 1992, India's traditional support for the two-state solution prevented its successive Prime Ministers from visiting Israel. However, the exchange of visits by ministers and armed forces officers took place at regular intervals. In the post-1992 period, India separated bilateral relations from the intricacies of the peace process without changing its voting patterns in international forums.

Post-1993, Israeli Foreign Minister Shimon Peres's visit to India helped in creating a strong foundation of economic and defence ties. A Memorandum of Understanding (MoU) was signed to deepen economic ties, and discussions were held on issues related to terrorism.[3] Subsequent visits including that of Israeli President, Ezer Weizman, to India (first visit by an Israeli President), L.K. Advani's visit to Israel in 2000 and Israeli Prime Minister, Ariel Sharon's visit to India in 2003, helped to cement the ties further. Sharon's visit was extremely significant since it witnessed the signing of six agreements focusing "on combating illicit trafficking of drugs, environment, health, education and culture," and deepened the defence ties further between the counties.[4]

In 2004, under the United Progressive Alliance (UPA) government, the "contacts with Israel became minimal and were largely confined to defence and security issues."[5] This was majorly attributed to the domestic and international opposition to Israel which emerged after the Al Aqsa intifada (September 2000). However, the UPA government tried to return to Nehru's pragmatic approach towards the West Asian region and adopted a more balanced policy with Israel in its decade-long tenure.[6]

Since 2014, India-Israel ties have reached a new era of more pronounced relations. Under the leadership of Narendra Modi, the bilateral relations have expanded across various sectors such as defence, innovation, trade, agriculture, and cyber security, to name a few. Both countries have intensified their defence relations through regular joint military exercises, procuring security equipment and weapons and technology sharing.

Similarly, agricultural ties have also witnessed significant advancements. In this regard, India has sought Israel's technological know-how in areas such as irrigation technologies, water management and agricultural productivity. Furthermore, both countries have initiated various collaborative projects and training programmes to improve agricultural practices and water-related issues in India. At the diplomatic level, regular high-level visits have been taking place between the two countries, the most recent being the visit by Israeli Foreign Minister, Eli Cohen to India on 9 May 2023. Cohen's visit opened avenues to expand the ongoing collaboration in agriculture and water between the two nations.

An important factor that has been a major catalyst in nurturing robust Indo-Israel ties is Prime Minister Modi's close personal relationship with Israeli leaders, including Benjamin Netanyahu. This can be inferred from the instance wherein both the leaders addressed each other by their first names, indicative of their informality and warmth. In light of the positive relations shared between the two, the countries have engaged with each other on several fronts. Currently, both countries are exploring joint collaboration in new areas such as cybersecurity, renewable energy and the establishment of a robust start-up ecosystem in India.

Factors Shaping India's Approach to Israel

The expansion of India's relations with Israel, especially under the leadership of Modi, has been influenced by several domestic and international factors. With respect to the deepening of defence ties between the two countries, the following factors have played a major and overpowering role: Firstly, the growing national security challenge faced by India from China and Pakistan has necessitated the modernisation of its armed forces in terms of acquisition of more advanced weaponry and technology. The intelligence failures during the Pathankot and Uri attacks and terror strikes in Mumbai in 2008 have highlighted gaps in India's intelligence system and coastal surveillance capabilities respectively. In addition, India's recent confrontation with China has underlined the urgent requirement of multiple security systems to safeguard Indian borders.[7]

Secondly, India's progress in the development of indigenous defence equipment and systems has been relatively slow.[8] For instance, the Report of the Comptroller and Auditor General (CAG) in 2018 highlighted the unwarranted interruption in the home-grown advancement in the development of unmanned aerial vehicles (UAVs) led by the Defence Research and Development Organisation (DRDO).[9] The Report further underscored that the UAVs so developed, failed to meet the user's requirements despite incurring a cost of INR 79.75

crore in their procurement.[10] Additionally, the setback in the progress of the Medium Altitude Long Endurance UAV system development had an adverse effect on the Indian Army's aerial surveillance capability.[11] Thus, India has sought more dependable partners such as Israel which has expertise in UAVs and surveillance systems.[12] India has also procured radars from Israel due to the unavailability of indigenous technologies to enhance surveillance on its borders.[13]

The economic factors have also contributed significantly in shaping India-Israel relations. Israeli technology and its advanced expertise in various sectors have benefited the Indian economy in areas such as water management, agriculture, cybersecurity and healthcare. The recognition of these benefits by the Indian policy makers has incentivised them to further explore avenues for deepening ties with Israel to provide solutions to problems associated with India's economic development.

In addition, certain changes in the geopolitical dynamics have dictated India's enhanced engagement with Israel. The gradual shift in the perception of the Arab countries regarding Israel has provided an opportunity for India to engage more freely with Israel. The reduced hostility towards Israel among the major Arab countries, such as Egypt, Jordan, Turkiye, UAE, Saudi Arabia, and Bahrain has changed the regional realities. A further impetus to the relations was provided by the signing of the Abraham Accords on 15 September 2020 between Israel and the UAE, followed by Bahrain. This removed the strategic obstacles for India to actively expand its ties with Israel and opened the doors for multilateral cooperation with the West Asian countries along with Israel as one of the partners. The inaugural virtual gathering in October 2021 featuring the foreign ministers of India, Israel, the UAE and the US (I2U2) followed the principles of the Abraham Accords.

In addition to aiding India's increased engagement with Israel, the growing convergence between Israel and the Arab countries has also made it easy for India to de-hyphenate its relations vis-a-vis Israel and Palestine. This has enabled India to have a relationship with Israel independent of its ties with the Palestinians, thereby being able to follow a more pragmatic policy focussing on its best interests.[14]

High-Level Visits Between India-Israel Since 2014

The initial encounter between the Prime Ministers of both nations, Narendra Modi and Benjamin Netanyahu, during the United Nations General Assembly (UNGA) in September 2014 signalled an era of deepened relations between both countries. During the meeting, Netanyahu highlighted the opportunities for collaboration between the two countries by saying that "sky's the limit" when it comes to cooperation between the two countries.[15] A year later, in March 2015, Modi met with the President of Israel, Reuven Rivlin, in Singapore.[16] At the meeting, the Israeli President reiterated an invitation to Modi to visit Israel. Henceforth, several other important visits by leaders from the two countries took place, including a visit by the Israeli Minister of Agriculture Yair Shamir (January 2015), Defence Minister Moshe Ya'alon (February 2015), Indian Union Home Minister Rajnath Singh (November 2015) and then Foreign Minister Sushma Swaraj (January 2016). All these early meetings were indicative of India's foreign policy shift towards Israel.

President Pranab Mukherjee's first visit to Israel in October 2015, signified another breakthrough in bilateral relations. This set the stage for the future visit by the Indian Prime Minister, Narendra Modi. During the visit, President Mukherjee addressed the Israeli Members of Parliament in a special Knesset session, expressing that his trip to Israel coincided with a period of increasingly positive developments in relations between the two governments.[17] Shortly after the visit of the President, External Affairs Minister Sushma Swaraj paid a visit to Israel in January 2016.[18] She met with Prime Minister Netanyahu and discussed various issues related to bilateral relations, particularly, security, science and technology, cyber security, education, research and innovation, water and agriculture. Both leaders also discussed possibilities to expand cooperation in business and education sectors.[19] The conducive environment being provided by the shift in perception among the Arab countries regarding Israel played an enabling role for India to productively engage with Israel.

Thus, within the first few months of Modi's premiership, Israel became an important part of India's "constructive engagement" with West Asia, and Israel was integrated within India's wider regional policy rather than being treated as a special case. Significant importance began to be given to expanding cooperation in the non-defence areas, such as science and technology, drinking water and sanitation, agricultural cooperation, space research, innovation and cyber security. This was clearly evident in the agreements and MoUs that both the countries signed in July 2017 during Modi's visit to Israel. Since this was the first time an Indian Prime Minister visited Israel, it marked a big shift in India's foreign policy towards Israel. Prime Minister Modi's decision of not to visit Palestine during the trip, broke all previous conventions and came to be described as the "de-hyphenation" of India's relations with Israel and Palestine.[20]

From 14 to 19 January 2018, Israeli Prime Minister Benjamin Netanyahu visited India to celebrate the silver jubilee of the India-Israel relationship and the growing partnership between the two. Accompanied by a 130-member business delegation, Netanyahu aimed at solidifying trade relations. On 15 January 2018, the leaders shared a joint statement and said that both countries "share a common vision for the relationship." In addition, both countries agreed that "in the next twenty-five years the two respective countries should strive to raise bilateral cooperation in diverse sectors to a qualitatively new level in consonance with our Strategic Partnership."[21] During the visit, Netanyahu held comprehensive talks with Modi and also visited his home state Gujarat, where the two leaders participated in a joint road show. Both the leaders signed "four government-to-government agreements on cyber security, oil and gas cooperation, film co-production and air transport, along with five other semi-government agreements."[22]

Netanyahu also delivered the keynote address at the Raisina Dialogue in 2018, organised by the Observer Research Foundation. In his speech, he emphasised on deepening collaboration in all the areas of cooperation. He also highlighted the common security challenges for both nations and emphasised on strengthening the "India-Israel alliance." The use of the term alliance was significant to understand the deepening ties between the two countries. The visit was the final step in the process of full normalisation of bilateral relations.

The developments before the visit, such as India's General Assembly vote on Jerusalem[23] and the signing of a US$ 2 billion rail deal with Iran,[24] highlighted that India was vigilantly balancing its policy with the other actors in the region as well. However, during Netanyahu's visit, both countries agreed to strengthen relations in areas that improve the well-being of people, such as agriculture, security and science and technology. Discussions were held on developing more Centres of Excellence, key pillars of agricultural cooperation, with the aid of sophisticated Israeli practices and technology. In addition, India also welcomed "Israeli companies to take advantage of the liberalised Foreign Direct Investments (FDI) regime to make more in India with Indian companies."[25] The visit emphasised on traditional domains of collaboration between India and Israel, including agriculture and defence, while also expanding cooperation into less explored sectors like energy resources (oil and gas), cybersecurity, start-ups, and the film industry.

As part of the visit, nine MoUs and agreements, including those on cyber-security, gas and oil sector, Amendments to the Air Transport Agreement, Agreement on Film co-production, cooperation in the field of Research in Homoeopathic Medicine, MoU on cooperation in the field of space, memorandum on investment, were signed.[26] A Letter of Intent (LoI) for "cooperation in the domain of metal-air batteries and concentrated solar thermal technologies" was also signed. As an encouragement to Indian innovation, Netanyahu and Modi dedicated iCREATE[27] to the nation in order to create an ecosystem in India to produce quality entrepreneurs.[28]

Indo-Israel relations which were previously limited mostly to defence collaborations, now expanded to non-defence areas with a major thrust given by India on leveraging the innovation capabilities of Israel in various fields and domains.

India-Israel Defence Cooperation

Since the recognition of Israel in 1950, defence ties have been the cornerstone of India-Israel relations, although marginally documented in the pre-normalisation period (1950-1992).[29] After the India-China War in 1962, India expressed its willingness to seek consultation from Israeli specialists regarding security matters. In the following years, the two nations shared frequent off-the-record visits of dignitaries including a secret visit by Moshe Dayan in 1977.[30] Both the countries also shared covert intelligence ties under the leadership of Prime Minister Indira Gandhi (1966-1977 and 1980-1984) and Rajiv Gandhi (1984-1989).[31] Since the normalisation of relations in 1992, defence ties have deepened consistently. In the mid-1990s, India bought Ramta two Super Dvora Mark II attack boats from the Israeli Aerospace Industries (IAI) and secured the "licence to build the remaining at Goa Shipyard in collaboration with Ramta in 1997."[32] Furthermore, India procured Electronic Support Measure Sensors, 32 IAI Searcher UAVs and Instrumentation simulator systems from Israel.[33] Israel has also played an instrumental role in upgrading Russian-made ground attack aircraft, MiG-21, for the Indian Air Force.[34] In 1999, Israel's vital support to India in the Kargil War made it a dependable partner for India's defence requirements.

In the post-normalisation period, India procured various equipment from Israel, including but not limited to, assault rifles (Tavor), Sniper rifles (Galil), Harpy and Harop loitering anti-radiation drones, Spike anti-tank missiles, Barak-1 air-defence missile, the Green Pine missile-defence radar, night/adverse weather precision-targeting pod, Spyder air-defence system, radars, Python-4 air-to-air missile, fire-control missiles, Phalcon airborne warning and control systems (AWACS).[35] From 1997 to 2000, India accounted for 15 per cent of total Israeli arms exports, which further increased to 27 per cent by mid-2000.[36]

The defence ties further deepened under Prime Minister Modi's leadership. Data on defence trade since 2014, compiled by the Stockholm International Peace Research Institute (SIPRI) indicates that approximately 42.1 per cent of Israel's arms exports have been directed to India, with Azerbaijan (13.9 per cent), Vietnam (8.5 per cent), and the US (6.2 per cent) constituting the other significant customers.[37] SIPRI also underlined that the weapon deliveries to India from Israel witnessed a 175 per cent increase in 2015-2019[38] rendering Israel the second largest supplier of major arms to India. In addition, exports from Israel increased by 19 per cent between 2012-16 and 2017-2021.[39]

From 2014, Israel has turned out to be an important player in India's defence market along with Russia and France. In October 2014, a contract for procurement of *Barak-1* missiles was signed with Rafael

Advanced Defence Systems Ltd.[40] The defence ties have further strengthened because of the joint development projects. For instance, in January 2006, the Defence Research and Development Organisation (DRDO) and the IAI, signed a contract to co-develop a long-range surface-to-air missile (LRSAM) for India's naval forces.[41] The first batch of five LRSAMs was handed over by DRDO in 2017.[42,43] In the same year, India also signed a MoU worth US$ 1.6 billion with Israel for the development of MRSAMs for the Indian ground forces, the first test of which was conducted in December 2020.[44]

In 2017, a joint venture between Indian and Israeli companies, namely, Kalyani Rafael Advanced Systems Ltd (KRAS) commenced manufacturing of *Spike* anti-tank guided missiles for Indian forces.[45] Reportedly, India procured over 200 *Spike* missiles and their launchers from Israel for the Indian Army through the emergency procurement route in February 2020.[46] In addition, India reportedly inked a US$ 200 million deal with Israel for the procurement of software-enabled radios, bomb guidance kits and anti-tank guided missiles (ATGMs).

Apart from radars, UAVs and missiles, India and Israel also deepened their relations in the fields of small arms and ammunition. Indian forces are using Israeli small arms such as Tavor, Uzi, Negev and Galil rifles. In 2020, India ordered 16,000 Negev NG-7 light machine guns (LMGs) to deal with increasing ceasefire breaches from Pakistan. Similarly, under Make in India initiative, Punj Lloyd is collaborating with Israel Weapon Industries (IWI) to produce small weapons (Tavor) in India under "a complete technology transfer arrangement."[47] Indian and Israeli armed forces collaboratively engaged in joint training exercises which helped in strengthening relations. In 2017, for the first time, an Indian Air Force (IAF) contingent comprising 45 members participated in the Blue Flag Exercise (A multilateral Exercise organised in Israel) along with France, Greece, Germany, Italy, the US and Poland.[48] In 2021, India again participated in the same Exercise and its contingent included Mirage 2000 and Rafale aircraft. Indeed, the joint military exercises have played a vital role in deepening the synergy between the two forces.[49]

In 2022, to boost defence ties and discuss avenues for further enhancing security relations, various high-level visits were made from India to Israel. This includes a visit by India's Chief of Air Staff Air

Chief Marshal Rakesh Kumar Singh Bhadauria (3 August 2021)[50] and Army Chief General Manoj Mukund Naravane's visit (15-19 November 2022).[51] Air Chief Marshal Bhadauria's visit to Israel was a significant milestone for the ties of the Air Forces of the two countries. During the visit, both countries discussed issues of mutual interest and bilateral defence cooperation. In addition, both also shared their vision for further strengthening of bilateral engagements and multidisciplinary professional exchanges. In November 2022, General Naravane's visit focused more on the aspects of border management and counter-terrorism practices.

In addition, a five-day visit to Israel was made by Indian External Affairs Minister, S. Jaishankar, in October 2021, marking a milestone in the relations between India and Israel with the announcement of the formation of the I2U2. During this visit, a decision was made to create a joint task force to identify new domains for defence collaboration through the formulation of a comprehensive ten-year roadmap.[52] On 2 June 2022, the visit of Israeli Defence Minister Benjamin Gantz played a significant role in deepening the defence ties. During the visit, both countries agreed to advance joint military training, weapons research and development.[53] To strengthen collaboration in the realm of Futuristic Defence Technologies, a Letter of Intent was also exchanged between the two Ministers.[54]

Table 4.1: Major Israel Weapons Used by Indian Armed Forces

	Weapon	*Description*
Ariel Vehicles	Searcher	UAV
	Heron	UAV
Air Defence Systems	SPYDER	SAM System
	BARAK-LR	SAM System
Missiles	BARAK-8	SAM
	Derby	BVRAAM
	Python-5	BVRAAM
	SPICE-2000	Guided Bomb
	Griffin	Guided Bomb
	Harop	Loitering Ammunition
	Crystal Maze	ASM
	Barak-1	SAM

	Weapon	*Description*
Sensors	EL/M 2075 Phalcon	AWACS
	EL/M 2032	Combat Aircraft Radar
	EL/M 2248 MF-STAR	Multi-function RADAR
	EL/M 2221 STGR	Fire Control RADAR
Small Arms	Carmel	Assault Rifle
	UZI	Submachine Guns
	ARAD	Multi-Caliber Assault Rifle
	Tavor	Assault Rifle
	Galil	Sniper Rifle
	UZI Pro	Sub Machine Gun
	Israeli Tavor X95	Assault Rifle
	Negev	Light Machine Gun

Source: SIPRI[55] and Middle East Eye.[56]

Cooperation in Security and Border Management

Internal security and border management are the two other areas of India-Israel cooperation. Common security challenges of terrorism and radicalisation impacting the people of both countries have provided a solid ground for robust cooperation in these areas. To deal with the threats posed by terror groups, the two countries formed a Joint Working Group for Counter Terrorism in 2002 and this group has served as a platform to share the field experiences on border security, suicide terrorism, terror financing and cyber warfare.[57] In October 2021, the 15th gathering of the Joint Working Group on Counter-Terrorism took place, during which India and Israel concurred to establish "a task force to formulate a comprehensive Ten-Year Roadmap to identify new areas of cooperation."[58]

The cooperation in areas of internal security has significantly improved since the Mumbai attacks of 2008. The attacks highlighted the challenges which India was facing in managing its borders and in dealing with the terrorist attacks. As a result, Israel came forward to help India by providing "satellite photo imagery, unarmed aerial vehicles, hand-held thermal imagers, night vision devices, long-range reconnaissance and observation systems (LORROS), and detection equipment for counterterrorism purposes."[59] In November 2016, during the Israeli President Reuven Rivlin's meeting with Modi on his visit to India, counter-terrorism was a focal point of the deliberations.[60] To expand the cooperation in Homeland and Public Security, an Agreement was signed in February 2014[61] in pursuance of which regular institutional interactions have taken place. The Agreement facilitated the formation of "four working groups in areas of border management, internal security and public safety, capacity building and police modernisation with the objective of preventing and combating crime and cybercrime."[62] The groups frequently hold meetings in both countries.

Border management is another area where Israel has shared its technological know-how with India. In November 2014, Home Minister Rajnath Singh reviewed the Israeli border management technology while visiting Israeli bordering territories along with the Israeli National Security Adviser, Yossi Cohen. Since then, there were media reports suggesting that India acquired "high-technology border-fencing solutions" from Israel which was later confirmed by the Director General Border Security Force (BSF), K.K. Sharma in July 2018. He confirmed that India was using Israeli technology and methods in the Comprehensive Integrated Border Management System (CIBMS), which was a pilot project started by the Government of India in 2016.[63]

India and Israel have close ties in the intelligence domain as well. The roots of intelligence cooperation can be traced to 1968 when India established the Research and Analysis Wing. According to the reports, its first director "R.N. Kao was tasked by Prime Minister Indira Gandhi to establish ties with Israel's Mossad."[64] However, details regarding the same are largely classified. Media reports suggest that India imported critical intelligence-gathering technologies from Israel and regularly exchanged officials from the intelligence community. Both nations also exchange real-time intelligence to combat the issue of terrorism.[65]

India-Israel Economic Ties

On the economic front, India-Israel bilateral trade has continued to grow. In 2022-23, the total trade between the two countries was worth US$ 10.8 billion, with the balance of trade in India's favour. The total trade has jumped from US$ 7.8 billion in 2021-22 to 10.8 billion in 2022-23.[66] While imports fluctuated, the Indian exports to Israel rose from US$2.8 billion in 2015 to US$ 3.7 billion in 2019. The period of COVID-19 pandemic resulted in a fall in total trade between the two countries (2019 to 2021). However, as the countries recovered, the value of total trade saw a major jump from US$ 4.6 billion in 2020-21 to US$ 10.8 billion in 2022-23. In addition to the increase in the value of total trade, there has been diversification in the products being traded between the two countries over the years, encompassing new goods and services such as pharmaceuticals, agriculture, homeland security and IT and telecom.[67]

In terms of cross-country investments, the inflow of Foreign Direct Investment (FDI) from Israel in India amounted to US$ 284.96 million from April 2000 to March 2022.[68] Indian investments in Israel as of June 2022 were to the tune of US$ 131.85 million.[69] In July 2022, Israel's Gadot Group and India's Adani Ports and Special Economic Zone Ltd (APSEZ) successfully secured the bid for privatising the Port of Haifa. By securing the tender of US$ 1.18 billion, "the Adani-Gadot consortium holds the right to buy 100 per cent shares of Haifa Port Company Ltd."[70]

Previously, some major Indian companies such as Infosys, Tech Mahindra and Wipro Infrastructure Engineering have also made significant acquisitions and investments in Israel during 2015-2016. In 2017, Saisanket Enterprises Private Limited, an Indian company, took over the Israeli firm Shtula, while in January 2019, India's Lohia Group assumed control of the Israeli defence company Light and Strong.[71] As far as investments from Israel into India are concerned, Government of India data shows that "more than 300 investments have been made especially in the high-tech and agricultural domain."[72]

Additionally, the countries are also negotiating a Free Trade Agreement (FTA) which will expand the volume of trade between the two. Thus, the economic engagements are not only making great strides in magnitude but also in terms of composition.

Table 4.2: India-Israel Bilateral Trade (in US$ Millions)

Sl. No.	Year	Export	Import	Total Trade
1	2014-2015	3,289.85	2,328.04	5,617.89
2	2015-2016	2,821.18	2,095.33	4,916.50
3	2016-2017	3,087.16	1,961.12	5,048.28
4	2017-2018	3,364.05	2,066.51	5,430.56
5	2018-2019	3,717.98	1,931.58	5,649.56
6	2019-2020	3,363.10	1,592.70	4,955.80
7	2020-2021	2,701.49	1,960.19	4,661.68
8	2021-2022	4,796.13	3,073.79	7,869.92
9	2022-2023	8,451.47	2,323.19	10,774.66

Source: Ministry of Commerce, Government of India.

Agriculture and Water Cooperation

The saga of India-Israel agricultural relations began after the signing of a comprehensive work plan for agricultural cooperation, on 10 May 2006. Thereafter, the relations in the agricultural domain have improved significantly. Since 2014, there has been growing cooperation between India and Israel in agriculture, as Israel is recognised for its unique expertise in the field. Both parties are collaboratively operating within the framework of a Five-Year Joint Work Plan for strategic cooperation in agriculture and water.[73]

As part of the three-year joint programme (2018-21), the Indo-Israel Agricultural Project (IIAP) set up 30 Centres of Excellence (CoE) across 21 Indian states, majorly focussing on vertical farming, soil solarisation and increasing productivity.[74] Additionally, two more such Centres are being opened in Jammu & Kashmir.[75] Through these CoEs, Israel shares its best practices and know-how and provides a suitable platform for technology transfer to Indian farmers. The Government of India and Israel's Agency for International Development Cooperation (MASHAV), are also in the process of expanding collaboration towards Indo-Israel Villages of Excellence (IIVOE) wherein CoEs, tailored to local conditions, shall disseminate Israel's novel technologies and methodologies. The goal is to reshape 74 villages in India. The IIVOE shall include modern agriculture infrastructure such as precision agriculture solutions, agro-machinery, cold chain facilities, etc.; capacity building through training of farmers and agribusiness training; and digital marketing platforms.[76]

In September 2022, a two-week training programme on horticulture management, "Horticulture Management: The Israeli Value Chain" organised by MASHAV, was concluded by a third major delegation of 19 agricultural officers from seven states in India. As a part of this, the delegation visited orchards, vegetable farms and nurseries, to explore the potential of importing Israeli planting varieties suitable for India.

Table 4.3: List of India-Israel Centre of Excellence in Indian States

Sl. No.	*State*	*Centre of Excellence*
1.	**Haryana (4)**	Vegetables, Karnal Fruits, Mangiana Mango, Ladwa Beekeeping, Ram Nagar
2.	**Gujarat (3)**	Mango, Junagarh, Talala Vegetables, Vadrad Date palm, Bhuj
3.	**Karnataka (3)**	Veg, Dharwad Pomegranate, Bagalkot Mango, Kolar
4.	**Maharashtra (4)**	Mango, Dapoli Citrus, Nagpur Pomegranate, Rahuri Mango, Aurangabad
5.	**Punjab (3)**	Fruits, Hoshiarpur Vegetables, Kartarpur Brackish Water, Bhatinda
6.	**Rajasthan (3)**	Citrus, Kota Pomegranate, Bassi Date Palm
7.	**Tamil Nadu (2)**	Floriculture, Thally Vegetables, Dindigul
8.	**Mizoram (1)**	Citrus, Lunglei
9.	**Uttar Pradesh (2)**	Vegetables, Kannauj Mango, Basti
10.	**Andhra Pradesh (1)**	Vegetables & Flowers, Kuppam
11.	**Telangana (1)**	Vegetables & Flowers, Jeedimetla
12.	**Bihar (2)**	Vegetables, Chandi-Nalanda Mango, Desri-Vaishali
13.	**West Bengal (1)**	Vegetables, Chinsurah, Hooghly

Source: Government of Israel.[77]

In water resource management, India is the only country where a Water Attache has been stationed by Israel at its Embassy. Israel is a world leader in water management and recycling. While India adopted Israeli drip irrigation in 1993, two major pacts were inked during the visit of Prime Minister Narendra Modi to Israel in 2017, including one on the National Campaign for Water Conservation in India and the other on the reform of state water utility in India, between the Uttar Pradesh Jal Nigam and the Ministry of National Infrastructure, Energy & Water Resources.[78] The countries also officially endorsed the Strategic Partnership on Water in 2018. Furthermore, technological know-how is being provided by 32 Israeli water projects in 13 Indian states. More than seven desalination plants in India are using Israeli technology.[79] In 2018, the Gal-Mobile, a desalination and purification jeep, was gifted by Israel to India, which was transferred to the BSF to help them avail high-quality drinking water during operations in difficult arid terrains. This can also be used during natural disasters and for providing drinking water to rural areas.[80]

Israel is also considering investing in the Bundelkhand region to solve the problem of water scarcity.[81] At the 17th Everything About Water Expo on 4 August 2022 to strengthen Indo-Israel cooperation in the water sector, the Israeli companies shared solutions related to water distribution and management, desalination, wastewater treatment and filtration.[82]

Cooperation in Health and Medicine during COVID-19

The expansion of ties in the areas of health and medicine is another milestone in India-Israel ties. The two countries inked an Agreement on Cooperation in the fields of Health and Medicine on 21 December 2020. The Agreement envisions deepening the partnership in "the health sector, including research and development, between the two countries."[83] According to the Agreement, the countries would exchange and train medical practitioners and other health professionals, share regulatory information regarding pharmaceuticals, medical devices, cooperate in developing climate-resilient hospitals along with promoting research and development in several relevant domains.[84]

Since the beginning of the COVID-19 pandemic, India and Israel have been closely cooperating with each other. During the initial and difficult period of COVID-19, Prime Minister Modi conversed with Netanyahu multiple times on telephone wherein both discussed possible areas of collaboration to fight the pandemic. Some of these areas include "improving the availability of pharmaceutical supplies, innovative use of high technology, cooperation in research and development efforts in the fields of vaccines, therapeutics and diagnostics." [85] Due to COVID-19 restrictions, interactions were "held virtual[ly] including the First India-Israel Policy Planning Dialogue on 21 October 2020 and the 16th Foreign Office Consultations on 7 December 2020."[86]

Amidst the COVID-19 crisis, both countries expressed solidarity with each other in their fight against the global pandemic. A shipment of medicines weighing five tonnes, which included the anti-malarial drug hydroxychloroquine, considered a potential treatment for COVID-19, was sent by India to Israel.[87] In July 2020, Israel reciprocated by sending a special flight with researchers, defence experts and advanced medical equipment (ventilators) on board, for India's aid.[88] The delivery was made following an exceptional approval from the Israeli Government. Additionally, scientists from both nations collaborated to create a rapid COVID-19 testing kit.[89] On 12 August 2020, as part of its pandemic aid to India, the Israeli Government provided state-of-the-art Artificial Intelligence technologies as well as high-end equipment to the All India Institute of Medical Sciences (AIIMS).[90] In addition, the Prime Ministers of both countries discussed ways to combat the pandemic at a meeting on the sidelines of the COP-26 climate summit in Glasgow on 2 November 2021.[91] Moreover, during Jaishankar's visit to Israel on 17-21 October 2021, both countries agreed to recognise each other's COVID-19 vaccine certificates.[92] By expressing solidarity towards each other during the testing times of COVID-19, India and Israel have displayed a stronger humane bond.

Science and Technology Cooperation

Under Prime Minister Modi's leadership, considerable emphasis has been placed on broadening collaboration with Israel in the fields of science and technology. In this regard, a MoU to establish the India-

Israel Industrial R&D and Innovation Fund (i4F) by the Department of Science and Technology (India) and the National Authority for Technological Innovation (Israel) was signed in July 2017 during Modi's visit to Israel. This Fund has sponsored more than ten projects so far including "the Apollo-Zebra Medical Artificial Intelligence-based project for the early detection of tuberculosis."[93]

Similarly, in September 2020, Israel's Start-Up Nation Central (SNC) and India's International Centre for Entrepreneurship and Technology (iCREATE) signed a bilateral programme to boost innovation and cooperation in the area of technology.[94] To achieve the objective of iCREATE, 93 problem statements from 25 Indian companies were gathered during the programme and after a tough shortlisting procedure, five innovators were selected for the first India-Israel Innovation Accelerator (i3A) that began on 22 February 2021.[95] By February 2021, iCREATE supported over 262 innovations and 20 patents,[96] to deliver commercially profitable innovative technological solutions.[97]

To promote innovation in start-ups, the DRDO and the Directorate of Defence Research & Development (Israel) entered into the Bilateral Innovation Agreement (BIA), which will help both countries to develop dual-use technologies.[98] The agreement fosters the development of cutting-edge technologies and products in domains like Drones, Artificial Intelligence, Brain-Machine Interface, Robotics, Biosensing and Natural Language Processing, to name a few.

To expand cooperation in the cyber domain, in July 2020, the Ambassador of India to Israel, Sanjeev Singla and Yigal Unna, Director General of Israel's National Cyber Directorate signed an agreement on cyber security. During Prime Minister Modi's visit to Israel in 2017, both nations acknowledged the significance of cooperation in the cyber domain, and in pursuance of the same, an agreement was signed during Netanyahu's India visit in 2018.[99] Currently, various cyber security start-ups are flourishing in India where people from both countries are working together, such as Coralogix and ThinkCyber.

Space Cooperation

Apart from innovation and cyber security, both countries have also widened the areas of cooperation to the realm of Space by signing a

MoU for cooperation in space exploration in January 2018. In March 2018, the Israel Space Agency (ISA) and the Indian Space Research Organisation (ISRO) completed a study on the joint work on electric propulsion for small satellites, and a Plan of Cooperation was entered into in April 2020. In addition, the Chairman of ISRO, K. Sivan and the Director of the ISA, Avi Blasberger, examined the progress made on these projects in July 2021.[100] In 2019, ISRO's launch of the Israeli satellite RISAT-2BR1[101] (November 2019) and Duchifat-3 (December 2019) from Sriharikota launch site, had been another notable collaboration between both nations.[102]

To enhance collaboration and find more avenues in this sphere, Israel's Ambassador Naor Gilon met ISRO Chairman, S. Somanath at the ISRO headquarters in Bengaluru on 22 February 2022.[103] Both agreed to collaborate and commemorate the 30th anniversary of diplomatic ties, through an event held jointly in 2022. India-Israel collaboration in the field of Space underlines the strong desire of the two countries to expand bilateral ties in new domains. Under the changed regional realities in West Asia after the signing of the Abraham Accords, India-Israel cooperation in the Space domain can be expanded to include countries such as the UAE. Although India and Israel have engaged in a few collaborative efforts in the Space domain, their partnership remains relatively limited compared to their respective collaborations with other countries. There is substantial scope in this domain to cooperate, considering the technological advancement in the Space domain between the two countries.

I2U2

While India has bilaterally engaged with the West Asian countries over these years, the Abraham Accords brought about a major change in the regional realities, thereby providing a boost to multilateral engagements of India with Israel and other Gulf countries. The formation of I2U2 in October 2021, was a milestone in this regard. India is aiming to utilise this forum to deepen its engagements with Israel without putting at risk its relations with the Arab nations. In addition, the grouping has also brought the member countries together to cooperate in key areas such as water, transportation, energy, food security, space and health.

The I2U2 grouping underlined a shift in India's approach towards West Asia and created a flourishing ground to advance cooperation in the human security domain.[104] The regional grouping provides India with a great opportunity to avail of "scientific and technological solutions along with foreign direct investments (FDI)" from the other member countries in areas such as water, transportation, food security and clean energy.[105] India can also benefit through strengthened trade relations with the Arab nations and simultaneously aid in the advancement of the economy, peace and prosperity of the region.

On 14 July 2022, the group held its first-ever Virtual Summit which witnessed the participation of Prime Minister Modi along with the Heads of State of Israel, the UAE, and the US. During the meeting, the leaders discussed issues of clean energy and food security. In addition, all four countries agreed on finding "innovative ways to ensure longer-term, more diversified food production and food delivery systems that can better manage global food shocks."[106] At the meeting, it was agreed to extend invitations to the private sectors of the US and Israel to share their knowledge and innovative approaches, thus contributing to the project's long-term viability. Regarding clean energy, it was decided to progress a hybrid renewable energy project in Gujarat, featuring a combined wind and solar capacity of 300 megawatts (MW) and an energy storage system powered by batteries. The feasibility study for the project, funded by the US Trade and Development Agency, received $330 million in funding. The UAE pledged to assist in identifying opportunities for investment partners, while Israel and the US committed to supporting India in exploring opportunities in the private sector.

On 22 February 2023, the four partnering nations discussed sustainable cooperation opportunities at the Abu Dhabi Business Forum, which saw the participation of public and private sector representatives from I2U2 countries.[107] In the same Forum, India also joined the Agriculture Innovation Mission for Climate initiative. On 19 April 2023, I2U2 member countries signed a MoU to form a joint business coalition to encourage the group's key initiatives namely, economic development and food security. The MoU aimed at gathering private sector support for a new economic partnership between the four countries. I2U2 will serve as a valuable platform for

India to attract West Asian businesses and investors to tap its large consumer market. In addition, the group will help India fortify its position in West Asia, both strategically and economically.

Israel-Palestinian Conflict and India

Since the evolution of the Palestinian issue, India has consistently maintained a favourable position towards Palestine. In 1947, when the UN General Assembly adopted Resolution 181, calling for the establishment of two states for Jewish and Arab people respectively, India voted against the resolution. However, over time, India's stance shifted, and it became empathetic towards the Palestinian cause. The Palestinian people have since become an integral part of India's foreign policy. India holds the distinction of being the first non-Arab state to recognize the Palestine Liberation Organisation (PLO) as the sole and legitimate representative of the Palestinian people in 1974. Additionally, India was among the earliest countries to recognize the state of Palestine in 1988. In 1996, India opened its Representative Office in Gaza, which was later relocated to Ramallah in 2003.

India has consistently maintained an independent and steadfast stance on the Palestinian issue, as reflected in its global positioning. This commitment is evident through its active support for the Palestinian cause at the international level. Notably, India co-sponsored the draft resolution affirming "the right of Palestinians to self-determination" and voted in favour of this resolution during the 53rd session of the United Nations General Assembly in 1998.[108] Similarly, India endorsed the UNGA resolution on 29 November 2012, which granted Palestine the status of a "non-member Observer state" at the UN, albeit without voting rights.[109]

Under the premiership of Modi, India has maintained its conventional position vis a vis Palestine, abreast strengthening relations with Israel. On 21 December 2017, India voted in favour of the resolution presented by Turkiye and Yemen in the UN, opposing the US decision to recognize Jerusalem as the capital of Israel.[110] Additionally, India supported the UNGA resolution titled "Protection of the Palestinian Civilian Population" on 13 June 2018.[111] On 16 May 2021, India's Permanent Representative to the United Nations,

T.S. Tirumurti, reiterated India's support for the "Palestinian cause" and its unwavering commitment to the two-state solution at the Security Council.[112] This position was reiterated by the Modi government at the COP28 meeting in Dubai on 1 December 2023, during his meeting with the Israeli President Isaac Herzog.[113] Under the leadership of Modi, India has consistently urged Israel and Palestinian groups, including Hamas and Islamic Jihad, to exercise restraint and refrain from attempting to unilaterally change the existing status quo. The country has also called for timely de-escalation of clashes that periodically erupt between Israel and Palestinian groups.

However, a shift was seen in India's position after the surprise attack on Israel by Hamas on 7 October 2023 wherein India described the attacks as "terrorist attacks", and expressed solidarity with Israel.[114] The promptness of Prime Minister Modi's remarks highlights the importance India accords to its relations with Israel and its zero-tolerance policy towards terrorism. In addition, its position during the ongoing conflict seems like a balancing act between both the parties wherein India supports Israel in its war against terrorism at the same time holding steadfast to its stand on a two-state solution between Israel and Palestine. This was reflected in India's positions in the UN over the issues related to the Israel-Hamas War. On 13 December 2023, India endorsed a UNGA resolution calling for an immediate humanitarian ceasefire in the Israel-Hamas conflict and the unconditional release of all hostages.[115] This marked the first instance of India supporting such a resolution since the war broke out more than two months ago. The same position was reiterated by the External Affairs Minister, Dr. S. Jaishankar, during the High-Level Segment of the 55th Session of the Human Rights Council on 26 February 2024, wherein he highlighted the need for a sustainable resolution to the Gaza crisis and emphasised on the unacceptability of terrorism and hostage taking.[116] Throughout the ongoing conflict, India maintained a cautious and traditional stance, aiming to avoid causing harm to both Israel and the Palestinians.

Conclusion

India's foreign policy acknowledges Israel's geo-political significance.

Since 1992, a gradual improvement was seen in the relations of the two countries especially in the areas spanning defence, health, education, Space, agriculture and water management, to name a few. A major shift has been seen in the relations since 2014, under Modi's leadership. The factors aiding this include a shift in perception about Israel among the Arab countries, as can be seen through the signing of the Abraham Accords. Furthermore, India's closeness has increased due to consistent support from Israel to deal with its security challenges and owing to Israel's technological know-how which has proved a boon for India's defence indigenisation campaign. Israel's backing of India on the Kashmir matter and India's need for modern defence equipment to tackle hostile neighbours and upgrade its military has further enhanced the relations between the two.

Recognising Israel's technological prowess, ranking in innovation and expertise in non-defence areas, India has entered into collaboration in the domains of water resource management, agriculture, health and medicine, science and technology and Space cooperation. Additionally, both countries extended help during the pandemic thereby indicating their increasing commitment to uphold the humanitarian principles while engaging with each other.

While bilateral relations have strengthened with time, the countries are also engaging with each other through multilateral groupings. The I2U2 platform has provided India and Israel a forum to enter into quadrilateral economic partnerships with the US and the UAE. Apart from focussing on defence security, the group aims to incentivise joint investments in the areas of water, transportation, energy, health, food security and Space and thus help India leverage the research and development know-how and promote knowledge and exchange of personnel between the member countries. In terms of geopolitics and geo-economics, being part of this forum shall strengthen India's position at the global level, especially among the West Asian countries, thereby allowing it to tap the economic opportunities in this region.

Since the two countries individually have invested significantly in transforming into knowledge-based economies, their efforts at working jointly on innovation and Research and Development in various fields shall be highly beneficial. In the defence sector, India can positively add to its military might with Israel's assistance, military hardware and weapons procurement. Additionally, India and Israel – with their extremely similar civilizational values of *Vasudhaiva Kutumbakam* (the world is one family) and *Tikun Olam* (heal the world) respectively – can strive to make the world a better place, with their cooperation being ample testimony.

NOTES

1 P.R. Kumaraswamy, "India and Israel: Evolving Strategic Partnership", Begin Sadat Centre for Strategic Studies, 1 September 1998, at https://besacenter.org/india-and-israel-evolving-strategic-partnership-2-2/ (Accessed 4 December 2022).
2 Ibid.
3 Nicolas Blarel, *The Evolution of India's Israel Policy: Continuity Change and Compromise Since 1992*, Oxford University Press, New Delhi, 2015.
4 "India, Israel sign six agreements", *The Times of India*, 9 September 2003, at https://timesofindia.indiatimes.com/india/india-and-israel-sign-six-agreements/articleshow/174162.cms (Accessed 4 December 2022).
5 P.R. Kumaraswamy, no. 1.
6 Nicolas Blarel, no. 3.
7 S. Samuel C. Rajiv, *The India-Israel Strategic Partnership: Contours, Opportunities and Challenges*, Pentagon Press, New Delhi, 2023, p. 19.
8 Ibid.
9 "CAG's Audit Report No. 13 of 2018 on Defence Services (Army)", Comptroller and Auditor General, Government of India, 7 August 2018, at https://cag.gov.in/uploads/PressRelease/PR-Press-13-of-2018-1-05f5f6fb85a2021-47277784.pdf (Accessed 25 December 2022).
10 Ibid.
11 Ibid.
12 S. Samuel C. Rajiv, no. 7, p. 22.
13 Ibid.
14 Herb Keinon, "What is India's de-hyphenation policy toward Israel and why does it matter?", *Jerusalem Post*, 18 January 2018, *at https://www.jpost.com/israel-news/india-israel/what-is-indias-de-hyphenation-policy-toward-israel-and-why-does-it-matter-538170 (Accessed 1 December 2022).*
15 "Home Minister Rajnath Singh to visit Israel," *Gateway House*, 6 November 2014, at https://www.gatewayhouse.in/events/home-minister-rajnath-singh-to-visit-israel/ (Accessed 4 December 2022).
16 P.R. Kumaraswamy, "Modi's stand-alone visit to Israel?", MP-IDSA Comment, 2 January 2017, at https://idsa.in/idsacomments/modi-stand-alone-visit-to-israel_prkumaraswamy_ 020117 (Accessed 4 December2022).
17 Ibid.
18 "Indian EAM Sushma Swaraj to visit Israel", Embassy of Israel New Delhi, 12 January 2016, at https://embassies.gov.il/delhi/NewsAndEvents/Pages/Minister%20of% 20External %20 Affairs%20Sushma%20Swaraj%20to%20visit%20Israel.aspx (Accessed 5 December 2022).
19 Ibid.
20 Kabir Taneja, "The nuances of India's de-hyphenated policy", *Livemint*, 5 Feb 2018, at https://www.livemint.com/Opinion/HcQJgc8h4klmaczOw4BWQM/The-nuances-of-Indias-dehyphenated-policy.html (Accessed 5 December 2022).

21 "India-Israel Joint Statement during the visit of Prime Minister of Israel to India", Ministry of External Affairs, Government of India, 15 January 2018, at https://www.mea.gov.in/bilateral-documents.htm?dtl/29357/IndiaIsrael_Joint_Statement_during_ visit_ of_ Prime_Minister_of_Israel_to_India_January_15_2018 (Accessed 12 November 2022).

22 "India-Israel Bilateral Relations", Ministry of External Affairs, Government of India, 1 June 2019, at https://www.mea.gov.in/Portal/ForeignRelation/India-Israel_relations.pdf (Accessed 1 November 2022).

23 Prabhash K. Dutta, "Why India voted against US, Israel on Jerusalem at United Nations," *India Today*, 22 December 2017, at https://www.indiatoday.in/world/story/why-india-voted-against-us-israel-on-jerusalem-at-united-nations-1114436-2017-12-22 (Accessed 1 December 2022).

24 "Iran Signs $2b Rail Deal with India", *Financial Tribune*, 13 January 2018, at https://financialtribune.com/articles/domestic-economy/79897/iran-signs-2b-rail-deal-with-india (Accessed 1 December 2022).

25 "Press Statement by Prime Minister during Visit of Prime Minister of Israel to India", Press Information Bureau, 15 January 2018, at http://pib.nic.in/PressReleseDetail.aspx? PRID=1516713 (Accessed 1 December 2022).

26 "List of MoUs/Agreements signed during the visit of Prime Minister of Israel to India", Official Website of Prime Minister of India, 15 January 2018, at https://www.pmindia.gov.in/en/news_updates/list-of-mousagreements-signed-during-the-visit-of-prime-minister-of-israel-to-india/ (Accessed 12 June 2023).

27 A centre established to foster entrepreneurship in the areas of food security, water, connectivity, cybersecurity etc., by leveraging creativity, innovation, engineering, product design and leveraging emerging technologies to deal with major issues such as food security, water, connectivity, cybersecurity, etc.

28 "PM Modi, Israeli PM Netanyahu inaugurate iCreate", Official Website of Prime Minister of India, 17 January 2018, at https://www.narendramodi.in/pm-modi-israeli-pm-netanyahu-inaugurate-icreate—538547 (Accessed 1 December 2022).

29 Manjari Singh, "India-Israel Defence Relations: From Longstanding to Robust", *Centre for Land Warfare Studies Journal*, 15(1), 2022, pp 129-139.

30 Jayita Sarkar, "India and Israel's Secret Love Affair", *The National Interest*, 10 December 2014, at https://nationalinterest.org/blog/the-buzz/india-israels-secret-love-affair-11831 (Accessed 12 June 2023).

31 P.R. Kumaraswamy, *India's Israel Policy*, Columbia University Press, New York, 2010, pp. 4-5.

32 "Indian Naval Fast Attack Craft (In Fac) T80 decommissioned after 23 years of service", Press Information Bureau, 8 October 2021, at https://pib.gov.in/PressReleaseIframePage. aspx?PRID=1762095 (Accessed 1 December 2022).

33 "India-Israel: Blowing hot and cold", *Business Standard*, 2 June 2015, at https://www.business-standard.com/article/current-affairs/india-israel-blowing-hot-and-cold-115060200510_1.html (Accessed 11 December 2022).

34 Ibid.

35 S. Samuel C. Rajiv, *The India-Israel Defence and Security Partnership At 30*, MP-IDSA Monograph Series No. 75, at https://www.idsa.in/system/files/monograph/monograph75. pdf (Accessed 6 December 2022).

36 Azad Essa, "India and Israel: The arms trade in charts and numbers", 1 June 2022, at https://www.middleeasteye.net/news/india-israel-arms-trade-(Accessed 6 December 2022). numbers#:~:text=A%20brief%20history,wars%20against%20China%20 and%20Pakistan (Accessed 6 December 2022).

37 Ibid.

38 "Trends In International Arms Transfers", *SIPRI Fact Sheet,* 1 March 2020, at https://www.sipri.org/sites/default/files/2020-03/fs_2003_at_2019_0.pdf (Accessed 5 November 2022).

39 Ibid.

40 S. Samuel C. Rajiv, no. 35.

41 Ministry of Defence, *Annual Report 2009-2010,* Government of India, at https://mod.gov.in/sites/default/files/AR910.pdf (Accessed on 13 June 2023).

42 Ministry of Defence, *Annual Report 2017-18,* Government of India, at https://www.mod.gov.in/sites/default/files/AR1718.pdf (Accessed on 12 June 2023).

43 S. Samuel C. Rajiv, no. 35.

44 Seth Frantzman, "Israel and India test MRSAM air defence system", *Defence News,* 5 January 2021 at https://www.defensenews.com/training-sim/2021/01/05/israel-and-india-test-ofmrsam-air-defence-system (Accessed 17 December 2022).

45 Azad Essa, "India and Israel: The arms trade in charts and numbers", *Middle East Eyes,* 31 May 2022, at https://www.middleeasteye.net/news/india-israel-arms-trade-numbers#:~:text=A%20brief%20history,wars%20against%20China%20and%20Pakistan (Accessed 6 December 2022).

46 "Tel Aviv completes Spike missiles supply to New Delhi: Rafael India head", *The Business Standard,* 5 February 2020, at https://www.business-standard.com/article/news-ani/tel-aviv-completes-spike-missiles-supply-to-new-delhi-rafael-india-head-120020501352_1.html (Accessed 6 December 2022).

47 Tunia Cherian, "Punj Lloyd ties up with Israeli co to manufacture assault rifles in India", *The Hindu Business Line,* 11 January 2018, at https://www.thehindubusinessline.com/companies/punj-lloyd-ties-up-with-israeli-co-to-manufacture-assault-rifles-in-india/article64269107.ece (Accessed 3 November 2022).

48 S. Samuel C. Rajiv, "Blue Flag 2017 and Beyond", MP-IDSA Comment, 1 December 2017, at https://idsa.in/idsacomments/blue-flag-2017-and-beyond_sscrajiv_011217#:~: text=A%2045%20member%20Indian%20Air,Israeli%20Air%20Force%20(IsAF). (Accessed 5 November 2022).

49 "Jaishankar visits Israel's Ovda Airbase to meet IAF contingent taking part in Blue Flag exercise", *The Hindu,* 19 October 2021, at https://www.thehindu.com/news/national/jaishankar-visits-israels-ovda-airbase-to-meet-iaf-contingent-taking-part-in-blue-flag-exercise/article37072122.ece (Accessed 5 November 2022).

50 "IAF Chief in Israel", *The Hindu,* 4 August 2021, at https://www.thehindu.com/news/national/iaf-chief-in-israel/article35732691.ece (Accessed 5 November 2022).

51 "Army Chief Gen. Naravane leaves for Israel on 5-day visit", *The Hindu,* 14 November 2021, at https://www.thehindu.com/news/national/army-chief-gen-naravane-leaves-for-israel-on-5-day-visit/article37484356.ece (Accessed 5 November 2022).

52 "Jaishankar visits Israel's Ovda Airbase to meet IAF contingent taking part in Blue Flag exercise", *The Hindu,* 19 October 2021, at https://www.thehindu.com/news/national/jaishankar-visits-israels-ovda-airbase-to-meet-iaf-contingent-taking-part-in-blue-flag-exercise/article37072122.ece (Accessed 5 November 2022).

53 Yaniv Kubovich, "China Tensions Top Israeli Defence Minister Gantz' India Visit", *Haaretz,* 23 January 2024, at https://www.haaretz.com/israel-news/2022-06-02/ty-article/.premium/israeli-defense-minister-gantz-visits-india-to-mark-30-years-of-security-ties/00000181-23b4-d366-a1f3-afbfa6150000 (Accessed 5 November 2022).

54 "Raksha Mantri Shri Rajnath Singh & his Israeli counterpart Mr Benjamin Gantz hold bilateral talks in New Delhi", Press Information Bureau, 2 June 2022, at https://pib.gov.in/PressReleasePage.aspx?PRID=1830445 (Accessed 5 November 2022).

55 "SIPRI Arms Transfer Database", 25 December 2022, at https://armstrade.sipri.org/armstrade/page/values.php (Accessed 25 December 2022).

56 Azad Essa, "India and Israel: The arms trade in charts and numbers", *Middle East Eye*, 31 May 2022, at https://www.middleeasteye.net/news/india-israel-arms-trade- (Accessed 1 November 2022)

57 Ely Karmon, "India's Counterterrorism Cooperation with Israel", *Perspectives on Terrorism*, 16(2), April 2022, pp. 1-12.

58 "5th India-Israel Joint Working Group meeting in Tel Aviv", Press Information Bureau, 29 October 2021, at https://pib.gov.in/PressReleaseIframePage.aspx?PRID=1767593 (Accessed 27 December 2022).

59 Vinay Kaura, "Indo-Israeli Security Cooperation: Onward and Upward", Begin-Sadat Centre for Strategic Studies, 8 July 2017, at https://besacenter.org/wp-content/uploads/2017/07/522-Indo-Israel-Security-Cooperation-Kaura-final.pdf (Accessed 27 December 2022).

60 Ibid.

61 "India-Israel Relations 2014", Ministry of External Affairs, Government of India, 1 August 2014, at https://www.mea.gov.in/Portal/ForeignRelation/Israel_December_2014.pdf (Accessed 28 December 2022).

62 "India-Israel Relations 2014", Ministry of External Affairs, Government of India, 1 December 2014, at https://www.mea.gov.in/Portal/ForeignRelation/Israel_December_2014.pdf (Accessed 28 December 2022).

63 "Israel fence systems, quick response team at Pakistan borders: BSF DG", *The Economic Times*, 13 July 2018, at https://economictimes.indiatimes.com/news/defence/israel-fence-systems-quick-response-team-at-pakistan-borders-bsf-dg/articleshow/60044263. cms?utm_source=contentofinterest&utm_medium=text&utm_campaign=cppst (Accessed 1 November 2022).

64 Somdeep Sen, "India's deepening love affair with Israel", *Aljazeera*, 9 September 2021, at https://www.aljazeera.com/opinions/2021/9/9/indias-deepening-love-affair-with-israel (Accessed 27 December 2022).

65 "India, Israel share similar challenges from radicalism, terrorism: Jaishankar", *The Economic Times*, 9 September 2021, at https://economictimes.indiatimes.com/news/defence/india-israel-share-similar-challenges-from-radicalism-terrorism-jaishankar/articleshow/87101672.cms?utm_source=contentofinterest&utm_medium=text& utm_campaign=cppst (Accessed 27 December 2022).

66 "Ministry of Commerce Trade data", Government of India at https://tradestat.commerce. gov.in/eidb/iecnt.asp (Accessed 1 November 2022).

67 "India-Israel Bilateral Relations", Ministry of External Affairs, Government of India, 1 January 2022, at https://mea.gov.in/Portal/ForeignRelation/ISRAEL_BILATERAL_brief_ final_2022.pdf (Accessed 1 November 2022).

68 "India-Israel Economic and Commercial Relations", Indian Embassy in Israel, at https://www.indembassyisrael.gov.in/pages?id=nel5a&subid=7 ax9b#:~:text=(c)%20 Israeli%20 investments%20in%20India,tech%20domain%2C%20agriculture%20and%20water (Accessed 1 November 2022).

69 "India-Israel Economic and Commercial Relations", Indian Embassy in Israel at https://www.indembassyisrael.gov.in/pages?id=nel5a&subid=7ax9b (Accessed 1 November 2022).

70 Ibid.

71 "India-Israel Bilateral Relations", Ministry of External Affairs, Government of India, June 2019, at https://www.mea.gov.in/Portal/ForeignRelation/India-Israel_relations.pdf (Accessed 14 December 2022).

72 Ibid.

73 "India, Israel working on 5-year cooperation plan for agriculture, water", *Business Today*, 16 January 2018, at https://www.businesstoday.in/industry/agriculture/story/india-israel-5-year-cooperation-plan-for-agriculture-water-99287-2018-01-16 (Accessed 1 November 2022).

74 Navdeep Suri and Hargun Sethi, "30 years of bilateral ties: What Indo-Israeli relations look like", Observer Research Foundation, 12 September 2022, at https://www.orfonline. org/expert-speak/30-years-of-bilateral-ties-what-indo-israeli-relations-look-like/ (Accessed 1 November 2022).

75 Sunil Bhat, "Israel to open 2 centres of excellence in Jammu and Kashmir as part of agriculture project", *India Today*, 8 November 2022, at https://www.indiatoday.in/india/story/israel-india-agriculture-project-centres-of-excellence-in-jammu-kashmir-2294928-2022-11-08 (Accessed 11 November 2022).

76 "Indo-Israel Villages of Excellence (Iivoe)", Israeli Embassy in India, at https://embassies.gov.il/delhi/Relations/Indo-Israel-AP/Pages/Villages%20of%20 Excellence.aspx (Accessed 1 December 2022).

77 "Indo-Israel Agricultural Project (IIAP) A Growing Partnership", Israeli Embassy in India at https://embassies.gov.il/delhi/Relations/Indo-Israel-AP/Pages/Centers%20of%20 Excellence.aspx (Accessed 21 December 2022).

78 "Water to space: India, Israel ink 7 key strategic pacts during Modi visit", *Business Standard*, 6 July 2017, at https://www.business-standard.com/article/economy-policy/water-to-space-india-israel-ink-7-key-strategic-pacts-during-modi-visit-117070501128_1.html (Accessed 1 December 2022).

79 Ron Malka, "Based on Israel's success story, we want to help India in its quest for water", *The Hindustan Times*, 24 November 2019, at https://www.hindustantimes.com/analysis/based-on-israel-s-success-story-we-want-to-help-india-in-its-quest-for-water-opinion/story-dG8BrpIBsYkH8hurynpyoK.html (Accessed 1 December 2022).

80 Kamaljit Kaur Sandhu, "From Israel to India: A desalination vehicle", *India Today*, 15 January 2018, at https://www.indiatoday.in/india/story/from-israel-to-india-a-desalination-vehicle-1146142-2018-01-15 (Accessed 1 December 2022).

81 "Israel's deal with UP to resolve Bundelkhand water crisis has a 3-pronged solution", *The Hindustan Times*, 20 August 2020, at https://www.hindustantimes.com/india-news/israel-signs-deal-to-resolve-bundelkhand-water-crisis-has-a-3-pronged-solution/story-606PQi6jfeZFoxRFcpq4ZM.html (Accessed 12 December 2022).

82 "India can learn from Israel about water management: Jal Shakti Ministry", *The Print*, 05 August 2022, at https://theprint.in/world/india-can-learn-from-israel-about-water-management-jal-shakti-ministry/1069764/ (Accessed 11 December 2022).

83 "India-Israel Bilateral Relations", Ministry of External Affairs, Government of India, at https://mea.gov.in/Portal/ForeignRelation/ISRAEL_BILATERAL_brief_final_2022.pdf (Accessed 1 November 2022).

84 "Agreement between India and Israel on Cooperation in the fields of Health & Medicine", Government of India, at https://www.indembassyisrael.gov.in/press?id=bqx2a (Accessed 1 January 2022).

85 "India-Israel Cooperation", 24 February 2022, at http://www.mei.org.in/india-speaks-150 (Accessed 1 March 2022).

86 Ibid.

87 "Netanyahu thanks PM Modi for delivering hydroxychloroquine to Israel", *India Toda*, 10 April 2020, at https://www.indiatoday.in/india/story/israel-pm-netanyahu-

thanks-india-pm-modi-delivering-hydroxychloroquine-to-israel-1665302-2020-04-09 (Accessed 11 December 2022).

88 "Supply of medical equipment to India reciprocation of earlier help: Israel", *Business Standard*, 28 July 2020, at https://www.business-standard.com/article/current-affairs/supply-of-medical-equipment-to-india-reciprocation-of-earlier-help-israel-120072800085_1.html (Accessed 10 December 2022).

89 "India, Israel collaborate to develop rapid testing for Covid-19 in under 30 seconds", *The Print*, 23 July 2020, at https://theprint.in/diplomacy/india-israel-collaborate-to-develop-rapid-testing-for-covid-19-in-under-30-seconds/467043/ (Accessed 8 December 2022).

90 Shailaja Tripathi, "Israel shares AI-based Technology, equipment with AIIMS for COVID-19 treatment", *Jagran Josh*, 12 August 2020, at https://www.jagranjosh.com/current-affairs/israel-shares-ai-based-technology-equipment-with-aiims-for-covid-19-treatment-1597233104-1 (Accessed 10 December 2022).

91 "Prime Minister's Meeting with Prime Minister of Israel on the sidelines of COP-26 in Glasgow, UK", Press Information Bureau, 2 November 2021, at https://pib.gov.in/Pressreleaseshare.aspx?PRID=1768998 (Accessed 15 December 2022).

92 "India and Israel agree to recognise corona vaccine certification of each other", *All India Radio*, 19 October 2021, at https://newsonair.gov.in/News?title=India-and-Israel-agree-to-recognise-corona-vaccine-certification-of-each-other&id=428237 (Accessed 10 December 2022).

93 "India-Israel Relations", Ministry of External Affairs, Government of India, at https://mea.gov.in/Portal/ForeignRelation/ISRAEL_BILATERAL_brief_final_2022.pdf (Accessed 11 December 2022).

94 "Israel, India sign MoU to collaborate in tech innovation and start up", *Asian News Agency*, 23 September 2020, at https://www.aninews.in/news/world/asia/israel-india-sign-mou-to-collaborate-in-tech-innovation-and-start-ups20200923005935/#:~:text=The%20 Memorandum %20of%20Understanding%20 (MoU)%20 was%20 signed%20between %20 Israel', projects %2C %20 according %20to%20a%20 statement. (Accessed 11 December 2022).

95 "iCreate helps Indian corporates find innovative solutions from Israel via a Joint Accelerator Programme with SNC of Israel", *Business Standard*, 12 April 2021, at https://www.business-standard.com/content/press-releases-ani/icreate-helps-indian-corporates-find-innovative-solutions-from-israel-via-a-joint-accelerator-programme-with-snc-of-israel-121041201278_1.html (Accessed 11 December 2022).

96 "iCreate and Start-Up Nation Central (SNC) kick off Accelerator Programme with 6 Israeli Start-up", 22 February 2021, at https://www.icreate.org.in/press/bwdisrupt-businessworld/ (Accessed 3 January 2023).

97 Pradipta Roy, "Benjamin Netanyahu's state visit to India," *Israel Affairs*, 25(5), 2019, pp. 788–802.

98 "DRDO & Directorate of Defence R&D, Israel signs Bilateral Innovation Agreement for development of dual use technologies," Press Information Bureau, 9 November 2021, at https://pib.gov.in/PressReleaseIframePage.aspx?PRID=1770299 (Accessed 11 December 2022).

99 "India and Israel sign agreement to expand collaboration in dealing with cyber threats", *India Today*, 16 July 2020, at https://economictimes.indiatimes.com/news/defence/india-and-israel-sign-agreement-to-expand-collaboration-in-dealing-with-cyber-threats/articleshow/76998307.cms?utm_source=contentofinterest&utm_medium=text&utm_ campaign=cppst (Accessed 11 December 2022).

100 S. Samuel C. Rajiv, no. 7.

101 U. Tejonmayam, "ISRO PSLV-C48/RISAT-2BR1 mission: PSLV milestone flight successful, 10 satellites placed in orbits", *The Times of India*, 11 December 2019, at https://timesofindia.indiatimes.com/india/isro-pslv-c48/risat-2br1-mission-pslvs-milestone-flight-successful-10-satellites-placed-in-orbits/articleshow/72472857.cms (Accessed 11 December 2022).

102 Pon Vasanth B. A., "Satellite built by Israeli students successfully put into orbit by ISRO", *The Hindu*, 13 December 2019, at https://www.thehindu.com/news/cities/chennai/satellite-built-by-israeli-students-successfully-put-into-orbit-by-isro/article30290548.ece (Accessed 11 December 2022).

103 "Ambassador of Israel to India met Chairman, ISRO/ Secretary, DOS", Indian Space Research Organisation, 22 February 2022, at https://www.isro.gov.in/Ambassador.htm l#:~:text=Naor%20Gilon%2C%20Ambassador%20of%20Israel, South%20India%20 accompanied% 20the%20Ambassador. (Accessed 6 December 2022).

104 Muddassir Quamar, "I2U2: A New Template for Cross-Regional Cooperation", Issue Brief, Manohar Parrikar Institute for Defence Studies and Analyses, 5 September 2022, at https://www.idsa.in/issuebrief/I2U2-A-New-Template-mm quamar-050922 (Accessed 6 December 2022).

105 Ibid.

106 "Joint Statement of the Leaders of India, Israel, United Arab Emirates, and the United States (I2U2)", Government of United States, 14 July 2022, at https://www.whitehouse.gov/briefing-room/statements-releases/2022/07/14/joint-statement-of-the-leaders-of-india-israel-united-arab-emirates-and-the-united-states-i2u2/ (Accessed 10 September 2022).

107 "I2U2 business forum holds inaugural meeting in Abu Dhabi", *The Hindustan Times*, 23 February 2023, at https://www.hindustantimes.com/india-news/i2u2-business-forum-holds-inaugural-meeting-in-abu-dhabi-101677123402503.html (Accessed 10 March 2023).

108 Seema Guha, "India's Shifting Stand on Israel-Palestine Reflects the Changing Contours of its Foreign Policy", *Outlook*, 12 August 2022, at https://www.outlook india.com/national/india-s-shifting-stand-on-israel-palestine-reflects-the-changing-contours-of-its-foreign-policy-news-215882 (Accessed on 1 January 2024).

109 "India-Israel Relations", Ministry of External Affairs, Government of India, at https://mea.gov.in/Portal/ForeignRelation/Bilateral_Brief-Sept_2019.pdf (Accessed on 2 January 2024).

110 "Why India voted against US, Israel on Jerusalem at United Nations", *India Today*, 22 December 2017, at https://www.indiatoday.in/world/story/why-india-voted-against-us-israel-on-jerusalem-at-united-nations-1114436-2017-12-22 (Accessed on 2 January 2024).

111 "India-Israel Relations", Ministry of External Affairs, Government of India, at https://www.mea.gov.in/Portal/ForeignRelation/Bilateral_Brief-Sept_2019.pdf (Accessed on 2 January 2024).

112 "UNSC Open VTC on The situation in the Middle East" Permanent Representative of India to the United Nations, 16 May 2021, at https://pminewyork.gov.in/IndiaatUNSC?id=NDI0OA (Accessed on 2 January 2024).

113 "PM Modi Meets Israeli President Isaac Herzog on Sidelines of COP28", NDTV World, 1 December 2023, at https://www.ndtv.com/india-news/pm-narendra-modi-meets-israeli-president-isaac-herzog-on-sidelines-of-cop28-4624964 (Accessed on 2 January 2024).

114 "Deeply shocked, says PM Modi on terrorist attack in Israel, says India stands in

solidarity with Tel Aviv", *Business Today*, 7 October 2023, at https://www.businesstoday.in/latest/story/deeply-shocked-says-pm-modi-on-terrorist-attack-in-israel-says-india-stands-in-solidarity-with-tel-aviv-401098-2023-10-07 (Accessed on 12 January 2024).

115 "India votes in favour of UN resolution demanding Gaza ceasefire: Everything you need to know", *Indian Express*, 14 December 2023, at https://indianexpress.com/article/explained/explained-global/india-vote-favour-un-resolution-gaza-ceasefire9066979/#:~:text=India%20on%20Tuesday%20(December%2013, unconditional%20release%20of%20all%20hostages (Accessed 3 January 2024).

116 "Statement by EAM Dr. S. Jaishankar at the High-Level Segment of the 55th Session of the Human Rights Council, Geneva", Ministry of External Affairs, Government of India, 26 February 2024, at https://www.mea.gov.in/Speeches-Statements.htm?dtl/37663/Statement+by+EAM+Dr+S+Jaishankar+at+the+HighLevel+Segment+of+the+55th+Session+of+the+Human+Rights+Council+ Geneva+February+26+2 024#:~:text=The%20humanitarian%20crises%20arising%20from,law%20must%20always %20be%20respected. (Accessed 27 February 2024).

5

India's Approach to Conflicts in West Asia and North Africa

Md. Muddassir Quamar

Introduction

West Asia and North Africa (WANA) region has been beset with conflicts. Some of these are protracted historical conflicts such as the Israeli-Palestinian conflict, the Turkiye-Cyprus conflict, the conflict in Western Sahara and the Kurdish struggle for self-determination. On the other hand, numerous limited conflicts have caused tensions in the region and beyond from time to time. Such conflicts include the four wars between Israel and the Arabs between 1948 and 1973, followed by wars between Israel and Lebanon (1982), Israel and Hezbollah (2006), and Israel and Hamas (2008 onwards) as well as the wars between Iraq and Iran (1980-88) and the Gulf War (1990-91). Besides these wars, almost all regional countries have at one time or another witnessed internal conflicts or/and civil wars with few exceptions. But since the Arab Spring uprisings that erupted in December 2010, regional conflicts, geopolitical rivalries, terrorist attacks and military interventions have threatened the security and stability of the region, and their ripple effects have been felt globally. The 7 October 2023 Hamas attack on Israel and the Israeli military incursion on Gaza in response have again underlined the proneness of the region to armed conflicts.

India too has been affected by the turmoil in the region. Although India does not have problems with any of the regional countries and maintains friendly ties with all of them, regional events acquire significance for India given its multifaceted stakes in the region. Among the key issues that concern India in WANA is the safety and security of its citizens living and working as expatriates in regional countries with a large concentration, estimated at 8.9 million as of 2022,[1] in the six Gulf Cooperation Council (GCC) countries. Besides, India overwhelmingly depends on the regional countries to fulfil its energy security needs and imports large quantities of oil and gas from Saudi Arabia, Iran, Iraq, the UAE, Qatar and other regional countries.[2] Further, WANA is one of the largest trading blocks for India with trade worth US$ 240.94 billion, which comprised nearly 20 per cent of India's total foreign trade in 2022-23.[3] The region is also crucial for the safety and security of maritime trade routes in the Western Indian Ocean vital not only for India's foreign trade but also for global energy supplies and the sea lines of communication (SLoCs) connecting North and South America, Europe and Africa.[4] Finally, WANA is critical for India and the world for containing and defeating global jihadi terror emanating from regional conflicts and turmoil.[5]

For India, therefore, it is vital to manage and minimize the impacts of conflicts in WANA that directly or indirectly affect its interests. Historically, India adopted a policy of maintaining neutrality in regional conflicts, avoiding any military commitments except in the case of United Nations (UN) peace forces[6] and advocating diplomacy and negotiations to resolve disputes and conflicts. These served India well and can be construed as the principle behind India's approach towards regional conflicts. Nevertheless, over the years, India has undertaken rescue and repatriation missions for its nationals stuck in the region in case of conflicts; the largest of which was carried out after Iraq invaded and annexed Kuwait in August 1990.[7] Furthermore, India has developed close maritime security partnerships with regional and global powers for the safety and security of the SLoCs in the Western Indian Ocean as well as for India's coastal security in the Arabian Sea.[8] Besides, there is the institutionalised mechanism for intelligence sharing and exchange of views with the WANA region, directed towards countering terrorism and combating radicalism.[9]

The increased intensity of India's engagements with important regional countries since 2014 has helped improve political, economic and security ties between India and WANA, and in the process has enhanced India's ability to safeguard its interests in the region. Under Prime Minister Narendra Modi, the Indian approach towards conflicts in the region has continued to follow the abiding principles of neutrality and promoting peace through diplomacy. India's growing global stature and improved strategic ties with the region have added weight to the Indian position. This chapter focuses on India's response to select ongoing conflicts in WANA within the context of the significance of the region for India's external relations. The conflicts have been chosen based on the degree of their impact on India's stakes and interests in the region. The chapter first gives a brief sketch of the relevance of the region in Indian foreign policy followed by a discussion on the response of the Government of India. It concludes that India has followed the abiding principles of its foreign policy when responding to conflicts in the region, and the growing strategic ties between India and WANA countries under Prime Minister Modi have helped it safeguard its interests from the adverse impacts of the conflicts.

WANA in Indian Foreign Policy

The WANA region finds a prominent place in Indian foreign policy. Post-independence, as India charted the course of evolving into a major global actor and a leader among newly independent countries, the Government of India gave due importance to developing closer political and diplomatic ties with WANA. Hence, in the early decades after independence, countries like Egypt and Iraq emerged as India's major partners.[10] Nonetheless, the Indian policy towards WANA countries was constrained by domestic, regional and international factors, limiting relations with countries such as Israel, Iran, Saudi Arabia and Türkiye.[11] After the Cold War ended, India gradually began recalibrating its foreign policy with the focus shifting to accelerating economic growth and leaving the trap of a low-income country behind. This required developing close global economic, trade and business ties including with the WANA region. With issues like energy security, migration and remittances, and bilateral trade at the forefront, the Gulf countries including the members of GCC – Bahrain, Kuwait, Oman, Qatar, Saudi Arabia and the UAE – and Iran and Iraq, emerged as India's most important partners in the region.[12] Meanwhile, India also developed closer ties with Israel, with an increased volume of defence trade and cooperation in areas like agriculture and science and technology.[13]

With better political and diplomatic contacts, trade and commercial ties began to develop. One of the key areas where India's trading ties with the region witnessed an increase was in imports of oil and gas. Most of the Gulf countries are rich in hydrocarbon reserves and their economies have revolved around the production and export of petroleum while India's fast-paced economic growth meant an increasing requirement for energy supplies. Domestic production was unable to meet this requirement. The Indian requirement and the Gulf's keenness to find markets formed a strong mutuality of interest. Hence, the Gulf region emerged as one of the most reliable suppliers of hydrocarbons to India and gradually energy security emerged as a pillar in Indo-Gulf relations.[14] As of 2022-23, the Gulf countries' share in India's oil and gas imports was close to 50 per cent. Besides energy security, the number of Indians migrating to the GCC countries increased rapidly in the 1990s to find work in the booming labour-incentive regional economies. Thus, the Indian expatriate population increased from 1.5 million in 1991 to 3.2 million in 2000 and reached nearly 6.5 million in 2010 and as of 2022, an estimated 8.9 million Indians resided in the Gulf.[15] Concurrently, the remittances sent by the expatriate community in the Gulf increased contributing as much as 50 per cent as of 2016-17, although according to media reports, this has declined to 30 per cent as of 2020-21.[16]

An important area where relations began to improve was trade and commerce. While the bulk of the trade was energy imports from the Gulf, Indian exports of food and agricultural products, jewellery, textile, machinery and petroleum products started to increase, resulting in significant growth in trade. Thus, India's bilateral trade with the WANA countries increased from a meagre US$ 9.59 billion in 1996-97 to US$ 240.94 billion in 2022-23.[17] Further, the share of the regional countries in India's foreign trade increased from 13 per cent to 21 per cent during the period. Besides trade, the two-way flow of investments has also been a major source of improved economic relations, particularly with the GCC countries. While the share of foreign direct investments (FDIs) from the region to India witnessed a sharp increase, especially since 2014-15,[18] the number of Indian businesses and investments in the WANA market too has increased significantly in recent years. This has led to a situation wherein trade, investments, energy, expatriates and remittances emerged as the driving force behind India's policy towards the WANA region.

In addition to economic relations, greater political contacts led to improved security and defence cooperation. Maritime security emerged as an important area of priority, given the increased significance of the Western Indian Ocean for India's trade with West Asia, Africa, Europe and North and South America.[19] Piracy in the Horn of Africa, off the coast of Somalia, further boosted maritime security cooperation with the regional countries.[20] Moreover, the need for India's enhanced coastal security in the Arabian Sea guided greater naval and maritime cooperation. Besides, threats from terrorism, radicalism and organised crimes led to improvement in security cooperation through intelligence sharing, institutionalised cooperation and extradition treaties.[21] Gradually, defence and military cooperation were also included, given the shared security interests and friendly relations.

Since 2014, under Prime Minister Modi, India accelerated its efforts towards improving relations with WANA countries. High-level political contacts played a key role with the Gulf countries, especially the UAE and Saudi Arabia, and Israel emerged as the key partner for India in WANA. Other regional countries, Iran, Qatar, Oman, Egypt, Bahrain, Syria, Morocco, and Jordan too featured prominently in India's engagement with the region under Modi. Greater political contacts boosted bilateral investments and closer security cooperation and created an opportunity for rapid growth in trade, besides opening up the defence and security sector for cooperation. The strategic component in India's engagement with WANA got a significant boost under Prime Minister Modi. Thus, India's 'Look West' policy acquired more robust 'Think West' and 'Act West' contours since 2014, with Modi making the Gulf and WANA region a foreign policy priority.[22]

Indian Response to Conflicts in WANA

To explain the Indian response to conflicts in WANA, it might be useful to classify the regional conflicts into three categories: (1) protracted historical conflicts; (2) civil wars or internal conflicts; and (3) conflicts or rivalries among regional countries. As noted earlier, it is not possible to take into account all the conflicts, hence only select conflicts have been chosen for analysis here, based on how significant they are in terms of India's stakes and interests in WANA. Among these are the protracted Israeli-Palestinian conflict, the internal crises in Iraq, Syria, Libya and Yemen and the intra-region rivalries and tensions between Iran and Saudi Arabia, Iran and Israel and the Qatar crisis. Overall, the Indian response has followed the broad principle of Indian foreign policy wherein neutrality, non-intervention and achieving peace through diplomacy form the core. Nonetheless, given the variation in the characteristics of these conflicts and the specific interests at stake, one can also find certain variations, adaptability and evolution in the Indian approach.

Israeli-Palestinian Conflict

Among the most contentious and protracted conflicts in WANA is the Israeli-Palestinian conflict. The complexity of the conflict can be gauged from the fact that it has historical, cultural, ethnic, racial, religious, political, geopolitical and socio-economic manifestations that have remained unresolved for close to a century. While the roots of the problem go much deeper, it was the disintegration of the Ottoman Empire after the First World War and the end of the European colonial enterprise after the Second World War that accentuated the conflict. It led to the first Arab-Israel War in 1948, when Egypt, Syria, Iraq and Jordan marched their militaries into the newly declared State of Israel to prevent the formation of a Jewish State and restore the Arab-Palestinian character of the territory that as of 2024 constitutes Israel, the West Bank, Gaza Strip and East Jerusalem. While Israel withstood the assault and emerged stronger from the War, the conflict did not end leading to many more wars, attacks and killings that continued into the third decade of the twenty-first century even when the regional political scene has changed significantly, with the gradual change in Arab approach towards Israel.[23] Hence from being an Arab-Israeli conflict at the start, the character of the conflict has changed to Israeli-Palestinian.

The 7 October 2023 attack from Gaza on southern Israel by Hamas and Islamic Jihad followed by the massive military operation by Israel Defence Forces (IDF) in response have once again underlined the potency of the conflict in destabilising the region and keeping the Israeli-Palestinian conflict alive. The fact that the Palestinian Authority (PA) led by President Mahmoud Abbas has not joined the conflict indicates the faction-ridden intra-Palestine politics but also underlines the possibility of a change in the character of the Israeli-Palestinian conflict into an Israel-Hamas conflict. Notwithstanding, it is clear that going forward, it is the non-state actors and proxies of Iran which are keeping the violent nature of the Israeli-Palestinian conflict alive. That none of the regional states–including Iran, the staunchest supporter of Hamas–joined the conflict while regional non-state actors (NSAs), such as Hezbollah in Lebanon and Houthis in Yemen, have come out in support of Hamas underlines the threats posed by armed NSAs in the region.[24]

The Indian response to the broader Israeli-Arab and Israeli-Palestinian conflict has been marked by a degree of continuity with a level of adaptability and evolution based on both its foreign policy changes as well as the changing nature of the conflict. One of the key issues that India has maintained since the beginning is its support for the Palestinian right to self-determination and the establishment of a Palestinian State.[25] In that context, since proposing a federal plan in 1947, India has consistently supported a two-state solution in accordance with the Resolutions adopted by the United Nations. Until 1992, when it established diplomatic relations with Israel, India remained closer to the Palestinian side. As relations between India and Israel began to improve, and as the Palestinian issue started to lose its primacy in the region, India's approach also evolved. The growing defence trade with Israel played an important role in changing the dynamics. India has, however, not given up support for Palestine providing aid for nation-building. Politically, it continues to support a two-state solution, even though under Modi, India de-hyphenated its relations with Israel and Palestine.[26] That is, the relations with the State of Israel and the support for Palestinian

Statehood were no longer considered mutually interlinked and now stand on their merit.

On the recurrent conflicts between IDF and Hamas since 2008, and the latest conflagration since October 2023, India maintains that fighting cannot resolve the conflict and leads only to loss of life and that the two sides should cease violence and engage in diplomacy to resolve the problems. India also advocates the revival of the peace process between Israel and Palestine to avoid escalation in violence between IDF and Hamas.[27] During each of the violent conflicts between IDF and Hamas, India has condemned the targeting of civilians and civil infrastructure by both parties. Nonetheless, one can also see a nuanced shift; whereas India was earlier more critical of Israeli actions and ignored Palestinian violence, under Modi, it has also underlined and condemned rocket attacks by Hamas on Israeli civilian targets such as in May 2021.[28] Hence, New Delhi was vocal in condemning the 7 October attack by Hamas as a terrorist act, but simultaneously it refused to condone the continued Israeli occupation and settlements in the Occupied Territories.[29]

Conflict in Iraq and the Rise of the Islamic State

Iraq has faced serious internal turmoil, violence and conflict since the toppling of the Saddam Hussein regime after the US invasion in 2003. The US military action in Iraq was a reaction to the 11 September 2001 attacks in the United States wherein the George W. Bush administration devised the global war on terror policy and attacked Afghanistan (2001) and Iraq (2003). Undoubtedly, the two wars proved disastrous from both American foreign policy and economic perspectives as well as global and regional geostrategic and geopolitical points of view.[30] But its impact on Iraq was even more devastating as it destroyed the country to the extent that it is yet to come out of the cycle of violence and turmoil. After the US forces removed Saddam Hussain, the country went through a brutal phase of insurgency and sectarian violence devolving into a civil war in 2006 that continued until 2008-09. While it was yet to recover from the violence, Iraq felt the ripple effects of the 'Arab Spring' protests leading to the 'Islamic State in Iraq' led by Abu Bakr Al Baghdadi starting a military pursuit to form a Sunni Islamic Caliphate in the

Levant.[31] The rise of the Islamic State (ISIS) terror group sent shock waves across WANA and the world, inspiring jihadi terrorist organisations and lone-wolf attacks in many places.

India also faced serious challenges. Among the pressing issues that emerged was the safety of Indians who were advised against travelling to Iraq.[32] After the abduction of 40 Indians working for an oil company in Mosul in 2014, India started diplomatic efforts to rescue them but could not succeed as they were killed by ISIS. In the meantime, India evacuated thousands of Indians stranded in Iraq. Eventually, in 2018, the Government of India facilitated the return of the remains of those abducted and executed by ISIS to their families after they were discovered in mass graves once ISIS was defeated by American, Iraqi, Kurdish and Iranian forces.[33] While this was one of the problems, India also faced the challenge of ISIS spreading its ideology inside the country through online propaganda and social media attracting scores of Indian Muslim youth towards its ideology. As reports of many Indians trying to migrate to Syria and Iraq to join ISIS began to emerge, Indian security forces took proactive measures to prevent them from going to ISIS territory and to counter the spread of the terrorist ideology among Indian citizens.[34] In addition to taking security-oriented measures, India also took diplomatic steps to engage with the regional countries towards countering terror and combating radicalisation.[35] These measures aided in minimizing the threats from ISIS to India, although the challenge from jihadi terror remains a potent one.

The Syrian Civil War

The crisis in Syria began with the eruption of protests against the Bashar Al Assad regime in March 2011, and within months Syria devolved into a civil war. The inability of the Syrian government to accommodate the protestors' demands and proclivity to use force to suppress dissent and the tendency of the opposition movement to take up arms and call for the fall of the regime worsened the crisis. Political and military interventions from regional powers and external players including Russia, Iran, Türkiye, the Gulf Arab countries and the United States accentuated the crisis. Syria eventually fell into one of the worst humanitarian crises of contemporary times and continues to struggle to come out of it.[36] However, as the civil war progressed, several factors, namely the inability of the opposition groups to put up a united front, the involvement of jihadist forces against the regime, the Iranian, Russian and Hezbollah military support for the Assad forces and the inability of the anti-Assad external forces to build a consensus, tilted the civil war in favour of the Assad regime.

From the Indian point of view, the Syrian crisis was a case of armed uprising and external intervention. India viewed the crisis from the lens of the violation of Syrian unity and sovereignty by both internal and external actors. The Government of India supported the regime from the beginning, underlining the need for an immediate ceasefire and argued against any external intervention even under UN sanction.[37] Through the crisis, India kept its mission in Damascus open and functional and continued to have political exchanges with the Syrian government with several high-level visits from the Syrian side since 2011.[38] In 2016, India sent its Minister of State for External Affairs M.J. Akbar to convey its support for the Syrian government. India's support for the Syrian government was based on friendly relations and the principle of resolution of any dispute in a peaceful and negotiated manner. India argued for a 'Syrian-led' political process for the resolution of the crisis.[39] Besides, India delivered aid worth US$ 6 million to Syria in the form of medicine and essential food items in 2018 to help the government ward off the humanitarian crisis.[40] India has also committed to helping the Syrian government in its effort towards education and capacity building of its youth to come out of the crisis as well as extended support in the fight against COVID-19.

Turmoil in Libya

The problem in Libya started with protests against Muammar Gaddafi's rule in February 2011 that soon devolved into an armed rebellion and a civil war. A North Atlantic Treaty Organisation (NATO) military intervention after the imposition of a United Nations-sanctioned no-fly zone over Libya in March 2011 led to the quick fall of the regime. Within months the rebels with NATO's military help forced Gaddafi to flee into hiding in his hometown in Sirte where he was eventually found and brutally killed in October.[41]

While the NATO intervention ended with the toppling of the Gaddafi regime, the trouble for Libya had just started. Tribal infighting began soon after, and local strongmen, militias and terrorist groups proliferated as the National Transition Council (NTC) was formed to take Libya to an elected and stable government, unable to wield power. A second civil war erupted in Libya in May 2014 and continued until October 2020 when an UN-led ceasefire transpired. However, the situation in Libya is far from stable, with different factions engaged in infighting and no consensus on the way forward. The threats of terrorist groups including ISIS persist while there is no central authority to govern. Involvement of external powers including Egypt, UAE, Russia, France, Italy, United States and Türkiye, has further worsened the quagmire.

India which has historically had friendly relations with Libya was from the start sceptical of the international response to the Libyan crisis. It counselled respecting Libyan sovereignty and avoiding external intervention. It also advocated for peaceful dialogue and a negotiated resolution of the problems. In March 2011, India abstained from the UNSC vote for the imposition of the no-fly zone.[42] It also underlined the need for NATO to stop airstrikes and wait for the government and rebels to come to a political solution.[43] After the end of the first Libyan civil war, India encouraged the Libyan factions to work towards a political solution and supported the NTC towards leading Libya to a stable government. It also provided humanitarian aid to the tune of US$ 2 million in medical and essential supplies through the UN Office of Commissioner for Humanitarian Aid (OCHA).[44] During 2011-12, India advised its citizens against travel to Libya, carried out rescue and repatriation of several thousand of its nationals stranded in the country, and temporarily closed its mission in Tripoli. The mission resumed work in 2012. When the second civil war erupted in 2014, India again had to carry out the rescue and repatriation of its nationals and eventually closed down its mission in April 2019. In August 2021, the Indian embassy in Tunis was concurrently accredited to Libya.[45]

The response to the crisis in Libya reinforced the Indian position of respecting state sovereignty and avoiding external intervention. It advocated the need for political dialogue and non-military solutions to differences and disputes. India was also mindful of the human and commercial costs to the country as well as to India.

Yemen Conflict

Yemen also felt the tremors of the Arab Spring protests in 2011. After months of protests and uncertainty, in February 2012 Ali Abdullah Saleh agreed to step down and hand over power to his deputy Abdrabbuh Mansur Hadi in a GCC-mediated transition. The hope for an elected and more representative government started to fade as no consensus emerged in the National Dialogue. Eventually, in 2014, an agreement was made for the way forward but within weeks the Houthi faction from northern Yemen backtracked and began marching towards Capital Sana'a in September. By January 2015, the Houthis had taken over government buildings in Sana'a and declared the formation of a parallel government forcing Hadi to flee to the southern city of Aden. The Houthi actions were bolstered by political and military support from Iran, while the Hadi government was hoping for Saudi-GCC support to help it maintain its control over Yemen. Hadi eventually fled to Riyadh in March 2015 leading a coalition force of regional allies led by Saudi Arabia to attack Yemen hoping for a quick turnaround forcing Houthis to retreat and enforcing a status quo ante. Nonetheless, nine years after the military intervention, the conflict in Yemen has only festered causing a humanitarian disaster of historical proportions.[46] The conflict has threatened to spread to the whole region with Iran using the situation in Yemen to settle scores with its smaller neighbours as well as with the United States. The internal conflict in Yemen also has manifestations of a proxy war between Iran and Saudi Arabia which has prevented any meaningful political resolution. As of 2024, the situation in Yemen remains uncertain but the change of guard in April 2022 pushing Hadi out of the office and the process of rapprochement between Iran and Saudi Arabia have generated some hopes.

The Indian response to the conflict has been guided by maintaining neutrality and underlining the need to avoid external military interventions. Like the case of Libya, India was forced to undertake a rescue and repatriation mission and brought back nearly 5,000 of its nationals and scores of foreign citizens from Yemen under *Operation*

Raahat.[47] An important Indian concern vis-à-vis the conflict in Yemen is the SLoCs passing through the Gulf of Aden and the choke point of Bab al-Mandab, underlining the need for greater multilateral cooperation for maritime security in the Western Indian Ocean. Despite its neutrality in the fighting, India has been clear that any terrorist actions or targeting of civilian and business infrastructure as has been done by the Houthis in Saudi Arabia and UAE is not acceptable. The Government of India has therefore condemned these attacks[48] and underlined the need for avoiding further escalation and resolving the conflict through the United Nations-led political process, which has achieved limited success in implementing a ceasefire between May and October 2022.

Qatar Crisis

The Qatar crisis started in June 2017 when three GCC members – Saudi Arabia, UAE and Bahrain – along with Egypt decided to impose a political, economic and diplomatic boycott of Qatar – a fellow Arab country and member of the GCC. This was one of the worst crises in the GCC, the only successful regional multilateral organisation in WANA. The main grievances of the Arab quartet were Doha's softer approach towards Iran, its support of regional Islamist organisations, especially the Muslim Brotherhood and its affiliates, Al-Jazeera's and other Qatari-funded media's coverage of internal issues in fellow Arab countries and contrarian foreign policy followed by Doha.[49] Qatar not only dismissed these allegations but termed the boycott as an assault on its sovereignty. It received regional and international support with Iran and Türkiye extending critical political and economic support. The two other members of the GCC, Oman and Kuwait, remained neutral with Oman emerging as an alternative to UAE for Qatar's external trade, while Kuwait led political and diplomatic efforts to resolve the crisis. With Qatar able to withstand the initial setbacks and refusing to give in to Saudi-Emirati demands, and the change in international and regional posture, eventually Riyadh took the lead to resolve the crisis in January 2021. The crisis came to a formal end with the signing of the Al-Ula Declaration,[50] though the tensions among the regional capitals might take longer to fade.

The Indian response to the crisis was prudent and mindful of its stakes and interests in the region. India took a neutral stand. A statement issued by the Ministry of External Affairs, Government of India noted the crisis and underlined that India is "of the view that all parties should resolve their differences through a process of constructive dialogue and peaceful negotiations based on well-established international principles of mutual respect, sovereignty and non-interference in the internal affairs of other countries (sic)."[51] It further noted the significance of peace and prosperity in the GCC countries for regional security and stability and also for the international community. Throughout the crisis, India managed to maintain its relations with individual countries and refused any temptation to attempt mediation or offer a diplomatic office for negotiations. Eventually, when the crisis came to an end, India welcomed it and underscored the importance of reconciliation for both the region and India's relations with the region.[52]

Saudi-Iran Tensions

Iran and Saudi Arabia are two important regional powers in the Gulf and WANA and have been geopolitical rivals for decades. Their relations became sour after the 1979 Islamic revolution in Iran and the two countries seldom see eye-to-eye on any important regional matter.[53] But the geopolitical tension and competition reached new heights during and in the aftermath of the Arab Spring, with both trying to outdo the other to undermine their interest and advance partisan influence. They also see each other as security threats. Both have allied with neighbouring countries and external powers and worked with non-state actors to strengthen their position against the other.[54] Any regional effort or international counsel has failed to bring the two to engage in a meaningful dialogue. For India, navigating this rivalry has required a degree of diplomatic dexterity and political maturity. Both are important bilateral partners and India has important stakes and interests with both of them. Hence, India has kept away from any intermixing of issues between the two Gulf neighbours maintaining a stoic silence on the rivalry and advancing relations with each on its merit. This has helped India to be in good stead and avoid any costly entanglement.

Iran-Israel Proxy War

The other important regional problem wherein Indian interests and stakes can be harmed is the ongoing proxy war between Israel and Iran. Again, both are important regional actors and partners of India. They see each other as serious security threats, and while Iran considers Israel as an illegitimate country formed by the colonial powers and supported by the United States to maintain its regional hegemony, Israel views Iran as an existential security threat because of its ideological rhetoric and arming of proxies such as Hamas and Hezbollah.[55] Israel has become more active in countering the Iranian military threat because of its presence in Syria and Iraq which have of late become the theatre for the fight between the two regional foes. The latest round of fighting between IDF and Hamas in Gaza in response to Hamas's attack on Israel in October 2023 is in some ways an extension of the Iran-Israel proxy conflict. India has to depend on its diplomatic and political capital with the two countries to avoid any entanglements and maintain relations with them mutually exclusive. There are certain challenges, especially as Indo-Israeli relations have thrived in recent years while relations with Iran have remained stagnant because of a variety of factors.[56] Nonetheless, India maintains political and diplomatic neutrality and has been careful not to make any statements on the attacks on Iranian targets in Iraq and Syria by Israeli forces.

Conclusion

The WANA region has been beset with conflicts, violence, civil wars, regional rivalries and geopolitical tensions and competitions. While this has been a problem historically, the situation has worsened during and after the Arab Spring protests. India has vital stakes in the region with energy security, expatriates and remittances, business, trade and investments, maritime security in the Western Indian Ocean, preventing terrorism, radicalism and organised crime making India's immediate priorities in the region. In light of this, the Government of India has invested significant diplomatic and political capital to develop and strengthen relations with the regional countries, and this process has intensified under Prime Minister Modi. Undoubtedly, the conflicts in the region are a threat to India in the sense that they can both, directly and indirectly, harm Indian interests as has been noted in this chapter. India has relied upon a time-tested policy of maintaining neutrality in external conflicts, avoiding and counselling against external interventions and calling for respecting the sovereignty of individual countries, and encouraging peaceful dialogue and political processes, with United Nations mediation, if needed, in responding to these conflicts. These in a way form one of the core principles of Indian foreign policy. At the same time, India has been reacting to specific conflicts and issues in a contingent manner to avoid any costly entanglements in regional conflicts. Hence, there are variations, adaptations and evolution on a case-to-case basis in Indian response to the conflict. The bottom line remains to safeguard Indian interests and maintain neutrality that has served India well in keeping its engagement with the WANA countries in good stead despite the multiple regional conflicts.

NOTES

1 "Population of Overseas Indians", Minister of External Affairs, Government of India, at https://www.mea.gov.in/population-of-overseas-indians.htm (Accessed 11 November 2022).

2 Department of Commerce, Ministry of Commerce and Industry, Government of India, Export Import Data Bank at https://tradestat.commerce.gov.in/eidb/Default.asp (Accessed 9 January 2024).

3 Ibid.

4 Amit A. Pandya, Rupert Herbert-Burns and Junko Kobayashi, *Maritime Commerce and Security: The Indian Ocean*, The Henry L. Stimson Center, Washington, D.C., 2011.

5 Fawaz A. Gerges, *The Far Enemy: Why Jihad Went Global*, Cambridge University Press, New York, 2009.

6 P.K. Chakravorty, "India's Contribution to Peacekeeping", *Journal of Defence Studies*, 16 (3), 2022, pp. 275-82.

7 J. Mohan Malik, "India's Response to the Gulf Crisis: Implications for Indian Foreign Policy", *Asian Survey*, 31 (9), 1991, pp. 847-61.

8 Gopal Suri, "India's Maritime Security Concerns and the Indian Ocean Region", *Indian Foreign Affairs Journal*, 11 (3), 2016, pp. 238-52.

9 Mohammed Sinan Siyech, "India-Gulf Counterterrorism Cooperation", Middle East Institute, Washington, D.C., 21 December 2017, at https://www.mei.edu/publications/india-gulf-counterterrorism-cooperation (Accessed 11 November 2022).

10 Najma Heptullah, *India-West Asia Relations: The Nehru Era*, Allied Publishers, New Delhi, 1991.

11 Prithvi Ram Mudiam, *India and the Middle East*, British Academy Press, London,1994.

12 Bansidhar Pradhan, "Changing Dynamics of India's West Asia Policy", *International Studies*, 41 (1), 2004, pp. 1-88.

13 P.R. Kumaraswamy, *India's Israel Policy*, Columbia University Press, New York, 2010.

14 Akhilesh C. Prabhakar, "India's Energy Security of Supply and the Gulf", *India Quarterly*, 60 (3), 2004, pp. 120-71.

15 Annual Reports, Ministry of External Affairs, Government of India, at https://mea.gov.in/Annual_Reports.htm?57/Annual_Reports; and "Population of Overseas Indians", Minister of External Affairs, Government of India, at https://www.mea.gov.in/population-of-overseas-indians.htm, (Accessed 11 November 2022).

16 "Remittances from Advanced Nations Beat Flows from Gulf Region in FY21", *The Hindu Business Line*, 17 July 2022, at https://www.thehindubusinessline.com/money-and-banking/share-of-inward-remittances-from-gcc-region-declined-to-30-in-2020-21/article65650279.ece (Accessed 11 November 2022).

17 Export Import Data Bank, Department of Commerce, Ministry of Commerce and Industry, Government of India, at https://tradestat.commerce.gov.in/eidb/Default.asp (Accessed 11 November 2022).

18 "FDI Statistics", Department for Promotion of Industry and Internal Trade, Ministry of Commerce and Industry, Government of India, at https://dpiit.gov.in/publications/fdi-statistics (Accessed 11 November 2022).

19 Abhijit Singh, "India's 'Look West' Maritime Diplomacy", *The Diplomat*, 4 October 2015, at https://thediplomat.com/2015/10/indias-look-west-maritime-diplomacy/ (Accessed 11 November 2022).

20 Shrikant Paranjpe "Maritime Security Issues in the Indian Ocean Region", *Journal of African Union Studies*, 2 (3/4), 2013, pp. 79–91.

21 Siyech, no. 9.

22 Anil Trigunayat, "India's Foreign Policy in West Asia", Lecture delivered at Indian Institute of Technology (IIT), Guwahati, 29 March 2019, at https://mea.gov.in/distinguished-lectures-detail.htm?809 (Accessed 11 November 2022).

23 Three accords beginning with the Camp David Accords in 1978, the Oslo Accords in 1993 and the Abraham Accords in 2020, underline the changing Arab approach towards Israel.

24 Md. Muddassir Quamar, "Armed Non-State Actors and Regional Stability in WANA," in Sujan Chinoy and Prasanta Kumar Pradhan (eds.), *India's Approach to West Asia: Trends, Challenges and Possibilities*, New Delhi: Manohar Parrikar Institute for Defence Studies and Analyses and Pentagon Press, New Delhi, 2024, pp. 56–79.

25 "India-Palestine Bilateral Relations", Ministry of External Affairs, Government of India, September 2019, at https://www.mea.gov.in/Portal/ForeignRelation/Bilateral_Brief-Sept_2019.pdf (Accessed 11 November 2022).

26 P. R. Kumaraswamy, "Modi Redefines India's Palestine Policy", IDSA Issue Brief, 18 May 2017 at https://www.idsa.in/issuebrief/modi-redefines-india-palestine-policy_prkumara swamy_180517 (Accessed 11 November 2022).

27 "India Calls for Direct Peace Talks between Israel, Palestine based on Global Consensus", *The Hindu*, 26 March 2021, at https://www.thehindu.com/news/international/india-calls-for-direct-peace-talks-between-israel-palestine-based-on-global-consensus/article34168200.ece (Accessed 11 November 2022).

28 "India Condemns All Violence in Israel, Gaza; Supports 'Just Palestinian Cause'", *Hindustan Times*, 16 May 2021, at https://www.hindustantimes.com/world-news/

india-condemns-all-violence-in-israel-gaza-supports-just-palestinian-cause-101621186766056.html (Accessed 11 November 2022).

29 "Question No–587 Israel – Palestine Conflict," Rajya Sabha, Unstarred Question, Ministry of External Affairs, Government of India, 7 December 2023, https://www.mea.gov.in/rajya-sabha.htm?dtl/37365/QUESTION+NO587+ISRAEL++PALESTINE+CONFLICT (Accessed 9 January 2024).

30 Paul Rogers, *Why We're Losing the War on Terror*, Polity Press, Cambridge, UK, 2008.

31 The Islamic State in Iraq and Levant (ISIL), also known as Islamic State in Iraq and Syria (ISIS) and by its Arabic acronym Da'esh.

32 "India-Iraq Bilateral Brief", Ministry of External Affairs, Government of India, February 2022, at https://mea.gov.in/Portal/ForeignRelation/India-Iraq_2022.pdf (Accessed 11 November 2022).

33 "Bodies of Indians Killed by ISIS in Iraq Return, Handed over to Family: Highlights", NDTV, 2 April 2018, at https://www.ndtv.com/india-news/live-updates-mortal-remains-of-indians-killed-by-isis-in-iraq-to-return-today-handed-over-to-family-1831518 (Accessed 11 November 2022).

34 Kalicharan V. Singam, "The Islamic State's Reinvigorated and Evolved Propaganda Campaign in India", *Counter Terrorist Trends and Analyses*, 12 (5), 2020, pp. 16-20.

35 Siyech, no. 9; Ely Karmon, "India's Counterterrorism Cooperation with Israel", *Perspectives on Terrorism*, 16 (2), 2022, pp. 2-11.

36 Dania K. Khatib (ed.), *The Syrian Crisis: Effects on the Regional and International Relations*, Springer, Singapore, 2021.

37 Embassy of India, Damascus, "India-Syria Bilateral Relations", at https://eoi.gov.in/damascus/?3078?000, (Accessed 11 November 2022).

38 Ibid.

39 Ibid.

40 Ibid.

41 Horace Campbell, *Global NATO and the Catastrophic Failure in Libya*, Monthly Review Press, New York, 2013.

42 "India Abstains from U.N. Vote on Libya", *The Hindu*, 19 March 2011, at https://www. thehindu.com/news/national/India-abstains-from-U.N.-vote-on-Libya/article14952398. ece (Accessed 11 November 2022).

43 Dipanjan Roy Chaudhary, "India, African union Call for End to Libya Air Strikes", *India Today*, 15 May 2011, at https://www.indiatoday.in/india/north/story/india-and-african-union-call-for-end-to-libya-airstrikes-134433-2011-05-25 (Accessed 11 November 2022).

44 "India-Libya Bilateral Relations", Embassy of India, Tunis, 31 May 2022, at https://www.embassyofindiatunis.gov.in/india-libya-bilateral-relations.php (Accessed 11 November 2022).

45 Ibid.

46 "Yemen: One of the World's Largest Humanitarian Crises", United Nations Population Fund, 11 October 2022, at https://www.unfpa.org/yemen (Accessed 11 November 2022).

47 "Evacuation Operation Yemen – Operation Rahat", Indian Navy, 6 April 2015, at https://www.indiannavy.nic.in/content/operation-evacuation-operation-rahat; Ministry of External Affairs, Government of India, "Suo-Moto Statement by Minister of External Affairs and Overseas Indian Affairs in Rajya Sabha on 'Recent Developments in the Republic of Yemen and Efforts Made for Safe Evacuation of Indian Nationals from There'", 27 April 2015, at https://mea.gov.in/lok-sabha.htm?

dtl/25129/SuoMoto+Statement+by+Mi nister+of+External+Affairs+and+Overseas+ Indian+Affairs+in+Rajya+Sabha+on+Recent+Developments+in+the+ Republic+ of +Yemen+and +Efforts+Made+for+ Safe+ Evacuation+ of + Indian+Nationals+ from+ There (Accessed 11 November 2022).

48 "India Condemns Missile Attack on Saudi Arabia Oil Facility", *Deccan Herald*, 1 December 2020, at https://www.deccanherald.com/national/india-condemns-missile-attack-on-saudi-oil-facility-922208.html (Accessed 11 November 2022).

49 Kristian Coates Ulrichsen, *Qatar and the Gulf Crisis*, Oxford University Press, New York, 2020.

50 Tuqa Khalid, "Full Transcript of AlUla GCC Summit Declaration: Bolstering Gulf Unity", *Al Arabiya News*, 6 January 2021, at https://english.alarabiya.net/News/gulf/2021/01/06/Full-transcript-of-AlUla-GCC-Summit-Declaration-Bolstering-Gulf-unity (Accessed 11 November 2022).

51 "India's Official Statement following the Recent Developments Related to Qatar", Ministry of External Affairs, Government of India, 10 June 2017, at https://www.mea.gov.in/press-releases.htm?dtl/28523/indias+official+ statement+ following+the+recent+developments+ related+to+qatar (Accessed 11 November 2022).

52 "Official Spokesperson's Response to Media Queries on the Reported Announcement of Restoration of Full Ties between Saudi Arabia/UAE/Bahrain/ Egypt with Qatar at the GCC Summit in Al-Ula, Saudi Arabia", Ministry of External Affairs, Government of India, 5 January 2021, at https://www.mea.gov.in/response-to-queries.htm?dtl/33369/official+spokespersons+ response+ to+ media+ queries+ on+the+reported+announcement+of+ restoration+ of+ full+ties+ between+saudi+ arabiauaebahrainegypt+with+qatar+at +the+gcc+summit+ in+ alula+ saudi+ arabia + on+5+january+2021 (Accessed 11 November 2022).

53 Simon Mabon, *Saudi Arabia and Iran: Power and Rivalry in the Middle East*, I.B. Tauris, London, 2013.

54 Ibid.

55 Daniel Avis, "Understanding the Shadow War between Israel and Iran", *Bloomberg*, 4 August 2021, at https://www.bloomberg.com/news/articles/2021-08-04/understanding-the-shadow-war-between-israel-and-iran (Accessed 11 November 2022).

56 See Jayant Prasad and S. Samuel C. Rajiv (eds.), *India and Israel: The Making of a Strategic Partnership*, Routledge, New Delhi, 2020; and P.R. Kumaraswamy and Meena Singh Roy (eds.), *Persian Gulf 2016-17: India's Relations with the Region*, Pentagon Press, New Delhi, 2018.

6

Security in West Asia and India: Shared Concerns and Converging Interests

Rajeev Agarwal

India and the West Asian region share a special bond and strong civilizational links nurtured over centuries. The idea of India has figured in the imagination of people in the region for centuries, and their civilisation has therefore effortlessly intersected with Indian civilization all these years. It is not merely a geographical fact or a coincidence that the Arabian Sea links the shores of our two regions. It is, in fact, a bridge across which people have found a common heritage and which has led to a rich exchange of ideas, beliefs, customs and language.

The British too saw common links between India and the region. British interest in the Persian Gulf region was also influenced by their strategic need to protect critical sea lanes back to Britain. They established a protectorate in Abu Dhabi in 1820, and captured Aden in 1839, incorporating them as provinces of British India. Later, they established protectorates over Oman, Qatar, Kuwait, Bahrain, and the States that today comprise the UAE.[1]

In the 21st century, as India looks beyond its immediate neighbourhood, West Asia forms a vital part of its strategic outlook and is crucial for its national interests. The region supplies about 50 per cent of India's crude requirements, over 70 per cent of natural gas requirements, hosts about 9 million Indians and accounts for a large percentage of remittances received in India annually. Instability in the region has a direct bearing not only on India's energy security but also on the safety and security of millions of Indians working and living in the region. From a strategic point of view, therefore, India has vital stakes in the stability, security and economic well-being of the region.

As India evolves into a major economic and military power and is exerting its influence beyond its shores, the West Asian region too is going through a phase of security transition and transformation and is seeking trustworthy and reliable security partners. The 'Arab Spring' in the previous decade, the 2019 crisis in the Persian Gulf, the Qatar crisis from 2017-21, the conflict and humanitarian crisis in Yemen, instability in Syria and Libya, episodic conflicts between Israel and Palestine or the uncertainty due to the Iran nuclear issue – have severely impacted the security dynamics of the region and are of deep concern to India. The reluctance of the US to be actively involved in security issues in the region coupled with the rise of terrorism emanating from countries in the region, adds to overall security concerns.

India's traditional foreign policy approach has been to remain non-intrusive, non-judgmental and non-prescriptive and strictly avoid taking sides in intra-regional disputes or exhibit partiality among regional countries. The fact that India is a power with no extra-territorial ambitions is widely appreciated in the region. While offering full support, India has always maintained that it is for respective countries to decide their destiny, without any external interference or diktats. This philosophy and India's unflinching commitment to sustaining and expanding relations with the region has helped build stronger ties in recent times, especially on security issues.

The constantly evolving security situation in the region and the fact that the guarantee of security through the US as in the past is no longer assured, has also resulted in an increased scope and space for India to play a constructive role in the region's security. India's growing security cooperation with the region covers a vast spectrum of issues like counter-terrorism, maritime security and anti-piracy as well as transnational crimes such as money laundering, fake currency, drugs, human trafficking etc. Safety of the Sea Lines of Communications

(SLOCs) too is of prime importance for India, as any disruptions here impact India's economy adversely, especially energy security. It is also important to keep the region free of influence of sea pirates and other disruptive non-State actors. Towards this, India has continuously deployed one naval ship since October 2008 in the Gulf of Aden for anti-piracy duties.[2] Security cooperation with the region is thus growing by the day as more and more countries recognise and embrace India as a reliable security partner. To evolve a better understanding of how India can enhance its security cooperation in the region, it is important to examine the fast-evolving security dynamics in the region.

Evolving Security Dynamics in the Region

The West Asian region has always been an area of conflict and competition, both internally between the regional powers and externally by the bigger players trying to establish influence and control. In modern times, we could go back to 1948, when the State of Israel was established which led to the first of many Arab-Israel conflicts in 1948. The Egypt-Israel Peace Treaty of 1979[3] may have ensured that there have been no more Arab-Israel wars, but conflicts with various Palestinian factions have continued. Among the recent conflicts was the one when Israel launched an offensive code-named "Operation Breaking Dawn"[4] on 5 August 2022 in the Gaza Strip targeting the Palestinian Islamic Jihad (PIJ). Again, in May 2023, Israel launched 'Operation Shield and Arrow' into the Gaza Strip, as Israel's response to an escalation of rocket and mortar fire by PIJ, which itself was a response to the death of a senior member of the group's West Bank branch while on hunger strike in an Israeli prison. The continued skirmishes and hostility, both in the West Bank as well as the Gaza Strip, along with shrinking land available for a viable Palestinian State due to ever-increasing Israeli settlements, offer very little hope for this conflict to end soon. The surprise terror attack by Hamas from the Gaza Strip into Israel on 07 October 2023 and the resultant Israeli offensive has put to rest any hopes of an early settlement of the issue, at least, in the short-term.

The other important security issue is the regional rivalry between Saudi Arabia and Iran, manifested in good measure after the Islamic

Revolution of Iran of 1979. Although both nations have not been involved in any direct military conflict yet, a number of proxies from both sides do keep creating disorder in the region from time to time. The most recent and prominent is Iran's support to the Houthis in Yemen who are fighting against the Saudi-led coalition since March 2015.[5] This, coupled with an intense debate and uncertainty over Iran's nuclear programme, has often drawn the US and other Western powers into the conflict. It manifested into the Persian Gulf Crisis of 2019,[6] which was triggered when four ships, including three oil tankers, were damaged in an attack on 12 May off the coast of the UAE.[7] On 13 June, a Norwegian and a Japanese tanker came under attack in the Gulf of Oman.[8] Fingers were immediately pointed at Iran, which denied it. However, when the Iranian military downed a US drone flying over its airspace on 20 June 2019, it brought the region close to an active military conflict. There were reports that the US President ordered retaliatory military strikes against Iran, to be executed at dawn on 21 June, before changing his mind at the last moment.[9] The killing of General Qasem Soleimani, the Iranian head of Al Quds Force at the Baghdad Airport on 03 January 2020 by a US Drone,[10] was again a strong provocation but the fragile cold peace has prevailed so far in the Persian Gulf. The ongoing Russia-Ukraine conflict and the fact that Iran has once again come under scrutiny and sanctions on supply of armed drones to Russia,[11] is keeping the security situation simmering in the region. The Saudi–Iran peace deal, brokered by China in March 2023, took the world by surprise. The agreement includes a deal to re-open their embassies and missions within two months. The agreement includes an affirmation of respect for the sovereignty of states and the non-interference in the internal affairs of states.[12] If successful, it has the potential to alter the security dynamics of the region, including an end to the war in Yemen.

Another major factor adding to the ever-fluctuating security dynamics in the region was the 'Arab Spring', a collective revolt by people in the West Asian region against 'dictators and oppressive regimes.' An incident on 17 December 2010 sparked unprecedented protests in the region when Mohammed Bouazizi, a Tunisian street vendor, set himself on fire in a show of public protest. Bouazizi's self-immolation triggered widespread unrest in Tunisia dubbed as the

'Jasmine Revolution'. Subsequently, when protests broke out in a number of other Arab countries, the phenomenon came to be termed as the 'Arab Spring.'[13]

It has been more than a decade since the 'Arab Spring', but the situation across the region is far from being normal. The only two countries who have 'stabilised' somewhat are Tunisia and Egypt. In Tunisia, President Ben Ali was forced to flee the country on 14 January 2011,[14] a month after the protests. However, in October 2011, in Tunisia's first free election, the Islamist group Ennahdha won 89 of 217 seats in a new Assembly.[15] Later, in January 2014, the new Constitution was adopted, leading to parliamentary and presidential elections later in the year. The cycle of election was repeated in 2019 and although not perfect, Tunisia is finding its own formula of governance.

In Egypt, after the initial turmoil and fall of President Hosni Mubarak's government, the Islamists came to power, electing Mohammad Morsi of the Muslim Brotherhood as the President in June 2012. He was ousted in June 2013 by a military coup led by General Fateh El Sisi.[16] However, thereafter, Sisi has stabilised the country and also won presidential polls twice in 2014, 2018 and again in December 2023.

Some of other countries in the region have not been so fortunate in coming to terms with the scars of the 'Arab Spring.' In Yemen, President Ali Abdullah Saleh was ousted when, under UN mediation, he signed a transfer of power agreement and relinquished the post of President, to hand over power to Vice-President Abdu Rabbo Mansour Hadi on 23 November 2011.[17] The transition process however got disrupted due to conflicts. In September 2014, the Houthis, an ethnic Shia group in Yemen seeking control and rule over Northern Yemen, took over the capital Sana'a.

Saudi Arabia, in consultation with regional Arab allies and the US, launched airstrikes in Yemen on 26 March 2015 in an air assault codenamed *Operation Decisive Storm*.[18] There have been a number of attempts towards negotiating peace in Yemen, a number of ceasefires as well as UN Resolutions, but a long-term solution still evades Yemen.

A new dimension was added to the Yemen conflict when the

Houthis attacked the Saudi airport at Abha and oil pipelines in May-June 2019, followed by drone strikes on Saudi Aramco facilities in September 2019. During the attacks on the Saudi cities of Riyadh, Nazran and Jizan on 23 June 2020, the Houthis claimed to have used *Quds* cruise missiles, *Zulfiqar* ballistic missiles and *Sammad-3* drones, all of Iranian origin. There have been repeated attempts by the UN to negotiate a ceasefire, including two during Ramadan in 2021 and 2022, without much success.

Syria is another country impacted by the 'Arab Spring' and is yet to stabilise. More than 12 years have passed since protests against President Bashar Al Assad's government erupted in March 2011 later turning into a full-fledged war pitching the US-led coalition on one side and the Russia-Iran coalition supporting Assad on the other. President Assad has survived and retained power. But the security situation is far from stable. The scars of the use of chemical weapons in August 2013[19] continue to haunt the Syrians while the Islamic State (IS) and the Kurdish rebels continue to attack government assets and machinery. The Kurdish forces have established an autonomous region in the north, creating serious security concerns in Turkiye, which is trying to create a buffer zone in Syria along its southern borders.

Libya too erupted in protests in early 2011 leading to mass reprisals by its dictator, Muammar Gaddafi. He was ousted after a bloody battle and finally killed in October 2011. However, Libya has not been able to stabilise. One of the other primary reasons for Libya's instability has been its failure to find a suitable political governance model and a common ground between the rival interests between competing tribal groups. After a protracted battle between the warring factions, the country is split down the middle, into eastern and western halves. The Government of National Accord (GNA) is based in Tripoli, whereas the House of Representatives (HoR) and the Libyan National Army (LNA) led by Khalifa Haftar, is in Tobruk, in the East. The lingering political tensions and frequent clashes are a challenge to the internal security and political stability of the country.

Iraq, though not directly impacted by the 'Arab Spring', was attacked by the then newly established Islamic State of Iraq and Syria (ISIS) or Daesh, a Sunni jihadist group led by Abu Bakr al Baghdadi. ISIS launched an attack on Mosul and Tikrit in June 2014. In response, a US-led coalition launched operations and airstrikes against ISIS in Iraq on 7 August 2014. Over the next year, the coalition launched more than 8,000 airstrikes, leading to huge losses to the ISIS. By the end of 2015, Iraqi forces had recaptured Ramadi and by December 2017, the ISIS had lost 95 per cent of its territory, including Mosul.[20] Iraqi Prime Minister Haider Al Abadi declared victory over the ISIS on 9 December 2017. Later, US Special Forces in northwestern Syria killed Abu Bakr Al Baghdadi in a raid on 26-27 October 2019.[21] Although ISIS has largely lost its cohesion, it remains active in small splinter groups across the region, especially Syria.

The security dynamics in the region, therefore, remain fluid and very fragile. Number of competing and conflicting interests prevent the establishment of lasting peace. Intra-regional rivalries, territorial disputes and terror have all contributed towards the prevailing situation. Dialogue and compromises are the only way to work out peace and is the need of the hour. India, with its goodwill and trust across the region, may have an important role to play in this regard in the future.

Existing Security Architecture in the Region and the Need for a Viable Alternative

Security threats in the modern era can quickly morph into multiple forms. Conventional military threats between nations are being constantly overshadowed by threats like cyber security, terror and human trafficking which transcend national boundaries and impact peace and security. The existing security dynamics in the West Asian region and the constantly evolving security threats in the region require a robust, reliable and an all-encompassing security framework.

However, the West Asian region has not yet been successful in either identifying common security threats or in coming up with a common security framework for the region. Across the region, only the GCC has a security component whereas the other two major regional frameworks, OIC and Arab League, are consultative frameworks on regional and political issues. Even the GCC is limited to six countries and does not include many important countries in the region like Egypt, Turkiye, Jordan, Yemen, Iraq, Syria, etc.

The GCC was formed in 1981, shortly after the Iranian revolution in 1979. The idea of the GCC was to bring together countries of the Gulf region against the threat from two perceived adversaries; Iran, an ideological rival, and Iraq, a belligerent military power. The birth of the GCC was thus based on fear (of Iran and Iraq), and exclusion (Iran and Iraq, along with embattled and weak Yemen). In its formation, the GCC however ignored the geographical and geopolitical realities of the region. Iran and Iraq together cover almost the entire northern coast of the Persian Gulf, and are critical links towards the Levant, Central Asia and South Asia. They also possess large reservoirs of natural resources. Geo-politically too, Iraq and Iran, being significant economic and military powers, cannot be ignored. On the other hand, Saudi Arabia is the only big country in the GCC. A very critical component of this framework was the US, which pledged to provide security guarantees to the GCC. In his 1980 State of the Union Address, in reaction to the 1979 Iranian revolution, President Jimmy Carter articulated this, stating:

> "An attempt by any outside force to gain control of the Persian Gulf region will be regarded as an assault on the vital interests of the United States of America, and such an assault will be repelled by any means necessary, including military force."[22]

The US, accordingly deployed the 'Rapid Deployment Force', and set up regional military bases, such as the ones in Masira and Bahrain.[23] In the following decades, several other security initiatives were experimented with in the region. After the Iraq war in 1991, the US also created a multilateral security framework known as the Madrid process,[24] within which it pursued a containment and deterrence strategy vis-a-vis Iraq and Iran.[25] In 1999, the US introduced a new strategy to minimise threats posed by Iran and Iraq. The Cooperative Defense Initiative (CDI) was a plan for the integration of the defence forces of the GCC, Egypt and Jordan; and coordinate intelligence sharing between them.[26] All GCC members signed a joint defence pact in December 2000. However, the 9/11 incident and the resultant war on terror in Afghanistan along with the war on Iraq in 2003 and the discovery of a 'covert' nuclear programme in Iran in 2002, once again changed the entire dynamics of security and US engagement in the region. The US found itself deeply involved in the security issues of the region. In May 2006, the US launched the Gulf Security Dialogue

(GSD). The core objectives of the Dialogue were the promotion of intra-GCC and GCC-US cooperation to meet common perceived threats.[27]

Later, the concept of a 'Gulf Union' was discussed at the GCC Summit in Bahrain in December 2012.[28] During the Manama Dialogue in December 2013 too, Saudi Arabia brought up this issue but failed to find traction among other partners. Oman was even quick to rubbish the idea with its Foreign Minister Yusuf bin Alawi stating, "We are against a union," further adding, "We will not prevent a union, but if it happens, we will not be part of it."[29]

At the US-GCC Summit in Riyadh in May 2017, a proposed regional alliance in the form of an 'Arab NATO' or 'Middle East Strategic Alliance' (MESA) was mooted. The alliance was projected to include nations of the GCC plus Egypt and Jordan.[30] However, soon thereafter, in June 2017, the diplomatic blockade against Qatar buried the concept before it could take any shape.

The Abraham Accords,[31] mediated by the US and signed between Israel and the UAE, Bahrain, Morocco and Sudan in September 2020, was another significant development. These were the first accords in the region since 1994, when Israel had signed a peace pact with Jordan[32] And could lead to the mainstreaming of Israel into West Asian framework in the future. The issue of Palestine and the sacred pledge of Arab countries to safeguard Palestinian interests is the most important factor in the way, although there has been a marked dilution in the stand by regional countries on Palestine issue in recent years. The Abraham Accords do not have any security component, at least as of now. However, if its coverage expands across the region, security cooperation too could get incorporated.

Another attempt towards making the existing GCC framework more inclusive across the region was witnessed during the GCC Summit at Jeddah on 16 July 2022 when, apart from GCC countries, the US and Egypt, Iraq and Jordan were invited. The final statement, "The leaders reiterated their condemnation of terrorism, and reaffirmed their keenness to strengthen efforts to combat terrorism and extremism, prevent the armament and financing of terror groups and confront all activities that threaten the region's security and stability",[33] had a clear security element embedded in it.

All regional security initiatives, right from the formation of GCC in 1981, have had two clear and critical consequences: first, Iran has been specifically targeted, second, the US, over the years, got more and more engaged in the security of the region. Regarding a viable regional security architecture, the most crucial is the question of regional participation. When examining it in the context of the West Asian region and specifically the GCC, the question is, can it afford to ignore the two largest countries north of the Persian Gulf, namely, Iran and Iraq in any viable security framework? The answer is clearly 'no'. Alluding to this important aspect in a speech at the Manama Dialogue in 2006, Bahrain's Foreign Minister, Sheikh Khalid Bin Ahmed Al Khalifa had stated: "In the Gulf, no sustainable long-term regional security arrangement can be envisioned without Iraq and Iran acting as two of its pillars."[34]

The GCC is, therefore, grossly insufficient and under-represented to address collective security concerns of the region. It also lacks a strong, viable and regionally representative armed force. The only military arm, the Peninsula Shield Force, consists primarily of troops from Saudi Arabia and therefore cannot be classified as credible or representative. The region therefore requires a security framework, which is larger in scope than the current GCC. It also needs to carve out a capability that is independent of the US, which is clearly unwilling to commit active resources for security in the region any more.

India, which has enhanced its engagement manifold with the region in the past decade, especially after the current government under Prime Minister Narendra Modi made West Asia a clear priority, could offer solutions to the region. A clear indication of India's increasing engagement with the region on security issues is illustrated by the growing defence and security cooperation, which could lay the foundation for a strong and viable regional security architecture in the future.

India's Defence and Security Cooperation with the Region

When compared with trade and people-to-people ties, India was slow off the blocks with its security and defence engagements with the West Asian region. This was attributed to a number of factors including

India's inward-looking policies and Pakistan-centric security outlook till the late 1990s. In addition, the traditional support and solidarity of the Arab countries to Pakistan came in the way. It was only after 9/11 that the world was forced to change its outlook on terror. The slow decoupling of India's security outlook away from Pakistan and also recognition of India as an emerging power by the countries of the region, helped India enhance its engagement in defence and security with the region. The start was modest and not much progress was made until 2014 when Narendra Modi was elected as the Prime Minister and the government thereafter prioritized its engagement with the region.

Oman

Within the region, Oman was amongst the first countries that signed the Agreement to Combat Terrorism and Organized Crime in Muscat with India in May 1999.[35] It was followed by the visit of Major General Ali bin Rashid Alkalbani, Commander of the Royal Army of Oman, to India in June 1999. MoU on defence cooperation was signed in December 2005[36] during the visit of the Omani minister responsible for defence affairs Sayyid Badr bin Saud bin Hareb al Busaidi. The MoU has since been operational and is extended every five years.[37] Oman is also the only country in the region with which India conducts regular biennial bilateral military exercises with all three services – with the Army (since 2015), the Navy (since 1993) and the Air Force (since 2009). In May 2016, Manohar Parrikar, the then Defence Minister, paid a three-day visit to Oman. During the visit, four MoUs/ agreements were signed, namely the MoU on Defence Cooperation between the Ministry of Defence of Sultanate of Oman and Ministry of Defence of Republic of India; the MoU between the Royal Oman Police (Coast Guard) and the Indian Coast Guard in the field of Marine Crime Prevention at Sea; the MoU between India and Oman on Maritime Issues, and the Protocol between the Omani Royal Air Force and the Indian Air Force on Flight Safety Information Exchange.[38]

In addition, there has been extensive cooperation between the two navies with the Indian Naval Ships often visiting ports of Muscat and Salah for Operational Turn Around and goodwill visits. On its part, India has been imparting regular training to Oman's naval personnel at its naval training institutes every year. During the visit of Prime Minister Modi to Oman in February 2018, India and Oman signed an Annexure to the MoU on military cooperation.[39] Under the Annexure, Oman is to provide logistical facilities to the Indian Navy in the Special Economic Zone and port of Duqm. Indian naval ships will also be able to use the port and dry dock for maintenance of ships. Duqm is strategically important due to its location right across the Indian coastline and overlooking the Gulf of Oman and the Arabian Sea and in close proximity to the Chabahar Port in Iran. It also allows India to keep a discreet watch on the growing naval activity of the Chinese People's Liberation Army (PLA) in the region.

Oman was also the first Gulf country to purchase the Indian Small Arms System (INSAS) assault rifle in 2010.[40] In September 2021, India and Oman signed an agreement on the exchange of white shipping information and to boost maritime security cooperation.[41] In February 2022, Oman's Secretary General of Defence, Mohammad bin Nasser bin Ali Al-Zabbi visited India where the two sides agreed to examine areas of mutual interest in forging joint ventures to enhance defence industry cooperation.[42] Admiral R. Hari Kumar, Chief of India's Naval Staff, undertook a three-day official visit to Oman from 31 July – 2 August 2023, which apart from high-level discussions, included a visit to the strategically important port of Duqm.[43] The State visit of Sultan of Oman, Sultan Haitham bin Tarik, on 16 December 2023 and the signing of joint vision document is an important landmark in India-Oman security partnership.

UAE

With the UAE, although a MoU on defence cooperation was signed in 2003, not much progress was made for almost a decade. During Prime Minister Modi's visit to the UAE in August 2015, a decision was taken to elevate the bilateral relationship to a 'comprehensive strategic partnership', in which security cooperation was an important element. Shortly thereafter, during the state visit of the UAE's Crown Prince Sheikh Mohamed bin Zayed Al Nahyan in February 2016, both sides agreed to conduct a regular security dialogue between their National Security Councils, to work closely on security issues, like counter-terrorism, maritime security, and cyber-security. Both sides also agreed to enhance cooperation in training, joint exercises, as well as identify options on the production of defence equipment in India.[44] The focus on security cooperation continued with the visit of Manohar Parrikar, India's Defence Minister, to the UAE in May 2016.[45] It was the first visit by any Indian Defence Minister to the UAE.

Cooperation in bilateral exercises forms an important component under which India and the UAE held the first Joint Navy Exercises 'Gulf Star 1' in Abu Dhabi in March 2018.[46] In March 2021, an Indian Air Force (IAF) contingent participated for the first time in *Exercise Desert Flag–VI*, an annual multilateral large force employment exercise, hosted by the UAE. The Exercise was conducted at the Al Dhafra Air Force Base, UAE. The IAF participated in this exercise for the first time, fielding Su-30MKI fighter aircraft.[47] The IAF again participated in Exercise Desert Flag–VII in UAE in March 2023, this time with five LCA Tejas and two C-17 Globemaster III aircraft. The first edition of joint military exercise 'Desert Cyclone' was held in January 2024 in the deserts of Rajasthan.

As part of cooperation in defence production, the Ordnance Factory Board (OFB) of India signed a contract with the UAE on 23 March 2017 for the supply of 40,000 rounds of 155 mm shells, followed by another 50,000 rounds in 2018.[48] There have been some reports in the media on the UAE expressing interest in the purchase of *Helina, Nag* and *Brahmos* missiles from India. India and the UAE have already agreed to cooperate in the field of Space as a part of their comprehensive strategic partnership.

Saudi Arabia

With Saudi Arabia too, there is an increased focus on defence and security cooperation. The 'Delhi Declaration'[49] signed during the visit of King Abdullah bin Abdulaziz Al Saud in 2006 and the 'Riyadh Declaration'[50] signed during Prime Minister Manmohan Singh's visit in March 2010, set the tone for revitalising the relationship. Later, a MoU on defence cooperation was signed during the visit of the then Crown Prince and Defence Minister Prince Salman bin Abdulaziz Al Saud to India on 27 February 2014.[51] However, it was the visit of Prime Minister Modi to Riyadh in April 2016[52] that holistically captured the spirit of enhancing cooperation in security and defence. During the visit, King Salman conferred on Prime Minister Modi the Kingdom's highest civilian honour, indicating the importance Saudi Arabia attached to its relations with India. The visit of Crown Prince Mohammad bin Salman to India later in February 2019 further cemented the engagement.

Saudi Arabia recognises India as one of its Strategic Partner countries under its "Vision 2030". Similarly, India is also seeking Saudi Arabia as a partner under its "Make in India" initiative in the field of defence production. Recently there were media reports which indicated that Kalyani Strategic Systems, a wholly owned subsidiary of Bharat Forge, has bagged an offer to sell its Bharat 52, a 155mm/52-calibre artillery gun to a friendly country in the 'non conflict zone.'[53] No names were revealed but the firm had been in talks with Saudi Arabia and it could have finally fructified. There have also been some inputs that Saudi Arabia has shown interest in the *Brahmos* missile system. In February 2022, Saudi Arabia was one of the 46 countries, which were invited to the Indian Navy's "Milan Exercise."[54] Earlier, in August 2021 the first-ever bilateral naval exercise between India and Saudi Arabia "Al Mohed Al Hindi 2021" was conducted off the King Abdulaziz Naval base in Al Jubail, Saudi Arabia.[55] The first edition of India-Saudi Arabia joint military exercise 'Sada Tanseeq' was held in the deserts of Rajasthan in January-February 2024.

A further testimony to strengthening defence relations has been a flurry of visits at the highest level of armed forces between the two countries in the recent past. On 14 February 2022, Lieutenant General Fahd Bin Abdullah Mohammed Al Mutair, Commander of the Royal Saudi Land Forces reached New Delhi on an official visit,[56] the first-ever visit by a serving Royal Saudi Land Forces Commander to India. Earlier, in December 2020, Chief of the Army Staff General M.M. Naravane visited Saudi Arabia on an official visit; once again, it was the first time that an Indian Army Chief had visited Saudi Arabia.

Egypt

Egypt is another country with which India has enjoyed close defence relations. Indo-Egypt defence ties go back to the 1960s-70s when Indian Air Force pilots trained Egyptian pilots and were a part of a joint venture to manufacture the Helwan-300 (Kahira) jet fighter.[57] Later, in 1998, during the visit of India's Chief of Air Staff, various proposals to enhance defence cooperation were proposed by both sides. The formation of a Joint Defence Committee was one such proposal. A Joint Defence Committee was proposed which was finally set up in August 2006 and its inaugural meeting was held in Cairo.

Ties with Egypt have received a fillip since 2014 when Prime Minister Modi and President Sisi both came to power in their respective countries. External Affairs Minister Sushma Swaraj paid a visit to Cairo in August 2015. Prime Minister Modi met President Sisi on the sidelines of the UNGA in New York in September 2015. Later, President Sisi paid a state visit to India in September 2016. The Joint Statement issued outlining the three pillars of cooperation, highlighted political-security cooperation as an important pillar. Egyptian Minister of Defence Sedki Sobhi later visited India in November 2017 and Minister of State for Military Production, General Mohamed El Assar was in India in April 2018, to participate in the DEF-EXPO at Chennai.[58]

During India's Defence Minister Rajnath Singh's official visit to Egypt in September 2022, the two countries signed a MoU on defence cooperation,[59] aimed to formalize and enhance bilateral defence cooperation, including expansion of their partnership in defence industries. As a part of the 'Make in India' initiative, Egypt could emerge as a lucrative market for Indian defence products, joint defence manufacturing and co-production units. Egypt is also one of the six countries interested in India's *Tejas* aircraft.[60] In addition, Egypt has reportedly shown interest in buying *Brahmos* missiles too. Most recently, the state visit of President Sisi in January 2023, as the Chief Guest at the Republic Day Parade and quick reciprocal visit by Prime Minister Modi to Egypt in June 2023, has further added impetus to the strengthening ties between the two nations.

Qatar

The India-Qatar Defence Cooperation Agreement was signed during Prime Minister Manmohan Singh's visit to Qatar in November 2008.[61] The Agreement is being implemented through a Joint Defence Cooperation Committee (JDCC), which held its fifth meeting in Doha on 27-28 November 2019.[62] The pace of engagement has however picked up in recent years. National Security Adviser Shri Ajit Doval visited Doha from 11-12 February 2015, the first such high-level visit from India after the Modi Government assumed office. The Emir of Qatar Sheikh Tamim Bin Hamad Al Thani paid a state visit to India in March 2015, his first visit to India. This was also the first visit of the Head of State of an Arab country after Modi became Prime Minister.[63] During Prime Minister Modi's reciprocal visit to Doha in June 2016, both countries agreed to provide impetus to defence cooperation, including through joint exercises and enhanced training of naval, air and land forces, as well as in the area of coastal defence. Qatar evinced interest in the opportunities under the 'Make in India' initiative for joint production of defence equipment in India.[64] Both sides agreed to enhance cooperation in maritime security in the Gulf and the Indian Ocean regions. A MoU on cooperation in exchange of intelligence related to money laundering, related crimes and terrorism financing was also signed.[65]

A number of high-profile visits have followed thereafter. The Chief of Staff of Qatar Armed Forces, Lt. Gen. (Pilot) Ghanim bin Shaheen Al Ghanim, visited India during19-22 June 2018. Khalid bin Mohammed Al Attiyah, Deputy Prime Minister and Minister of State for Defence Affairs visited India in February 2020. Staff Maj Gen (Navy) Abdulla Hassan M A Al Sulaiti, Commander of the Qatar Amiri Naval Forces (QENF) visited India from 02 to 05 April 2019.[66]

From the Indian side, there have been regular visits to Qatar from the armed forces. Indian Navy's warships, *INS Mumbai* and *INS Trikand* docked at Hamad port in 2018 and 2019. The Indian Coast Guard Ship *Samudra Paheredar* also docked at Doha Port in 2020 as part of its goodwill visit to the Gulf region. Indian Air Force C-17 Aircraft landed in Doha in May-June 2021 to transport cryogenic containers as part of COVID-19 relief operations. *INS Kolkata, INS Tarkash, INS Trikand* and *INS Shardul* docked at Hamad Port Doha in May and June 2021 to undertake shipping of medical supplies for COVID-19 relief from Qatar as part of *Operation Samudra Setu-II.*

India has offered training modules and facilities to Qatar for its armed forces personnel and Coast Guard. A number of Qatari officers have attended the Defence Services Staff College Course at Wellington. A customised course was conducted at Kochi in July 2019 for Qatari

Naval officers. With Qatar importing most of its defence equipment and India emerging as a significant producer, there is a lot of potential for enhanced engagement in defence and security with Qatar. The visit of Prime Minister Modi to Qatar on 14 February 2024 and the release of the Indian ex-navy personnel, who were on death sentence in Qatar, is an important confidence building measure in the bilateral partnership in general, and security cooperation in particular.

Iran

With Iran, India signed a MoU on defence cooperation in 2001,[67] but could not progress it further. Iran is very important to India due to its location, its relevance to peace in the Gulf and its centrality to peace in Afghanistan. Both countries are looking at the appropriate time to revitalize this relationship. In light of the security and geo-political dynamics, which have evolved over the past two decades in Iran, it is perhaps the right time to pursue closer defence and security ties with Iran. In this context, the visit of India's Defence Minister Rajnath Singh to Tehran in September 2020[68] and that of the Iranian Defence Minister to India in March 2021[69] are indicative of this. Most recently, the Iranian Deputy Foreign Minister Ali Bagheri visited India on 24 November 2022.[70] The Saudi-Iran peace deal of March 2023 too promises towards larger inclusion of Iran in the region and may facilitate closer ties with India too, in defence and security sphere. The visit of Dr. S. Jaishankar to Tehran in December 2023 and the focus on regional security is an important indicator towards increasing cooperation.

Israel

Defence cooperation with Israel is unique in nature when compared with other countries in the region. While India drives the contours of defence cooperation with most countries in the region, with Israel, due to its technological superiority, Israel is in a position to assist India and augment its defence preparedness. Both countries, surrounded by hostile neighbours and victims of frequent terror attacks, have often sought convergence on a number of security and defence issues. While the two sides established diplomatic relations in 1992, it was the Kargil War of 1999, which cemented the ties when Israel emerged as one of the very few countries to rush to India's aid and provide direct military assistance. It also brought to the fore Israel as a reliable, trustworthy and a technologically superior partner on defence and security, critical for India's defence preparedness.

During these last 30 years, Israel has provided India with a number of cutting-edge technologies, weapons and surveillance platforms like UAVs, missiles, Special Forces equipment and radar systems. An important part of this collaboration has also been joint production, within which the *Barak-8* air and missile defence system, co-developed by the Israel Aerospace Industries (IAI) and India's Defence Research Development Organisation (DRDO), is one such success story. During the visit of Israel's Defence Minister Benjamin Gantz to New Delhi in June 2022, both sides decided to work together to enhance cooperation in all forums of defence and security. The 'India-Israel Vision on Defence Cooperation' was adopted during the visit and a Letter of Intent on enhancing cooperation in the field of Futuristic Defence Technologies was also exchanged.[71] Israel's Ambassador to India, Naor Gilon, speaking to the media in September 2022, underlined the importance of this partnership when he reiterated that defence cooperation between the two sides is a long and successful one and that Israel is happy to be a strong partner in areas like UAVs, rockets, missiles and whatever defence system India needs.[72]

Others

With Bahrain, Yemen, Iraq and Kuwait, there are no formal defence and security agreements in place. There are ongoing discussions with Kuwait and Bahrain towards formalizing defence cooperation in the future. Turkiye-India ties are often overshadowed by Turkey's close ties with Pakistan, especially the military and Turkey's oft-repeated statements and comments on India's internal affairs, especially Kashmir.

India's defence and security cooperation with the region is therefore a work-in-progress but has gained significant momentum in the past decade. In addition to core defence issues, there is strong support for India in countering terror and unanimous acceptance of India's position on terror. Whether it was Uri or Pathankot, all the Gulf countries, especially Saudi Arabia, the UAE, Bahrain and Qatar condemned the attacks strongly. In fact, the UAE and Bahrain even supported active military action by India to confront, eradicate and fight terrorism. On the attack on a convoy of security forces in Pulwama on 14 February 2019, all the Gulf countries were prompt in their condemnation of the terror attack. There has also been strong support to the adoption of India's proposed Comprehensive Convention on International Terrorism in the United Nations.

Operation Raahat, conducted to evacuate Indians and foreign nationals stranded in conflict-ridden Yemen during March-April 2015 is yet another example of strong security coordination with countries in the region. This operation conducted over land, air and sea through multiple countries was a resounding success. Not only were 4,700 Indians safely evacuated but more than 1,950 foreign nationals from 48 countries were also brought to safety under most difficult circumstances.[73]

Areas of Convergence and Recommendations for the Future

India considers West Asia as its extended neighbourhood and "home away from home'[74] and accords priority to peace and security in the region. Under Prime Minister Modi's vision of India's overseas engagement, India's ties with the countries in the region has grown manifold in the past few years. Minister of State for External Affairs, M.J. Akbar, during the annual Manama Dialogue in December 2017, stated, "India recognises and stands by the Gulf region in its efforts to counter emerging security threats. However, while engaging with the Gulf countries, India's approach has remained and will remain non-intrusive, non-judgmental and non-prescriptive. We do not take sides in intra-regional disputes."[75] It is this specific philosophy of India's regional outlook that the countries in the region appreciate and therefore place their trust in exploiting the potential for greater and a more intensive security engagement with India in the region.

In doing so, India's engagement options on defence and security need to be evaluated against her core interests in the region, the capacity to engage actively, external pressures and more importantly, depth and scope of the 'strategic reach and vision.' Most countries in the region are looking for reliable partners and security assurances and therefore look at India as a safe and reliable partner, particularly after the US made it clear that it no longer has the appetite for any active military engagement in the region, especially involving boots on the ground. In such a scenario, India needs to explore options of engagement on a bilateral as well as multilateral/regional basis. While bilateral engagements provide the initial foothold and establish mutual confidence, multilateral engagements could give India an increased visibility as a security collaborator in the region.

Defence Wings

For any effective defence cooperation, India has to extend its Defence Wings to each of the countries in the region. In countries where the engagements are intense, personnel of more than one service could form part of the defence wings. With India enhancing its capabilities in defence production and seeking export destinations, a suitably equipped and a proactive defence wing at our embassies abroad is a must.

Maritime Agreements

India has signed specific agreements on maritime security with Qatar and Oman. These agreements provide India an opportunity to cooperate in combating a variety of maritime threats of terrorism, piracy as also security of offshore oil installations. India should sign similar maritime security agreements with other countries in the region too. In addition, the Indian Navy should increase its frequency of port calls, naval basing, joint exercises and missions to ensure an enlarged Indian foothold in the region. Logistics and basing facilities akin to Duqm in Oman need to be extended to other select countries in the region too.

Counter Piracy Cooperation

A large percentage of India's trade, including crude oil, natural gas and fertilizers, passes through the Persian Gulf and Gulf of Aden. As a part of the counter-piracy mission in the region, India has been operating independently in the region since 2008 in close coordination with the Bahrain-based and US-led multilateral Combined Maritime Force (CMF).[76] Recently, based on an agreement during the India-US 2+2 Dialogue in April 2023, India has formally commenced cooperation with the CMF as part of its widening military diplomacy and strengthening regional security cooperation.[77]

Counter Terrorism Engagement

Terrorism is a common concern that India shares with the region. Counter-terror cooperation already forms part of existing security protocols with some countries of the region. India needs to deepen this engagement by signing similar protocols with others in the region. Intelligence sharing and extradition of terror accused should form important elements of such cooperation. India could offer to train troops from these countries in counter-terror operations or even set up a regional Counter Terrorism School in the UAE or Oman. India could pitch for setting up a 'Regional Counter Terrorism Command Centre' in the region, which could be manned by intelligence personnel of these countries and India, for real-time intelligence sharing and coordination.

Regional Military Engagement

India should expand interaction with regional militaries through visits and courses/training, port visits, military exercises, intelligence sharing, joint production of weapon platforms and munitions. Regular bilateral or multilateral training exercises, training of their personnel – especially officers – in India should form an essential part of such an engagement. Maintaining regular contact with officers who have trained in India should be encouraged through our defence wings. Such officers should be specially invited to Embassy events and even regular reunions in India. This would help in building long-term relationships and comraderies for future engagements between the two armed forces. With these forms of engagements, India has the potential to emerge as an acceptable and successful 'security collaborator' in the region (especially the Gulf region).

Role in Regional Security

In addition to its role as a 'security collaborator' with individual nations, India could play an important role in the regional security structures too. An observer role in the GCC, or establishment of a 'regional military communication and liaison command post', comprising of officers from regional countries along with India, could not only facilitate training and sharing of experience between armed forces of regional countries and India, but could also help avert potential military situations by timely reporting and sharing of inputs, helping in diffusing the situation before it goes out of control. As such structures mature in time, it could help avert any potential crisis as also overcome the present atmosphere of hostility and mistrust between various camps, something extremely vital to regional security. India, with its vast experience of military conflicts and peacekeeping missions, could play a significant role.

Conclusion

As India's security ties with the nations in the region evolve, India will have to remain vigilant to some important issues. Balancing and managing conflicting and often contradictory, stands on regional security issues (Saudi Arabia versus Iran or Israel versus Iran etc.), would be a challenge. Also, given the nature of regimes in the region, defence cooperation could mean dealing with an ex-military ruler (Egypt) or with monarchies (GCC countries), which come with their own dynamics. However, India with its goodwill and trust across ideologies in the region, should be able to navigate such issues deftly.

India under Prime Minister Modi has made the West Asian region a critical part of its outreach into its extended neighbourhood and security cooperation has formed an important part of it which is clearly reflected in the growing defence and security cooperation with countries of the region in the past decade. Cooperation with the UAE has been the frontrunner with a number of bilateral initiatives. A MoU on cyberspace, signed in January 2017, upgrading security dialogue at the level of the National Security Adviser as well as agreement for joint defence production in India and purchase of important military equipment from India (*Brahmos* missile and 155 mm Artillery shells) are some of the important agreements with the UAE. Saudi Arabia, which is one of the largest purchasers of defence equipment globally (over US$ 80 billion annually), has been invited to join the 'Make in India' initiative. Saudi Arabia has also agreed to commence joint naval exercises. During the Prime Minister's visit to Qatar in June 2016, both sides agreed to give impetus to defence ties, including through joint exercises and enhanced training of naval, air and land forces, and also in the area of coastal defence. Kuwait has offered to sign a Defence Cooperation Agreement. The MoU on Duqm Port during the Prime Minister's visit to Oman in February 2018 is a historical landmark in India's security cooperation. Continued cooperation with Israel, the recent upswing in ties with Egypt and talk on revival of security cooperation with Iran during the recently held visits are a positive indicator of India's security outreach. Continuing Indian naval deployment in the anti-piracy operations across the Gulf of Aden and off the coasts of Oman and Yemen is another reflection of strong security cooperation with the region.

As India looks beyond its immediate neighbourhood, the West Asian region provides the perfect platform to expand its reach beyond its shores as a regional player and as a viable 'security collaborator.' Defence and security cooperation would play a pivotal role in this engagement.

NOTES

1 Akhilesh Pillalamarri, "India and the Gulf States Share a Long History", *The Diplomat*, 10 June 2016, at https://thediplomat.com/2016/06/india-and-the-gulf-states-share-a-long-history/ (Accessed 15 November 2022).

2 FAQs, Ministry of Defence, Government of India, at https://www.mod.gov.in/dod/faq?page=1 (Accessed 15 November 2022).

3 "Treaty of Peace between the Arab Republic of Egypt and the State of Israel", available at https://peacemaker.un.org/sites/peacemaker.un.org/files/EG%20IL_790326_Egypt%20and%20Israel%20Treaty%20of%20Peace.pdf (Accessed 15 November 2022).

4 Rajeev Agarwal, "Israel-Palestine Episodic Conflicts Deepening Divide", *Bharat Shakti*, 17 September 2022, at https://bharatshakti.in/israel-palestine-episodic-conflicts-deepening-divide/ (Accessed 15 November 2022).

5 "War in Yemen", Global Conflict Tracker, Council of Foreign Relations, at https://www.cfr.org/global-conflict-tracker/conflict/war-yemen (Accessed 21 November 2022).

6 Rajeev Agarwal, "Escalating tensions and threat of military conflict in the Gulf region: Who has the Edge?", 1 July 2019, Vivekananda International Foundation, at https://www.vifindia.org/article/2019/july/01/escalating-tensions% E2% 80% 93and-threat-of-military-conflict-in-the-gulf-region (Accessed 21 November 2022).

7 "Two Saudi oil tankers among 'sabotaged' ships off UAE coast", *Al Jazeera*, 13 May 2019, at https://www.aljazeera.com/news/2019/5/13/two-saudi-oil-tankers-among-sabotaged-ships-off-uae-coast (Accessed 21 November 2022).

8 "Tankers struck near Strait of Hormuz amid Iran-U.S. tensions", *PBS News*, 13 June 2019, at https://www.pbs.org/newshour/world/tankers-struck-near-strait-of-hormuz-amid-iran-u-s-tensions (Accessed 21 November 2022).

9 Rajeev Agarwal, no. 6.

10 Rajeev Agarwal, "As the Killing of Top Iran General marks a Tipping Point in the Crisis in the Middle East, Who has the Most to Fear", Vivekananda International Foundation,, 6 January 2020, at https://www.vifindia.org/article/2020/january/06/as-the-killing-of-top-iran-general (Accessed 21 November 2022).

11 "Russia, Iran defiant amid UN pressure over Ukraine drones", *Al Jazeera*, 20 October 2022, at https://www.aljazeera.com/news/2022/10/20/russia-iran-defiant-amid-un-pressure-over-ukraine-drones (Accessed 24 November 2022).

12 "Saudi Arabia and Iran agree to restore diplomatic relations", *Saudi Gazette*, 10 March 2023, https://www.saudigazette.com.sa/article/630567/SAUDI-ARABIA/Saudi-Arabia-and-Iran-agree-to-restore-diplomatic-relations (Accessed 4 August 2023).

13 Rajeev Agarwal, "Arab Spring: Aspirations Met Or Dreams Unfulfilled? ", MP-IDSA Comment, 26 October 2012, at https://www.idsa.in/issuebrief/ArabSpringAspirationsMet OrDreamsUnfulfilled_RajeevAgarwal_261012 (Accessed 24 November 2022).

14 "Tunisia's president flees the country", *Washington Post*, 15 January 2011, at https://www.washingtonpost.com/national/tunisias-president-flees-the-country/2011/01/14/ABynwhD_story.html (Accessed 24 November 2022).

15 "Tunisia, 10 years since its Arab Spring revolt", *The Times of India*, 26 July 2021, at https://timesofindia.indiatimes.com/world/rest-of-world/tunisia-10-years-since-its-arab-spring-revolt/articleshow/84748815.cms (Accessed 26 November 2022).

16 "Egypt crisis: Army ousts President Mohammed Morsi", *BBC News*, 4 July 2014, at http://www.bbc.com/news/world-middle-east-23173794 (Accessed 26 November 2022).

17 "Yemen's Saleh signs deal to give up power", *Reuters*, 23 November 2011, at https://www.reuters.com/article/us-yemen-idUSTRE7AM0D020111123 (Accessed 26 November 2022).

18 J.S. Sodhi, "Saudi Arabia and the Security Scars", *Indian Defence Review*, 1 April 2022, athttp://www.indiandefencereview.com/saudi-arabia-and-the-security-scars/ (Accessed 4 December 2022).

19 "Timeline of Syrian Chemical Weapons Activity, 2012-2022", *Arms Control Association*, athttps://www.armscontrol.org/factsheets/Timeline-of-Syrian-Chemical-Weapons-Activity (Accessed 4 December 2022).

20 "Timeline: the Rise, Spread, and Fall of the Islamic State", Wilson Centre, 28 October 2019, at https://www.wilsoncenter.org/article/timeline-the-rise-spread-and-fall-the-islamic-state (Accessed 4 December 2022).

21 "Islamic State vows revenge against U.S. for Baghdadi killing", *Reuters*, 31 October 2019, athttps://www.reuters.com/article/us-mideast-crisis-baghdadi-confirmation-idUSKBN 1XA25A (Accessed 4 December 2022).

22 "The Gulf Security Architecture: Partnership with the Gulf Cooperation Council, A Majority Staff Report Prepared for the use of the Committee on Foreign Relations United States Senate One Hundred Twelfth Congress Second Session, 19 June 2012, p. 7 (Accessed 6 December 2022).

23 Andrew Rathmell, Theodore Karasik and David Gompert, "A New Persian Gulf Security System", Issue Paper, RAND, 2003, at https://www.rand.org/pubs/issue_papers/IP248.html (Accessed 6 December 2022).

24 The Madrid Conference, 1991, Office of the Historian, at https://history.state.gov/milestones/1989-1992/madrid-conference (Accessed 6 December 2022).

25 Michael Kraig, "Assessing Alternative Security Frameworks for the Persian Gulf", *Middle East Policy*, 11 (3), Fall 2004, pp. 147-148 (Accessed 4 December 2022).

26 Patrick Knapp, The Gulf States in the Shadow of Iran, *Middle East Quarterly*, Winter

2010, pp. 49-59 (Accessed 6 December 2022).

27 Christopher M. Blanchard and Richard F. Grimmett, "The Gulf Security Dialogue and Related Arms Sale Proposals", CRS Report for US Congress, October 2008, https://sgp.fas.org/crs/weapons/RL34322.pdf (Accessed 8 December 2022).

28 "Saudi Arabia calls for 'strong and solid' Gulf union", *Al Arabiya*, at http://english.alara biya.net/articles/2012/12/24/256782.html (Accessed 8 December 2022).

29 "Oman opposes Gulf union", *Arab News*, 8 December 2013, at http://www.arabnews.com/news/488956 (Accessed 8 December 2022).

30 Rajeev Agarwal, "Arab NATO: A Reality Check", CLAWS, at https://archive.claws.in/1938/arab-nato-a-reality-check-rajeev-agarwal.html (Accessed 10 December 2022).

31 The Abraham Accords Declaration, US Department of State, at https://www.state.gov/the-abraham-accords/ (Accessed 10 December 2022).

32 Text of Treaty of Peace between the State of Israel and the Hashemite Kingdom of Jordan, at https://peacemaker.un.org/sites/peacemaker.un.org/files/IL%20JO_941026_ Peace TreatyIsraelJordan.pdf (Accessed 10 December 2022).

33 "Arab leaders, US President Biden affirm common vision for region at Jeddah summit", *Arab News*, 20 July 2022, at https://www.arabnews.com/node/2123541/saudi-arabia (Accessed 10 December 2022).

34 Sam Sasan Shoamanesh, "A New Security Order for the Middle East", 4 October 2012, at http://globalbrief.ca/blog/2012/10/04/a-new-security-order-for-the-middle-east/ (Accessed 10 December 2022).

35 Ministry of External Affairs, Government of India, Annual Report 1999-2000, P. 34, available at https://idsa.in/system/files/MEA_AnnualReport1999-00.pdf (Accessed 10 December 2022).

36 "India, Oman sign MoU on defence cooperation", *Zee News*, 7 December 2005, at https://zeenews.india.com/news/nation/india-oman-sign-mou-on-defence-cooperation_260824. html (Accessed 17 December 2022).

37 "India, Oman Extend MOU on Military Cooperation to 2015", PIB Press Release, 28 December 2011, at https://pib.gov.in/newsite/PrintRelease.aspx?relid=79251; "India & Oman renew MoUs on military cooperation & maritime issues", PIB Press Release, 20 May 2021, at https://pib.gov.in/PressReleaseIframe Page. aspx?PRID=1720411 (Accessed 17 December 2022).

38 "Defence Minister Manohar Parrikar Visits Oman", Press Information Bureau, Government of India, 22 May 2016, at http://pib.nic.in/newsite/PrintRelease.aspx?relid=145533 (Accessed 17 December 2022).

39 "India-Oman Joint Statement during visit of Honourable Prime Minister", Embassy of India, Oman, at https://www.indemb-oman.gov.in/page/visit-of-prime-minister-of-india-to-oman-2018/ (Accessed 17 December 2022).

40 "Oman army all set to use India's INSAS rifles", *The Hindustan Times*, 22 April 2010, at https://www.hindustantimes.com/india/oman-army-all-set-to-use-india-s-insas-rifles/story-MRxpigdWBkn5NEpS3TZCfI.html (Accessed 17 December 2022).

41 "India, Oman sign pact to boost maritime security cooperation", *Business Today*, 28 September 2021, atchttps://www.businesstoday.in/latest/economy/story/india-oman-sign-pact-to-boost-maritime-security-cooperation-307802-2021-09-28 (Accessed 17 December 2022).

42 "Secretary general of Oman's defence ministry calls on Rajnath Singh", *The Times of India*, 1 February 2022, at https://timesofindia.indiatimes.com/india/secretary-general-of-omans-defence-ministry-calls-on-rajnath-singh/articleshow/89281949.cms (Accessed 17 December 2022).

43 Ministry of Defence Press Release, PIB, 31 July 2023, at https://pib.gov.in/PressRelease Page.aspx?PRID=1944358 (Accessed 4 August 2023).

44 "India-UAE Joint Statement during the State Visit of Crown Prince of Abu Dhabi", Ministry of External Affairs, Government of India, at https://www.mea.gov.in/bilateral-documents.htm?dtl/26349/India_UAE_Joint_Statement_during_the_State _ Visit_of_ Crown _ Prince_of_Abu_Dhabi (Accessed 19 December 2022).

45 Ministry of External Affairs, Government of India, Press Release, at https://mea.gov.in/Portal/CountryNews/6277_Press_Release_23.5.2016.pdf (Accessed 19 December 2022).

46 "Naval Ships exercise to boost UAE-India ties", *Khaleej Times*, 18 March 2018, at https://www.khaleejtimes.com/uae/naval-ships-exercise-to-boost-uae-india-ties (Accessed 19 December 2022).

47 "Exercise Desert Flag-VI", Indian Air Force, at https://indianairforce.nic.in/exercise-desert-flag-vi/ (Accessed 19 December 2022).

48 "In its largest ever export order, OFB to supply 50,000 Bofors shells to UAE", *The Economic Times*, at https://economictimes.indiatimes.com/news/defence/in-its-largest-ever-export-order-ofb-to-supply-50000-bofors-shells-to-uae/articleshow/70501461.cms?from=mdr (Accessed 19 December 2022).

49 "Delhi Declaration, Signed by King Abdullah bin Abdulaziz Al Saud of the Kingdom of Saudi Arabia and Prime Minister Dr. Manmohan Singh of India, Embassy of India Riyadh", 27 January 2006, at https://www.eoiriyadh.gov.in/page/delhi-declaration/ (Accessed 19 December 2022).

50 "Riyadh Declaration: A New Era of Strategic Partnership", Embassy of India, Riyadh, 28 February 2010, at https://www.eoiriyadh.gov.in/page/riyadh-declaration/ (Accessed 19 December 2022).

51 "India, Saudi Arabia sign defense agreement", *Al Arabiya News*, 28 February 2014, at https://english.alarabiya.net/News/world/2014/02/28/India-Saudi-Arabia-sign-defense-agreement (Accessed 19 December 2022).

52 "India-Saudi Arabia Bilateral Relations", Ministry of External Affairs, Government of India, February 2022, https://mea.gov.in/Portal/ForeignRelation/India-Saudi_Arabia__1_. pdf (Accessed 19 December 2022).

53 "Indian company bags $155.5 million export order for artillery guns", *The Hindustan Times*, 10 November 2022, at https://www.hindustantimes.com/india-news/indian-company-bags-155-5-million-export-order-for-artillery-guns-101668019885550.html (Accessed 19 December 2022).

54 Ravi Sharma, "Saudi Army Chief on a historic visit to India", *The Frontline*, at https://frontline.thehindu.com/dispatches/saudi-army-chief-on-a-historic-visit-to-india/article65220306.ece (Accessed 19 December 2022).

55 Ravi Sharma, "Indian and Saudi navies hold the first-ever bilateral naval exercise in Port Al-Jubail, Saudi Arabia", *The Frontline*, 12 August 2021, at https://frontline.thehindu.com/dispatches/indian-and-saudi-navies-hold-the-first-ever-bilateral-naval-exercise-in-port-al-jubail-saudi-arabia/article35878352.ece (Accessed 19 December 2022).

56 "Saudi Army Chief on a historic visit to India", *The Frontline*, 16 February 2022, at https://frontline.thehindu.com/dispatches/saudi-army-chief-on-a-historic-visit-to-india/article65220306.ece (Accessed 19 December 2022).

57 "India-Egypt Defence Relations", Indian Embassy Cairo, at https://www.eoicairo.gov.in/eoi.php?id=Defence#:~:text=It%20was%20decided%20that%20a, in%20Cairo%20in% 20Aug%202006 (Accessed 23 December 2022).

58 "India-Egypt Bilateral Relations", Ministry of External Affairs, Government of India, July 2019, at https://mea.gov.in/Portal/ForeignRelation/Bilateral_brief_ for_

website.pdf (Accessed 23 December 2022).

59 "India, Egypt sign MoU to further defence cooperation", *The Hindu*, 20 September 2022, at https://www.thehindu.com/news/national/india-egypt-sign-mou-to-further-defence-cooperation/article65913296.ece (Accessed 23 December 2022).

60 "US, Australia among 6 countries interested in Tejas: Govt", *The Economic Times*, 5 August 2022, at https://economictimes.indiatimes.com/news/defence/us-australia-among-6-countries-interested-in-tejas-govt/articleshow/93371035.cms?from=mdr (Accessed 23 December 2022).

61 "India, Qatar ink key defence pact, Financial Express", 10 November 2008, at https://www.financialexpress.com/archive/india-qatar-ink-key-defence-pact/383907/ (Accessed 23 December 2022).

62 "India Qatar Bilateral Relation", Ministry of External Affairs, Government of India, 12 July 2021, at https://www.mea.gov.in/Portal/ForeignRelation/Qatar_2021_new.pdf (Accessed 23 December 2022).

63 Ibid.

64 "India-Qatar Joint Statement during the visit of Prime Minister to Qatar", PIB Note, 6 June 2016, at https://pib.gov.in/newsite/printrelease.aspx?relid=145991 (Accessed 23 December 2022).

65 Ibid.

66 "Staff Maj Gen (Navy) Abdulla Hassan M A Al-Sulaiti, Commander, Qatar Emiri Naval Forces visits India" PIB Press Release, 6 April 2019, at https://pib.gov.in/PressReleasePage.aspx?PRID=1570089 (Accessed 23 December 2022).

67 Monika Chansoria, "India Iran Defence Cooperation", *Indian Defence Review*, 17 February 2012, at http://www.indiandefencereview.com/interviews/india-iran-defence-cooperation/ (Accessed 27 December 2022).

68 Abhijnan Rej, "Indian Defense Minister Visits Tehran Amid Predictable Complications in Ties", *The Diplomat*, 7 September 2020, at https://thediplomat.com/2020/09/indian-defense-minister-visits-tehran-amid-predictable-complications-in-ties/ (Accessed 27 December 2022).

69 "India-Iran Military Cooperation: Analysing Iranian Defence Minister's Visit to India", *The Diplomatist*, 12 March 2021, at https://diplomatist.com/2021/03/12/india-iran-military-cooperation-analysing-iranian-defence-ministers-visit-to-india/ (Accessed 27 December 2022).

70 Iran, India complete each other: Iranian Deputy Foreign Minister, ANI News, 24 November 2022, https://www.aninews.in/news/world/asia/iran-india-complete-each-other-iranian-deputy-foreign-minister20221124144548/ (Accessed 27 December 2022).

71 "Discuss ways to enhance cooperation in all domains with focus on R&D in future technologies & defence co-production, India-Israel Vision on Defence Cooperation adopted to further strengthen existing framework", PIB Press Release, 2 June 2022, at https://pib.gov.in/PressReleseDetailm.aspx?PRID=1830445 (Accessed 3 January 2023).

72 "Israel can be very strong player in Make-in-India plan, says envoy", *ANI News*, 26 September 2022, at https://www.aninews.in/news/world/asia/israel-can-be-very-strong-player-in-make-in-india-plan-says-envoy20220926101528/ (Accessed 3 January 2023).

73 "Yemen evacuation operation was 'resounding success': Sushma Swaraj", *Economic Times*, 27 April 2015, at https://economictimes.indiatimes.com/news/politics-and-nation/yemen-evacuation-operation-was-resounding-success-sushma-swaraj/articleshow/47071300.cms?from=mdr (Accessed 3 January 2023).

74 "India, UAE to work together to fulfil Indian diaspora dreams: Modi", *Business Standard*, 11 February 2018, at https://www.business-standard.com/article/news-ians/india-uae-to-work-together-to-fulfil-indian-diaspora-dreams-modi-118021100256_1.html (Accessed 3 January 2023).

75 Minister of State M. J. Akbar's speech on India's International Partnerships at Manama Dialogue 2017 Bahrain, Ministry of External Affairs, Government of India, at https://www.mea.gov.in/Speeches-Statements.htm?dtl/29285/Minister_of_State_Shri_M_J_ Akbars_ speech_on_Indias_International_Partnerships_at_Manama_Dialogue_2017 BahrainDecember_09_2017 (Accessed 3 January 2023).

76 "CTF 150: Maritime Security", at https://combinedmaritimeforces.com/ctf-150-maritime-security/ (Accessed 3 January 2023).

77 Peri Dinakar, "India begins cooperation with Bahrain-based Combined Maritime Forces", *The Hindu*, 8 August 2022, at https://www.thehindu.com/news/national/india-begins-cooperation-with-bahrain-based-combined-maritime-forces/article65741512.ece (Accessed 3 January 2023).

7

India's Counter-Terror Cooperation with West Asia and North Africa

Saman Ayesha Kidwai

Introduction

India's counter-terrorism partnership with West Asian and North African (WANA) countries has strengthened significantly in recent years. In the decades following India's independence, its relationship with the WANA countries was dominated by bilateral trade, energy cooperation, and the presence of Indian manpower in the region. Cooperation on defence, security and strategic affairs has been a comparatively recent phenomenon in the India-WANA relationship. Since Prime Minister Narendra Modi assumed office, India has given renewed attention to strengthening defence and security cooperation with the region, which India believes is its 'extended neighbourhood.' Prime Minister Modi has visited a number of countries in the region and interacted with their leaders. The issue of terrorism has been a dominant issue in India's engagements with the countries of the region. India's belief that joint international efforts are required to fight the global networks of terror has found resonance in the WANA countries. As a result, there is a growing convergence between India and the WANA countries on the issue. Thus, among other issues of cooperation, countering terrorism has emerged as one of the key elements of engagement between India and the region in recent years. Several aspects of counter-terror cooperation such as stopping the flow of money to the hands of terrorist organisations, de-radicalisation, education, military training, exchange of information, and intelligence sharing, are key features of India's counter-terror cooperation.

Driving Factors of India-WANA Counter-Terror Partnership

Terror Attacks and Radicalisation

On the one hand, the 9/11 attacks profoundly impacted the Western countries' perception of the scale and reach of transnational terrorism. It also created a backlash within their societies towards the WANA countries, particularly Saudi Arabia, where most of the perpetrators were initially based. This backlash manifested in the form of visible racial violence but, most importantly, a drastic shift in the US-Gulf foreign policy framework.

Islamist terrorism's nature and the lethality of al-Qaeda signalled to the American leadership that the above-mentioned attacks were the resultant impact of undemocratic systems in the WANA region. The Saudi Kingdom's support and reliance on Islamist groups in the past to advance its broader interests further created a rift with its Western ally. Additionally, the regional countries gradually began to look at the US as a disruptor instead of a stable guarantor of security any longer with its dwindling commitment towards regional issues. As a result, questions arose about the American foreign policy's ability to ensure a balance of power among the regional stakeholders. Therefore, it is unsurprising that WANA States began cultivating closer ties, including counter-terrorism, with alternative actors, such as India.[1]

On the other hand, India's tilt towards WANA countries presumably was driven by the fact that radicalisation in the WANA region always has a bearing on South Asian events. It is even believed that a deep relationship exists between the "interpenetration of religion and politics between Middle East and South Asia ... given the history of cross-border terrorism and radicalization supported by Pakistan and other jihadist groups."[2] Therefore, Indian officials might have found it prudent to forge closer ties with countries in West Asia and North Africa.

Moreover, during the 26/11 attacks, several casualties were reported among individuals who had travelled to Mumbai from several WANA countries. Given this situation, India's cooperation with West Asian countries became necessary to extradite perpetrators of the attack, such as Abu Jindal. Also, suspects who have been ISIS sympathisers or involved in terror financing have also been extradited from Gulf States, including UAE and Saudi Arabia, to India.[3] Finally, as discussed below, Israel is a key partner for India in the security sector. Tel Aviv has even provided New Delhi with key counter-terrorism measures and weaponry.

Arab Spring and Geopolitical Developments

The beginning of the Arab unrest brought unprecedented changes and turbulence in the Arab world. One of the most disturbing phenomena amid the Arab Spring was the emergence of a number of terrorist organisations and radicalised groups in different parts of West Asia. These groups severely threatened the national security of some of these countries and the region as well. Furthermore, the widening regional sectarian conflicts, socio-political and economic instability further introduced instability with global ramifications.

In the throes of uprisings across the region, organisations like Hayat Tahrir Al Sham, ISIS, Al Qaeda in the Arabian Peninsula and Al Nusra Front began to fill the vacuum by seizing territories and through recruitment and radicalisation of the erstwhile demonstrators who participated in the Arab Spring protests. This happened as efforts to institute democratic regimes in the region gave way to uncertainty, power struggles, and protracted civil wars. Furthermore, each conflict zone gradually became a theatre of proxy conflicts, and sectarian rivalries between Shia and Sunni Muslim communities pitted domestic and regional stakeholders against each other.[4] Iraq, with ISIS' rise and the Saudi-Iran proxy conflict in the Yemeni war, are critical examples here.

Countries worldwide, particularly in the WANA region, began to be rapidly exposed to violence, instability, and devastation caused by ISIS' campaign to establish its "caliphate."[5] Transnational threats in a globalised world order, such as terrorism, never remain confined to a specific geographical location. It makes it necessary for States to counter this challenge through increased cooperation. Therefore, it makes sense that India and WANA countries have worked closely together to address critical security threats. Their cooperation has been underlined below.

The Arab Spring was followed by a spurt in proliferation of terrorism carried out by violent non-State actors.[6] This was exacerbated due to the combination of the influence of social media forums, an influx of foreign fighters from all corners of the globe to fight in active combat zones, and violent extremist ideologies. These factors possibly began to be perceived by India and its WANA partners as detrimental to their national security interests. The chaos that followed spurred India to evacuate its citizens from countries like Yemen and Libya and coordinate with regional countries bordering the conflict zones.[7]

Finally, the presence of the Indian diaspora throughout the region, valuable remittances worth millions of US dollars sent to India, and the energy trade anchoring India-WANA ties have been a subject of great debate in the face of these challenges.[8] They have made it all the more critical for partner countries to ensure stability becomes the norm rather than the exception for all the stakeholders. Furthermore, these factors appear to have cultivated robust security engagements between them.

Despite the instability and rise in oil prices caused in some countries following the Arab Spring protests, India and WANA officials participated in high-level ministerial visits, investments, and trade and signed bilateral agreements.[9] This undoubtedly must have provided continuity for the regional actors amid all the uncertainty and instilled profound trust and cooperation towards India.

ISIS and Mutual Threat Perceptions

The emergence of the ISIS Caliphate by carving out territories in Iraq and Syria brought direct challenges to the regional countries as well as India. ISIS targeted Indian nationals in Iraq and Libya. A few Indians also travelled to Iraq and Syria to join the Caliphate. A number of ISIS sleeper cells were busted by the security forces in different parts of India as well. The presence of ISIS in India's neighbourhood is also a matter of grave concern for India's national security.[10] Therefore, it signed several agreements with Gulf States to share vital intelligence regarding notorious terrorists. In addition, it positioned itself as one of the key advocates of a joint global response to neutralise the threat posed by ISIS.[11]

There has been a convergence of interests between India and the West Asian countries to fight and defeat ISIS. For example, by exercising influence over actors fighting ISIS, Qatar has proven itself a capable partner in the fight against it. In addition, India looked to the Gulf State to locate Indian construction workers whom ISIS had taken hostage. The convergence was further amplified as India and WANA countries realised the impact of ISIS' online recruitment tactics on their populations should they let the matters go unchecked any further.[12] On the one hand, India has been a favoured partner in this regard due to its vast experience in countering online radicalisation. On the other hand, a number of Indians who joined ISIS travelled through Kuwait, Oman, Bahrain, and UAE as transit points.[13] Thus, the WANA stakeholders became crucial partners for India in its fight against terrorism. These factors have brought these actors closer to confronting and defeating a violent enemy.

Growing Trade and Investment

In the economic sphere, trade and investment between India and the WANA countries are increasing significantly each year. India relies on the Gulf countries for the supply of oil and gas. For the Gulf countries, India remains a long-term and reliable market for their oil. Thus, there is a convergence of economic interests between the two. It is in the interest of both to protect and further promote such huge economic interests and not allow the terrorist groups in India or in West Asia to disrupt that flow. The total trade between India and WANA countries has increased by 80.17 per cent in the last two years alone.[14] However, India's energy security and their (WANA and India) commercial interests can only be sustained by providing maritime security in areas such as the Strait of Hormuz.[15] This maritime domain is one through which India has imported at least half of its natural gas and oil from the resource-rich Arab States.[16]

Simultaneously, India and UAE are part of the I2U2 format which is designed to "...tackle some of the greatest challenges of confronting our world, with a particular focus on joint investments and new initiatives in water, energy, transportation, space, health, and food security."[17] How this grouping aims to establish a linkage between their start-ups and I2U2 investments and how it assesses collective financing opportunities is equally critical.[18] Additionally, UAE and India agreed on a Free Trade Agreement in February 2022.[19] This grouping will open its doors to Saudi Arabia and Egypt in the foreseeable future. Furthermore, Petronet, an Indian company, will import 7.5 million tonnes of Liquefied Natural Gas from Qatar until 2028.[20]

These aspects have ensured that counter-terrorism ties between India and WANA stakeholders have a solid foundation (given their long-standing and diversified relationship) to anchor them and deepen their partnership further. These actors must continue strengthening their counter-terror relationship by investing further in their bilateral energy trade and through commercial investments.

India-WANA Counter-Terror Cooperation

Israel

Even before the formalising of diplomatic ties, the India-Israel relationship was bolstered in the defence sector, including during the Kargil War. Today, India is the largest purchaser of Israeli weapons. However, their counter-terrorism ties gained prominence mainly after the 26/11 attacks. In 2008, Nariman House, a Jewish outreach centre in Mumbai, came under attack by Pakistani terrorists. During that incident, six people died, including the couple who ran the centre, Rabbi Gavriel Holtzberg and his wife, Rivka. This brought to light the urgency with which India and Israel had to come together to fight the menace of terrorism, regardless of their geographical positioning. Israeli technological advancements in combating terrorist threats play a critical role in this regard.

However, the origins of their counter-terrorism ties lie in the immediate aftermath of former Prime Minister Indira Gandhi's assassination in 1984 and the attack on Israeli tourists in Kashmir by a group proclaiming itself to be the 'Defenders of the Islamic Revolution,' amidst which Indian soldiers reportedly underwent counter-terrorism training in Israel.[21] In 2001, they set up a Joint Working Group to counter threats concerning cyber security, terror financing, border security, and suicide bombing. While India brings to the table its share of dealing with cross-border terrorism, Israel has the experience of facing threats posed by Hezbollah and Palestinian Islamist militants. Israel had offered its support and expertise to India to help strengthen its border security along the Line of Control after the Uri attacks in September 2016.[22] Having frequently experienced attacks on its border from Hamas and Hezbollah, Israel has sufficient experience in this matter. A renewed emphasis is placed on their bilateral ties with Israel, particularly after former Israeli President Reuven Rivlin's visit to New Delhi in November 2016 and Prime Minister Modi's visit to Tel Aviv as the first Indian Prime Minister to do so, in July 2017.

Terrorism and counter-terrorism initiatives have frequently featured as two primary aspects of bilateral discussions between leaders on various levels. The joint statement issued during PM Modi's visit focused on combating global terrorism in various domains, including cyberspace. The leadership at both ends even emphasised the need for their Working Group on Homeland and Public Security to implement key agreements regarding terrorism-based issues.[23] On his numerous visits as India's Minister of External Affairs, Dr. S. Jaishankar, has reiterated how India and Israel confront the twin challenges of terrorism and radicalisation. Over the years, both countries have forged a deeper partnership, having faced security threats from their hostile neighbourhood.[24]

Israel has committed to providing India with equipment to enhance the latter's counter-terrorism measures, such as thermal sensors, long-range reconnaissance and observation systems, and thermal imagers. This has allowed India to adopt pre-emptive measures to prevent any other significant terrorist attacks on its soil.[25] In addition, while both countries have shared relevant real-time intelligence with each other, India has also procured precision-guided Spice-2000 bombs and missile supplies. The bombs have been used to successfully retaliate against the Jaish-e-Mohammed (JeM) terrorist camps in Pakistan after the 2019 Pulwama attacks.[26] The Phalcon AWACS system also played a crucial role during the strikes in

Balakot.[27] To foil infiltration bids from cross-border terrorists, Indian armed forces posted in Jammu and Kashmir, rely on Israeli foliage-penetrating radar and surveillance technology.[28]

Kingdom of Saudi Arabia

Saudi Arabia has been no stranger to terrorist attacks aimed at undermining its national security. In the past, it has faced attacks from Al Qaeda, which has repeatedly targeted the Kingdom. Al Qaeda in Arabian Peninsula (AQAP), which operates out of neighbouring Yemen, remains a key security threat to the Kingdom. In recent years, ISIS has been trying to find a foothold for itself in Yemen, which is yet another challenge for Saudi Arabia. Besides, since the beginning of the coalition military strikes on Yemen, the attack on the Saudi Kingdom launched by the Houthis from Yemen has increased significantly. The Houthis have been able to target critical infrastructure in the Kingdom including airports, oil installations as well as the security forces. Repeated drone strikes on its oil, military, and civilian infrastructure by Houthi rebels have amplified its vigilance to guard its territorial integrity and populace.

In the Riyadh Declaration signed in 2010, the two countries decided to band together, condemn terrorism in all its forms and manifestations, and rejected attempts to link it to any religion or race. They mutually agreed to enhance cooperation in the sphere of intelligence sharing about narcotics and human trafficking and signed the Extradition Treaty and the Agreement for Transfer of Sentenced Persons.[29] The Treaty was ratified in 2011, with one of the earliest instances of extradition taking place in 2012. That year, Saudi authorities handed over to India, Zabiuddin Ansari alias Abu Hamza – responsible for instructing the ten terrorists who waged the coordinated assaults during 26/11, to converse in Hindi, including Ajmal Kasab.[30]

The Riyadh Declaration elevated the India-Saudi relationship to a strategic level and laid a strong foundation for counter-terror cooperation between the two countries.

Prime Minister Modi has further engaged with the Kingdom on the issue and there has been continuous engagement between the two at the political and official levels. Over the years, India's National

Security Advisor Ajit Doval and Prime Minister's Special Envoy on Counter-Terrorism, Syed Asif Ibrahim, have frequently travelled to West Asia to bolster regional counter-terror ties with India and discuss key security threats.[31] India has made great efforts to take the Kingdom into confidence regarding its implemented counter-terrorism measures.[32]

In 2016, the two countries, through a MoU, committed themselves to share relevant intelligence about terrorist threats.[33] This pact cemented Saudi Arabia's commitment to supply India with terror financing data and vice-versa, trace the paper trail of terrorists' money laundering methods and those covertly or passively supporting violent extremist propaganda within their countries. One of the other key developments, due to the 2016 MoU, was the formation of a Joint Working Group, similar to what India has instituted with Israel and Bahrain.[34]

A comprehensive dialogue at the level of National Security Advisors, to deal with terrorism and evolving challenges took place in February 2019. During this visit, the joint statement declaring that conducive conditions must be cultivated for Indo-Pak dialogues to resume presumably reflected the Kingdom's tacit acknowledgement that unless Pakistan's support for anti-India terrorist groups ends, there can be no resumption of talks.[35] In September 2019, approximately two weeks after the drone attacks on Saudi Arabia's Aramco oil facilities, India-Saudi bilateral ties in the counter-terrorism arena were further upgraded. The relationship now includes joint efforts to eliminate terror financing channels, intelligence sharing, and information exchanges. There have also been bilateral discussions about strengthening bilateral ties in spheres such as maritime and cyber security.

Due to growing bilateral engagements, Saudi Arabia has moved away from the Organisation of Islamic Cooperation's (OIC) virulent rhetoric about Jammu and Kashmir, becoming more aware of the security threats India faces in the Union Territory.[36] It has also become more empathetic of India's actions in the Valley and strongly condemned events like the Pulwama attack, which proved to be one of the worst terrorist attacks faced by armed forces in recent history. It even disallowed Pakistan's attempts to organise discussions on

Kashmir at the OIC's Foreign Ministers' Meeting in 2020. This denoted another shift in Saudi Arabia's approach towards India vis-à-vis Pakistan.

In August 2021, bilateral naval exercises, 'Al Mohed Al Hindi 2021,' which were shore and sea-based, were conducted amid deepening ties and in the light of the drone attack on Mercer Street Vessel. Vice Admiral Majed Al Qahtani, Saudi Arabia's Eastern Fleet Commander, termed these exercises the 'first of their kind.'[37] These were within the realm of their counter-terrorism initiatives.

UAE

Like Saudi Arabia, Yemeni Houthis have attacked the UAE. It is deeply concerned about the threat of terrorism and finds India to be a reliable partner in counter-terrorism. India and the UAE signed a Defence Cooperation Agreement in 2003 and a Security Cooperation Agreement in 2011. In recent years, there have been serious efforts on the part of the UAE to cooperate with India in several fields including counter-terrorism.

The radical transformation of ties has mainly taken place since 2015 after Modi chose the Emirati State to be his first foreign visit among the Gulf countries after he was sworn in after the 2014 general elections, as part of his foreign policy strategy. His visit was critical because it was the first visit by an Indian Prime Minister after more than three decades. It was also during the above-mentioned meeting that the two sides issued a joint statement, committing their countries to cooperation in arenas such as de-radicalisation and cyber security.[38]

Additionally, during Modi's visit to the UAE in April 2016, the two countries signed a MoU concerning terror financing and money laundering. Both sides have been affected by State-sponsored terrorism and have therefore shown great initiative in expanding their ties in the security domain.[39]

This was followed by the 2016 Comprehensive Strategic Partnership Agreement, which focused on India and the UAE's collective efforts to engage in counter-terrorism and maritime security, among other significant matters. It was also the first official visit by an Indian Defence Minister, Manohar Parrikar, to the Emirati State.

Furthermore, Pakistan's refusal to participate, announced after a unanimous decision in its parliament in 2015, in the Saudi-led coalition in Yemen also fractured its ties with the Emirati leadership.[40]

In January 2017, the two sides agreed to enhance their issue-based counter-terrorism ties focused on promoting collaboration in cyberspace, money laundering (with an impact on terrorist groups' radicalisation activities), arms, narcotics, and human trafficking, and maritime security, during President al Nahyan's visit to India.[41]

During the February 2018 virtual summit, Prime Minister Modi and President Sheikh Mohamed bin Zayed al Nahyan, committed their countries to collectively work towards countering terrorism. This development came on the heels of the July 2018 visit of the President to India, during which they upgraded their relationship to a comprehensive strategic partnership. However, the other significant highlight of this visit was the joint statement that the leaders issued. Both leaders condemned the efforts of any country to polarise political issues along sectarian or religious lines and underlined the culpability of State leaders to curb activities of the non-State actors under their control. They also called for ending any means through which terrorists could carry out their destabilising objectives against other States.[42]

The UAE has tacitly condemned Pakistan's policy of State-sponsored terrorism directed at undermining India's national security without laying it out publicly in explicit terms. It has, on numerous occasions, expressed 'unconditional' support for India's efforts to counter terrorism.

Both countries have supported each other's call for formulating a comprehensive strategy of disruption of the use of cyberspace and social media forums to radicalise and indoctrinate vulnerable youth by terrorist groups to advance their nefarious objectives. Additionally, the Indian efforts at lobbying the UAE have resulted in the latter maintaining a relatively neutral position on the Kashmir issue and agreeing to include several Pakistani terrorist groups within its gambit of terrorism, like the LeT, Haqqani network, and Indian Mujahideen (IM).

The deepening counter-terrorism cooperation has also yielded results in the extradition of known terrorists like Asadullah Akhtar, Abdul Sattar, and Yasin Bhatkal, associated with the proscribed organisation, IM.[43] The Extradition Treaty between the UAE and India was operationalised in 1999, and instruments of ratification were exchanged the following year. The first instance of extradition dates to 2002.[44] The IM has been culpable for the 2008 Ahmedabad bombings and the 2006 train attacks in Mumbai. Furthermore, terrorists affiliated with other banned organisations like LeT have also been detained and extradited to India. On the other hand, their fruitful partnership resulted in Yasin Mansoor Mohamed Farooq alias Farooq Takla's – accused of the 1993 blasts in Mumbai and Dawood Ibrahim's aid – extradition to India in May 2018.

In the past, both countries have called on all States to 'fully respect and sincerely implement their commitments to resolve disputes bilaterally and peacefully, without resorting to violence and terrorism,' covertly laying the blame for regional security challenges on Pakistan's policy of perpetuating terrorism through proxy groups.[45]

Kuwait

Kuwait's sympathetic stance and proactive participation in international matters concerning terrorism stem from its historical trauma. Beginning in the 1970s, it began experiencing a spate of terrorist attacks by Islamist militant groups allied with groups such Hezbollah, Peninsula Lions, Mujahideen of Kuwait, and the Muslim Brotherhood.

However, the worst attack on its soil occurred in June 2015, when an ISIS suicide bomber killed at least 27 and wounded no less than 227 individuals after an attack on the Imam Sadiq Mosque.[46] Following this attack, the former Indian President, Pranab Mukherjee, while expressing his concern and condolences over the incident, condemned 'all acts of terror and mindless violence' while underscoring that humanity can only move forward through an amalgamation of brotherhood, unity, non-violence, and peace, affirming support for Kuwait's efforts to counter terrorism.[47]

The above-mentioned attack (June 2015) proved even more of a jolt for India, as it lost two of its citizens – Ibne Abbas and Rizwan Hussain – who were offering mid-day prayers when the blast occurred. This is one of the several instances which have demonstrated why India and Kuwait, united by shared grief, have found ways to come together in the fight against terrorism.

One of the earliest instances of significance attached to India-Kuwait counter-terrorism cooperation includes the February 2010 meeting conducted between former External Affairs Minister S.M. Krishna and the Kuwaiti delegation, wherein the latter expressed a desire to see India play a more extensive role in international relations. In March 2018, a Kuwaiti Defence Ministry delegation led by Brigadier General Khaled Bilal Al Obaidi, was one of the key participants in the International Counter-Terrorism Conference held in Gurugram, India, revolving around themes such as terrorist trends and ideological challenges.[48]

Kuwait, after the Pulwama attack, condemned the attack, and in May 2019, during its tenure as a non-permanent member of the United Nations Security Council, designated Masood Azhar, JeM's Chief, as a global terrorist. The latter had long been a demand raised by India in the United Nations' corridors.

Qatar

India firmly believes that terrorism is a menace that can only be eradicated through the international community's collective efforts; therefore, Qatar is also one of its preferred partners in this fight. The latter has experienced relatively few terrorist attacks in the past, with only a small number of its citizens joining ISIS' ranks. Nonetheless, it remains well versed in the devastating impact of terrorist acts. For example, its Al Udeid base, housing the American military and Qatari air force, has repeatedly come under attack. Additionally, in March 2005, a suicide attack at the Doha Players Theatre injured 12 people and killed one.[49]

While their counter-terrorism partnership has intensified after Modi was sworn in, it has a long-standing precedent. For example, in November 2008, both countries inked a strategically important defence pact, under which naval officers were trained to combat international piracy, and a mechanism for sharing a database on threats detailing information posed by violent extremists to their security, was laid down.

On the other hand, in a joint statement issued at the end of Prime Minister Modi's visit to Qatar in June 2016, the two sides delineated that:

> 'Both sides noted that addressing the menace of global terrorism should be based on a comprehensive approach which should include the following measures:
> (a) countering violent extremism,
> (b) combating radicalisation and recruitment,
> (c) disrupting terrorist movements,
> (d) stopping all sources for financing of terrorism,
> (e) stopping the flow of foreign terrorist fighters,
> (f) dismantling terrorist infrastructure, and
> (g) countering terrorist propaganda through the internet.'[50]

During the above-mentioned visit, out of the seven pacts signed by the two sides, one of them has its basis in counter-terrorism initiatives. The agreement was signed between the Qatar Financial Information Unit and India's Finance Intelligence Unit. It aims at clamping down on terror financing affecting their countries' stability. As per its clauses, both sides will swap relevant intelligence to counter monetary offences and illegal transfers of money by terrorists. During this visit, the joint agreement highlighted the determination to pool resources and fight terrorism in all its forms and manifestations.

Furthermore, in December 2016, India and Qatar signed a MoU to enhance security and defence ties and combat terror financing. Exchange of information also occurred regarding these issues between Qatari and Indian teams at the latter's Ministry of Home Affairs.[51]

On the other hand, in November 2019, the Qatari and Indian naval officers were involved in a three-day joint maritime exercise to enhance interoperability and defence cooperation to counter maritime piracy and terrorism.[52]

Qatar has also acted as an important facilitator of dialogue with insurgent groups-turned government leaders like the Taliban whose political office in Doha acted as a conduit for all international stakeholders who invested in the Afghan peace process, including India.

Understanding that combating terrorism requires a holistic

approach, the two sides have, under Modi's leadership, called for conducting dialogue between their intellectual eminent religious scholars to promote inclusivity and peace instead of violence and terror. Similar to India's relationship with Kuwait, its ties with Qatar in counter-terrorism domain are driven by prevention of use of cyberspace to contain online radicalisation.

Bahrain

Like Kuwait and Qatar, Bahrain has also maintained a steadfast partnership with India in countering terrorism and violent extremism. In 2016, India and Bahrain inaugurated their first Bahraini-Indian Joint Steering Committee, which focused on reinforcing bilateral cooperation in the domain of counter-terrorism.[53] Rejecting the notion of 'your terrorist versus my terrorist,' they also pledged to campaign for conducting seminars and training modules to aid their collective fight in combating unconventional security challenges.

Incidentally, in December 2015, they assured their commitment to partake in global efforts to counter narcotics, human and arms trafficking, organised crime, counter-terrorism, and promote intelligence sharing. During Modi's visit to Manama in August 2019, where he met Bahraini Prime Minister Prince Khalifa bin Salman Al Khalifa, the two leaders issued a joint statement that implicitly targeted Pakistan for its support for subversive acts like cross-border terrorism within Indian territory while agreeing to strengthen cooperation in areas such as intelligence sharing and security. Some of the key features of their joint statement addressed the following:

(a) Condemning the policy of using terrorism against a fellow nation-state.
(b) Eradicating terrorist networks and infrastructures.
(c) Ceasing support to terrorist groups working against the interests of other States.
(d) Bringing terrorists to justice.[54]

They have also actively campaigned to adopt the United Nations Comprehensive Convention on International Terrorism and sanction terrorists and their affiliated organisations without delay. Incidentally, like in the above case studies, cyber security features predominantly in the India-Bahrain counter-terrorism partnership, with both actors emphasising preventing misuse of cyberspace, which can otherwise be used for online radicalisation and undermining social harmony.

Equally significant is the two sides' cooperation on maritime piracy and security, recognising in April 2021, how their bilateral dialogues have been instrumental in strengthening bilateral defence and security cooperation as a result of frequent interactions across counter-terrorism, maritime security, and piracy domains, and 'institutionalising cooperation in the area of intelligence sharing.[55]

Iran

While India and Iran's bilateral relationship has mainly revolved around the Chabahar Port's construction and oil imports, they have also displayed a united front regarding their mutual fight against Pakistan-sponsored terrorism. Within a span of a day, in February 2019, Indian armed forces and members of Iran's Revolutionary Guard Corps were attacked by JeM and Jaish Al Adl terrorists, respectively, in Pulwama and Khash-Zahedan (Sistan-Balochistan).[56] While 40 Indian officers were martyred in the fatal attack, Iranians lost 27 soldiers.

Stopping short of carrying out a surgical strike as India did in Balakot, Iranians lambasted the Pakistani nexus – civilian, military, and intelligence – for the attack on its armed officers, claiming that the security apparatus remained aware of Jaish Al Adl's safe house. Incidentally, Iran went so far as to threaten those involved with definitive measures to crack down on terrorists who act on behalf of trans-regional and regional countries' spy agencies, as mercenary officers.[57]

In May 2016 and February 2018, India and Iran, after Modi's bilateral meeting with former President Rouhani, released the same concise and rhetorically harsh joint statement. They called for:

(a) Eliminating the process of providing havens and any support to terrorists and their affiliated organisations
(b) Being critical of states who, in any manifestation or through various means, choose to support terrorism.[58]

By September 2016, as conflicts in Syria and Yemen arrived at their climax, India, and Iran, with strategic and civilisational ties with those countries, arrived at a mutually acceptable agreement to share intelligence and prevent the spillover of terrorism. ISIS' violent and destabilising activities featured prominently in Modi's discussions with his then counterpart in Tehran during that period. Additionally, the former Iranian Foreign Minister Zarif, during his visit to New Delhi in August 2016, emphasised the security concern facing India and Iran due to the emergence of the Islamic State Khorasan Province (ISKP) in Afghanistan.[59] These two bilateral visits highlighted how a terrorist organisation or its affiliates could threaten the national security of multiple countries simultaneously.

On the other hand, in September 2018, India, Iran, and Afghanistan held their initial tripartite meeting, focused on enhancing counter-terrorism cooperation, economic growth, curbing narcotics trafficking, and infrastructural initiatives.[60] Moreover, since Iran remained one of the few countries not to shut down its embassy doors in Kabul, along with China, Russia, and Pakistan, it has been able to preserve open communication channels with the Taliban regime.

As India has begun to diplomatically engage the interim administration, almost a year after it withdrew its diplomatic corps, Iran's continued, and much deeper ties with Afghanistan's new rulers could serve India's long-term goals well in the country. This is mainly because under President Rouhani and Raisi's tenures, Iranian regimes have welcomed India's participation in stabilising Afghanistan through non-military means. Since their bilateral cooperation regarding Afghanistan-centric issues has precedent, they (Indian leaders) can leverage those ties to ensure that the Taliban do not allow groups like JeM to conduct training camps in Afghanistan in preparation of any attacks. Iran has even backed India's stand at various international forums like the United Nations about how there must be no distinction between terrorists, for they are one and the same, with each activity carried out by them as unjustified.

Iraq

Iraq and India have forged their ties through diaspora, energy trade and the common threat posed by domestic terrorist groups. Concerned about its citizens joining ISIS, India stood steadfast alongside Iraq in its efforts to rally the international community at the United Nations to counter the terrorist outfit's rapid military offensive. Its defence delegations made three visits to Iraq from July 2017 to January 2018, after Mosul was recaptured from the Islamist militants, to express their solidarity in the fight against terrorism and towards stabilising the post-ISIS era.[61]

At one point, the Indian and Iraqi intelligence agencies were also deeply involved in tracing and freeing 39 Indians who were taken hostage by ISIS and used as slave labour. Falih Al Fayyadh, the former Iraqi National Security Advisor, had earlier called on his country and India to have robust counter-terrorism ties based on their shared experiences of being impacted by the scourge of terrorism.

During his visit to the Manohar Parrikar Institute for Defence Studies and Analyses in December 2013, the Institute signed a MoU with Al Nahrain Center for Strategic Studies for enhanced academic cooperation between the two organisations.[62] Al Fayyadh's views expressed during the above-mentioned visit to India concerning capacity building and intelligence sharing being two crucial aspects of their bilateral counter-terrorism relationship have continued to hold and resonate on both sides of the spectrum.

Jordan

There is deep-seated synergy between Jordanian and Indian perspectives on countering terrorism, both arguing that the fight against terrorism and radicalisation is not synonymous with the fight against any specific religion. Instead, it is aimed at countering those who mislead impressionable individuals to commit atrocities against humankind, particularly through the Aqaba Process (of which India is a participating member). This process involves an exchange of knowledge and expertise to prevent the expansion of terrorism.[63]

In October 2015, former Indian President Pranab Mukherjee rejuvenated long-standing historical ties between the two countries during his visit to Amman, making this the second visit by an Indian leader to Jordan since former Prime Minister Rajiv Gandhi's visit in 1988. Emphasising their shared perspectives on the fight against terrorism, President Mukherjee and King Abdullah II agreed to bolster their counter-terrorism partnership and defence cooperation mechanisms.

In Jordan, there is a great deal of appreciation for India's involvement in global counter-terrorism initiatives; since the Hashemite Kingdom has been at the forefront of the international coalition against ISIS, it is cognisant of terrorism's devastating impact. During the Jordanian monarch's visit to India, the 12 agreements signed by PM Modi and King Abdullah II in March 2018 focused primarily on bolstering bilateral defence cooperation. As per the MoU on Defence Cooperation, they focused on 'defining the scope of such cooperation and making provisions for the implementation of the cooperation in some of the recognised areas like training; defence industry; counter-terrorism; military studies; cyber security; military medical services, peace-keeping, etc.'[64] The leaders also highlighted the need to disseminate ideas about Islam's moderate version, religious plurality, interfaith dialogues between their communities, and a coordinated approach to ward off violent extremism.[65]

Morocco

Positioned at the crossroads of the Mediterranean Sea and the Atlantic Ocean, the Moroccan Kingdom has become a key strategic and counter-terrorism partner for India, particularly due to the proactive efforts of the Modi government. Approximately 22 high-level visits have taken place, and 35 MoUs regarding security and economic issues have been signed since October 2015.[66] Both India and Morocco have been affected by terrorism-related issues at different intervals. Therefore, due to the Kingdom's moderate interpretation of Islam and relatively successful de-radicalisation programmes, it is arguably a key ally in the fight against violent extremism and terrorism.[67]

During the former Indian Defence Minister Nirmala Sitharaman's visit to Morocco in 2018, the two sides identified counter-insurgency and counter-terrorism as two key areas of further cooperation.[68] In February 2019, India and Morocco signed a MoU to establish a Joint Working Group to combat terrorism by acquiring and exchanging relevant information.[69] This working group was created to address challenges emanating from cross-border terrorism, weaponisation of social media by terrorists, and terror financing. Additionally, it is meant to intensify their security cooperation on such matters in organisations such as the United Nations.[70]

The two countries have also collaborated to prevent a second round of terrorist attacks in Sri Lanka after the Easter bombings by providing credible leads that resulted in the arrest of potential attackers.[71] Furthermore, efforts are underway to develop a joint legal framework to deal with issues related to crime and violent extremism.[72]

Syria

The historical, civilisational ties between India and Syria received a boost in August 2016 when, in light of increasing ISIS-related threats, they agreed to strengthen their security ties through information sharing.[73] Their collective experience of being threatened or attacked by Islamist jihadist groups like LeT, Al Qaeda, and ISIS binds them, driving their strategy of upgrading their bilateral ties. For example, the IED blast near Damascus on 13 October 2022 killed 18 Syrian soldiers while wounding 27 others.

Furthermore, similar to arguments raised by Kuwait, Bahrain, and Qatar, Syria has also backed India's claims that there can be no differentiation, such as 'my terrorist versus your terrorist' made, to defeat this international menace since it has faced the brunt of groups like ISIS. Syria has also consistently supported India's position and initiatives regarding Kashmir. In return, while advocating for a peaceful resolution to the Syrian conflict, India has supported President Assad's stance against domestic terrorists. This position was in line with Indian External Affairs Minister S. Jaishankar's remarks made during a meeting with his Syrian counterpart, Faysal Mikdad, where he affirmed India's support for Syria in its counter-terrorism practices and territorial integrity.[74] Riad Abbas, the former Syrian Ambassador to India, believes that India and Syria's bilateral counter-terrorism ties can be strengthened further by tapping its experience in countering terrorism.[75]

Oman

Oman has remained clear of significant terrorist attacks while frequently serving as a mediator or peacemaker for disputing countries. Overlooking the Indian Ocean and the Arabian Sea, Oman has served as a critical partner for Indian anti-piracy operations and remains the sole country with which all three wings of the Indian armed forces conduct bilateral training and exercises.

Since the Muslim Brotherhood's plan to overthrow former Sultan Qaboos bin Said was uncovered by authorities in 1994, Oman has decisively stood against radicalism and terrorism in all its manifestations. It has even extended the same support to India, a country that has, on numerous occasions, faced the devastating impact caused by terrorist activities.

Principally taking a stand against terror financing during Modi's visit to Oman in February 2018, their joint statement comprised three crucial points, underscoring how Pakistan has implicitly been cornered in their decisive fight against global terrorism:

> "They reiterated their strong condemnation of terrorism in all its forms and manifestations, wherever committed and by whomever, and declared that there could be no justification for any act of terrorism anywhere.... The two sides also emphasised upon the need to isolate the sponsors and supporters of terrorism and ... agreed to coordinate efforts to counter extremism and radicalization and misuse of religion by groups and countries for inciting hatred and perpetrating acts of terrorism."[76]

Under the Modi government, both the countries have been concerned with bolstering their counter-terrorism efforts by sharing intelligence and via capacity building. Incidentally, the Omani ports, including the one based in Salalah, allowed Indian naval ships easy access to the Gulf of Aden and carried out effective counter-piracy operations, because of which pirates have been captured and piracy has declined.

Like Bahrain, Oman has also actively supported India's call for the swift adoption of the Comprehensive Convention on International Terrorism in the United Nations and working towards ending the misuse of cyberspace for subversive acts. These countries have deep regard for, and are cognisant of, the collective efforts of key global powers in the fight against eliminating terrorism.

In September 2017, Oman played a pivotal role in freeing Father Tom Uzhunnalil from ISIS' captivity. He was taken hostage in March 2016 after terrorists raided a home for the elderly in Aden, where he was residing. Both Indian and Omani leadership have frequently emphasised the need to isolate sponsors of terrorism and build inclusive societies as part of effective de-radicalisation and counter-terror measures.[77]

On 13 August 2022, India and Oman concluded the fourth phase of their joint counter-terrorism military exercise, referred to as 'Al Najah.' The most recent phase of the Al Najah exercise focused on counter-terrorism and counter-insurgency operations within semi-urban settings, as per the United Nations mandate. The core features of this exercise included counter-terrorism operations, organisation of collective drills and procedures, peacekeeping and regional security operations, etc.[78]

Egypt

Egypt is no stranger to terrorism, and the similar experiences of India make the two countries natural allies. In 2018, Indian and Egyptian National Security Advisors signed a MoU, following which both countries formally initiated the process of sharing pertinent information to eliminate terrorist threats and established a Joint Working Group to combat terrorism, similar to what India shares with Israel.[79]

Terror financing, money laundering, violent extremism, radicalisation and cross-border terrorism are some of the key drivers of the India-Egypt partnership and have deepened their bilateral ties over the years.[80] Since both countries continue to be affected by these challenges, they will presumably remain the cornerstone of their counter-terror ties.

During President Fattah El Sisi's visit to India in September 2016, he and Prime Minister Modi agreed to upgrade their counter-terrorism partnership with three key pillars – counter-radicalisation of youth, sharing of intelligence, and operational cooperation. Appreciating Egyptians as the moderate voice of Islam, the Prime Minister has underlined that he and his counterpart arrived at the conclusion that threats emanating in cyberspace would feature predominantly in their counter-terrorism partnership.[81]

Furthermore, in September 2020, during former Defence Minister Nirmala Sitharaman's visit to Cairo, Egypt and India agreed to upgrade their defence and security ties by committing their countries to joint military exercises and domain awareness in the maritime sphere.[82]

Their bilateral partnership has also served both countries well in the United Nations Counter-Terrorism Committee, in their efforts to rally member states around joint international efforts to counter terrorism, as per Indian officials' statements in the past. In September 2022, India's Defence Minister Rajnath Singh visited Egypt where his interaction with President al-Sisi focused on enhancing defence cooperation and the need to intensify cooperation regarding the exchange of successful practice and expertise to counter terrorism.[83]

Conclusion

Among WANA countries, Israel remains at the top in terms of counter-terrorism cooperation and is followed by Gulf Cooperation Council (GCC) countries, especially Saudi Arabia and the UAE. There is huge potential for cooperation on counter-terrorism with other regional countries, namely Iran, Egypt, Iraq, Syria, Jordan and Morocco who share the same concern with India. Dialogues, security agreements, counter-terrorism exercises, and extradition of criminals and terrorists have served as cornerstones of their evolving ties.

Undoubtedly, India's cooperation with the regional countries has, to a considerable extent, been successful in countering terror. The extradition of some terrorists to India from Saudi Arabia and the UAE reflects the success of counter-terror cooperation between these countries. Behind the scenes, there are a number of initiatives and continuous efforts among the security agencies such as sharing information and intelligence about the organisations, their leadership, ideology, the flow of money and the movement of terrorists, which have deterred terrorist attacks and busted their sleeper cells.

Three crucial factors would arise if one were to analyse the ebbs and flows of India-WANA counter-terrorism cooperation. Firstly, significant convergence is running across each partnership India shares with the regional States, from counter-terrorism to energy and defence security. Secondly, the implementation of the credible initiatives undertaken has accelerated under Modi's leadership. Thirdly, despite the constraints and challenges at both ends, greater cooperation in counter-terrorism is a step in the right direction. Furthermore, India and its WANA partners can explore economic and trade diversification, enhance defence and energy cooperation and cyber-technological exchanges, as measures to bolster and rejuvenate their ties.

NOTES

1 Pramit Pal Chaudhuri, "The balance of power in the recent past", Delhi Policy Group, 2015, at https://www.delhipolicygroup.org/uploads_dpg/arch_publication_file/west-asia-in-transition-1003.pdf (Accessed 11 January 2023).

2 Jon B. Alterman, "India's Middle East strategy", CSIS, 13 December 2022, at https://www.csis.org/analysis/indias-middle-east-strategy (Accessed 11 January 2023).

3 Rajesh Ahuja and Jayanth Jacob, "Of 24 terror suspects turned in by Gulf countries to India since 2012, 18 are from UAE and Saudi", *Hindustan Times*, 24 August 2018, at https://www.hindustantimes.com/india-news/of-24-terror-suspects-turned-in-by-gulf-countries-to-india-since-2012-18-are-from-uae-and-saudi/story-225ND 6iI OaWrD9m YZYRFLL.html (Accessed 11 January 2023).

4 Raed Fawzi Ihmoud Ihmoud, "Extremism and terrorism, challenges and impact on India-West Asia ties", Observer Research Foundation, 5 February 2016, at https://www.orfonline.org/wp-content/uploads/2016/02/transformations-in-west-asia-regional-perspectives.pdf (Accessed 11 January 2023).

5 Talmiz Ahmad, "Sectarianism and security implications for West Asia", in Prasanta Kumar Pradhan (ed.), *Geopolitical shifts in West Asia*, Pentagon Press, New Delhi, 2016, pp. 61-78.

6 Vincent Durac, "The role of non-state actors in Arab countries after the Arab uprisings", European Institute of the Mediterranean, 2015, at https://www.iemed.org/publication/the-role-of-non-state-actors-in-arab-countries-after-the-arab-uprisings/ (Accessed 11 January 2023).

7 "Rescue operations by India", Press Information Bureau, 23 December 2015, at https://pib.gov.in/newsite/PrintRelease.aspx?relid=133841 (Accessed 12 January 2023).

8 Arvind Gupta, et al. "Arab Spring: Implications for India", MP-IDSA Policy Brief, 2 January 2014, at https://www.idsa.in/policybrief/ArabSpringImplicationsfor India _westasia_020114 (Accessed 11 January 2023).

9 Prasanta Kumar Pradhan, "India's relationship with West Asia: Facing the challenges of Arab Spring", in Prasanta Kumar Pradhan (ed.), *Geopolitical shifts in West Asia*, Pentagon Press, New Delhi, 2016, pp. 227-240.

10 Adil Rasheed, "India was of little value to ISIS. That's all set to change now", *The Print*, 22 May 2019, at https://theprint.in/opinion/india-was-of-little-value-to-isis-thats-all-set-to-change-now/238361/ (Accessed 11 January 2023).

11 Pradhan, no. 9.

12 Kabir Taneja, "India's Middle East policy gathers momentum", *The Diplomat*, 8 March 2015, at https://thediplomat.com/2015/03/indias-middle-east-policy-gathers-momentum/ (Accessed 12 January 2023).

13 Mohammed Sinan Siyech, "India-Gulf counter terrorism cooperation", Middle East Institute, 21 December 2017, at https://www.mei.edu/publications/india-gulf-counterterrorism-cooperation (Accessed 12 January 2023).

14 "Foreign trade (WANA)", Department of Commerce, Ministry of Commerce and

Industry, Government of India, at https://commerce.gov.in/about-us/divisions/foreign-trade-territorial-division/foreign-trade-wana/ (Accessed 12 January 2023).

15 Ra'ed Fawzi Ihmoud Ihmoud, "Extremism and terrorism, challenges and impact on India-West Asia ties", Observer Research Foundation, 5 February 2016, at https://www.orfonline.org/wp-content/uploads/2016/02/transformations-in-west-asia-regional-perspectives.pdf (Accessed 11 January 2023).

16 "India faces biggest impact of tensions in Strait of Hormuz", *Economic Times*, 20 July 2019, at https://economictimes.indiatimes.com/news/economy/foreign-trade/india-faces-biggest-impact-of-tensions-in-strait-of-hormuz-iea/articleshow/70301376.cms?from=mdr (Accessed 12 January 2023).

17 Seema Guha, "Beyond religion, remittances: India's relationship with West Asia has transformed into partnership of mutual interests", *Outlook*, 10 January 2023, at https://www.outlookindia.com/national/beyond-religion-remittances-india-relationship-with-west-asia-has-transformed-into-partnership-of-mutual-interests-news-252247 (Accessed 12 January 2023).

18 "I2U2 Summit: UAE to invest $2 billion to develop integrated food parks in India", *Indian Express*, 14 July 2022, at https://indianexpress.com/article/india/i2u2-summit-uae-to-invest-2-billion-to-develop-integrated-food-parks-across-india-8029382/ (Accessed 12 January 2023).

19 "Comprehensive Economic Partnership Agreement (CEPA) between the Government of the Republic of India and the Government of the United Arab Emirates (UAE)", Ministry of Commerce and Industry, Government of India, 27 March 2022, at https://commerce.gov.in/international-trade/trade-agreements/comprehensive-economic-partnership-agreement-between-the-government-of-the-republic-of-india-and-the-government-of-the-united-arab-emirates-uae/ (Accessed 12 January 2023).

20 Seema Guha, "Beyond religion, remittances: India's relationship with West Asia has transformed into partnership of mutual interests", *Outlook*, 10 January 2022, at https://www.outlookindia.com/national/beyond-religion-remittances-india-relationship-with-west-asia-has-transformed-into-partnership-of-mutual-interests-news-252247 (Accessed 12 January 2023).

21 Ely Kamon, "India's counterterrorism cooperation with Israel," *Perspectives on Terrorism*, 16(2), April 2022, pp. 2-11.

22 Alvite Ningthoujam, "The upward trajectory of India-Israel relations", South Asian Voices, 6 April 2017, at https://southasianvoices.org/upward-trajectory-india-israel-relations/ (Accessed 27 November 2022).

23 Efraim Inbar, "Modi's Visit to Israel – The view from Jerusalem," MP-IDSA Comments, 10 July 2017, at https://www.idsa.in/idsacomments/modi-visit-the-view-from-jerusalem_e-inbar_100717 (Accessed 25 November 2022).

24 "India, Israel share similar challenges from radicalisation, terrorism: Jaishankar", *Economic Times*, 18 October 2021, at https://economictimes.indiatimes.com/news/defence/india-israel-share-similar-challenges-from-radicalism-terrorism-jai shankar/articleshow/87101672.cms (Accessed 4 September 2022).

25 Ely Kamon, no. 21.

26 Robert Fisk, "Israel is playing a big role in India's escalating conflict with Pakistan", *Independent*, at https://www.independent.co.uk/voices/israel-india-pakistan-conflict-balakot-arms-trade-jaish-e-mohammed-a8800076.html (Accessed 4 September 2022).

27 Pradipta Roy, "Debunking the Myths of Conflicting Nationalism Between India and Israel", 15 October 2020, at https://www.spmrf.org/debunking-the-myth-of-conflicting-nationalism-between-india-and-israel/ (Accessed 26 November 2022).

28 Somdeep Sen, "India's deepening love affair with Israel", *Al Jazeera*, 9 September 2021, at https://www.aljazeera.com/opinions/2021/9/9/indias-deepening-love-affair-with-israel (Accessed 5 September 2022).

29 "Riyadh Declaration", Embassy of India Riyadh, at https://www.eoiriyadh.gov.in/page/riyadh-declaration/ (Accessed 2 September 2022).

30 Surabhi Malik and Mala Das, "The Abu Hamza trail: How US thwarted Pakistan's attempts to get him deported", *NDTV*, 27 June 2012, at https://www.ndtv.com/india-news/the-abu-hamza-trail-how-us-thwarted-pakistans-attempts-to-get-him-deported-490068 (Accessed 30 August 2022).

31 Md. Muddassir Quamar, "Indo-Saudi Relations under the Modi government", at https://www.e-ir.info/2017/03/13/indo-saudi-relations-under-the-modi-government/ (Accessed 26 November 2022).

32 Omair Anas, "India-West Asia relations under the nationalist Modi government", *International Studies*, 58 (1), January 2021, pp. 59-79.

33 "Saudi Arabia to enhance anti-terror cooperation with India: Envoy", *Economic Times*, 25 September 2019, at https://economictimes.indiatimes.com/news/defence/saudi-arabia-to-enhance-anti-terror-cooperation-with-india-envoy/articleshow/71291017.cms?from=mdr (Accessed 2 September 2022).

34 Prasanta Kumar Pradhan, "Mohammed bin Salman walks the India-Pakistan tightrope", MP-IDSA Comments, 25 February 2019, at https://www.idsa.in/idsacomments/saudi-india-pakistan-tightrope-pkpradhan-250219 (Accessed 25 November 2022).

35 "India-Saudi Arabia Joint Statement during the State Visit of His Royal Highness the Crown Prince of Saudi Arabia to India", Press Information Bureau, 20 February 2019, at https://pib.gov.in/newsite/PrintRelease.aspx?relid=188826 (Accessed 25 November 2022).

36 Kinda Bakr, "Saudi Arabia-India: Strategic partnership"' Gulf Research Centre, 4 May 2021, at https://www.grc.net/single-commentry/31 (Accessed 2 September 2022).

37 "India and Saudi Arabia hold first-ever naval exercises in the Arabian Gulf", *Middle East Eye*, 10 August 2021, at https://www.middleeasteye.net/news/india-and-saudi-arabia-hold-first-ever-naval-exercises-arabian-gulf (Accessed 2 September 2022).

38 "Joint statement between the United Arab Emirates and the Republic of India," Ministry of External Affairs, Government of India, 17 August 2015, at https://www.mea.gov.in/bilateral-documents.htm?dtl/25733/Joint_Statement_ between _ the_United_ Arab_ Emirates_and_the_Republic_of_India (Accessed 3 September 2022).

39 S. Samuel C. Rajiv, "Modi's Act West policy in motion", 15 March 2017, at https://www.spmrf.org/modis-act-west-policy-motion/ (Accessed 27 November 2022).

40 "UAE officials slams contradictory Pakistan vote", *Al Arabiya*, 20 May 2020, at https://english.alarabiya.net/News/middle-east/2015/04/11/UAE-FM-Pakistan-needs-a-clear-a-position-on-Yemen-conflict- (Accessed 26 November 2022).

41 "India, UAE to cooperate on counterterrorism, increase trade by 60 per cent", *Deccan Chronicle*, 26 January 2017, at https://www.deccanchronicle.com/nation/current-affairs/260117/india-uae-to-cooperate-on-counterterrorism-increase-trade-by-60-per-cent.html (Accessed 3 September 2022).

42 Md. Muddassir Quamar, "India and the UAE: Progress towards comprehensive strategic partnership", MP-IDSA Comments, 5 July 2018, at https://www.idsa.in/issuebrief/india-and-the-uae-progress-strategic-partnership-mmquamar-050718 (Accessed 25 November 2022).

43 Jhinuk Chowdhury, "India and UAE: A partnership against terrorism", *Swarajya Mag*, 11 February 2016, at https://swarajyamag.com/world/india-and-uae-a-partnership-against-terrorism (Accessed 3 September 2022).

44 Amitabh Bhaumik, "UAE extradited 19 in 16 years; 2 since 2014", *Deccan Herald*, 5 December 2018, at https://www.deccanherald.com/national/uae-extradited-19-india-18-yrs-706556.html (Accessed 27 November 2022).

45 "Joint statement between the United Arab Emirates and the Republic of India", Ministry of External Affairs, Government of India, 17 August 2015, at https://mea.gov.in/articles-in-foreign-media.htm?dtl/25733/Joint+Statement+between+the +United+ Arab+ Emirates+and+the+Republic+of+India (Accessed 28 November 2022).

46 "Kuwait: Extremism and terrorism", Counter Extremism Project, at https://www.counter extremism.com/countries/kuwait-extremism-and-terrorism (Accessed 30 August 2022).

47 "President of India expresses deep concern over terrorist attack at a mosque in Kuwait", Press Information Bureau, at https://pib.gov.in/newsite/PrintRelease.aspx?relid=122845 (Accessed 30 August 2022).

48 "Kuwait participates in international counter-terrorism conference in India", *Arab Times*, 15 March 2018, at https://www.arabtimesonline.com/news/kuwait-participates-in-international-counter-terror-conference-in-india/ (Accessed 30 August 2022).

49 "Qatar: Extremism and terrorism", Counter Extremism Project, at https://www.counterextremism.com/countries/qatar-extremism-and-terrorism (Accessed 31 August 2022).

50 "India, Qatar pledge to fight terrorism, internet propaganda", *Business Standard*, 5 June 2016, at https://www.business-standard.com/article/news-ians/india-qatar-pledge-to-fight-terrorism-internet-propaganda-116060500602_1.html (Accessed 31 August 2022).

51 "India-Qatar agrees on joint action plan to counter terrorism", United News of India, 3 December 2016, at http://www.uniindia.com/india-qatar-agrees-on-joint-action-plan-to-counter-terrorism/india/news/707011.html (Accessed 31 August 2022).

52 "Joint exercise between the Qatari Emiri Navy and the Indian Navy Forces (the Roar of the Sea)", Press Information Bureau, 18 November 2019, at https://pib.gov.in/PressRelease Page.aspx?PRID=1591973 (Accessed 31 August 2022).

53 "India-Bahrain relations", Ministry of External Affairs, Government of India, January 2020, at https://mea.gov.in/Portal/ForeignRelation/India-bahrain_Bilateral_Brief_ JAN_2020.pdf (Accessed 31 August 2022).

54 "India, Bahrain call on global community to reject use of terrorism against other countries", *The Hindu*, 28 November 2021, available at https://www.thehindu.com/news/national/india-bahrain-call-on-global-community-to-reject-use-of-terrorism-against-other-countries/article61580225.ece (Accessed 31 August 2022).

55 "Joint statement on third India-Bahrain high joint commission meeting", FSI, 7 April 2021, at https://fsi.mea.gov.in/bilateral-documents.htm?dtl/33777/Joint _ Statement _on _Third_ IndiaBahrain_High_Joint_Commission_Meeting_ 7_ April _ 2021 (Accessed 31 August 2022).

56 "India, Iran agree on close cooperation to fight terrorism", *Economic Times*, 17 February 2019, at https://economictimes.indiatimes.com/news/defence/india-iran-agree-on-close-cooperation-to-fight-terrorism/articleshow/68038205.cms?from=mdr (Accessed 31 August 2022).

57 "After India, Iran threatens Pakistan for harbouring militants, asks how many of your own people killed in terrorist operations", 4 March 2019, at https://www.india.com/news/world/after-india-iran-threatens-pakistan-for-harbouring-militants-asks-how-many-of-your-own-people-killed-in-terrorist-operations-3594668/ (Accessed 31 August 2022).

58 Shubhajit Roy, "India, Iran agree to eliminate forces that support terror", *Indian Express*, 17 February 2018, at https://indianexpress.com/article/india/india-iran-agree-to-eliminate-forces-that-support-terror-5068055/ (Accessed 31 August 2022).

59 Alvite Singh Ningthoujam, "A renewed Indo-Iranian security cooperation in the offing", *Vivekananda International Foundation*, 7 September 2016, at https://www.vifindia.org/print/3257?via=at (Accessed 27 November 2022).

60 "India, Iran, Afghanistan to boost economic, counter-terrorism cooperation", *Business Standard*, 11 September 2018, at https://www.business-standard.com/article/news-ians/india-iran-afghanistan-to-boost-economic-counter-terrorism-cooperation-118091100700_1.html (Accessed 1 September 2022).

61 Farzad Ramezani Bonesh, "How India views Iraq and important areas of cooperation between the two countries", Bayan Center, at https://www.bayan center.org/en/2022/03/3181/ (Accessed 1 September 2022).

62 "India and Iraq must cooperate to counter terrorism: National Security Advisor of Iraq", MP-IDSA, 20 December 2013, at https://idsa.in/pressrelease/Indiaand IraqMustCooperate toCounterTerrorism (Accessed 1 September 2022).

63 Ashok Sajjanhar, "India-Jordan Relations: An ascendant partnership", MP-IDSA Comments, 26 February 2018, at https://www.idsa.in/idsacomments/india-jordan-relations_asajjanhar_260218 (Accessed 25 November 2022).

64 "India and Jordan strengthen ties with a focus on defence cooperation", *The Wire*, 1 March 2018, at https://thewire.in/diplomacy/india-jordan-defence-cooperation (Accessed 1 September 2022).

65 Fazzur Rahman Siddiqui, "The visit of King Abdullah of Jordan to India: Its meaning and implications", Academia, 26 April 2018, at https://www.academia.edu/36547855/The_visit_of_King_Abdullah_of_Jordan_to_India_Its_Meanings_and_Impli cations (Accessed 28 November 2022).

66 "India-Morocco bilateral relations", Ministry of External Affairs, Government of India, 31 July 2022, at https://mea.gov.in/Portal/ForeignRelation/Bilateral_brief-31July_2022.pdf (Accessed 26 November 2022).

67 Meena Singh Roy, "India's Outreach to North Africa: Advancing the India-Morocco Partnership", MP-IDSA, January-February 2019, at https://idsa.in/system/files/profile/6-waw-2-1-MSR.pdf (Accessed 26 November 2022).

68 "India, Morocco enter into bilateral deals", 26 September 2018, at https://indbiz.gov.in/india-morocco-enter-into-bilateral-deals/ (Accessed 26 November 2022).

69 "Cabinet approves MoU between India and Morocco for setting up of a Joint Working Group on Counter-Terrorism", Press Information Bureau, 13 February 2019, at https://pib.gov.in/Pressreleaseshare.aspx?PRID=1564358 (Accessed 26 November 2022).

70 "Morocco, India poised to foster their counterterrorism cooperation", *North Africa Post*, 19 February 2019, at https://northafricapost.com/28179-morocco-india-poised-to-foster-their-counterterrorism-cooperation.html (Accessed 26 November 2022).

71 Dipanjan Roy Chaudhury, "India, Morocco prevent further terror strikes in Sri Lanka", *Economic Times*, 3 May 2019, at https://economictimes.indiatimes.com/news/defence/india-morocco-prevent-further-terror-strikes-in-sri-lanka/

articleshow/69163536.cms?from=mdr (Accessed 26 November 2022).

72 Ihssane Guennoun, "India and Morocco's new cooperation areas: Focusing on security and preventing violent extremism", Policy Center for the New South, 2 October 2019, at https://www.policycenter.ma/opinion/india-and-morocco's-new-cooperation-areas-focusing-security-and-preventing-violent-extremism (Accessed 26 November 2022).

73 "India-Syria to upgrade security consultations over Isis threat", AGI, 22 August 2016, at https://international.agi.it/international/india-syria_to_upgrade_ security_ consultations_ over_isis_threat-1021183/news/2016-08-22/ (Accessed 2 September 2022).

74 "Mikdad meets Jaishankar; India supports Syria in war against terrorism", Syrian Arab News Agency, 26 September 2021, at https://sana.sy/en/?p=249492 (Accessed 1 September 2022).

75 Dipanjan Roy Chaudhury, "Syria eyes to expand counter-terror ties; develop energy partnerships with India: Envoy", *Economic Times*, 30 October 2021, at https://economictimes.indiatimes.com/news/india/syria-eyes-to-expand-counter-terror-ties-develop-energy-partnership-with-india-envoy/articleshow/87391035.cms? from =mdr (Accessed 1 September 2022).

76 "India Oman joint statement during visit of Prime Minister to Oman", Ministry of External Affairs, Government of India, 12 February 2018, at https://www.mea.gov.in/bilateral-documents.htm?dtl/29479/India%B1Oman%B1Joint%B1Statement%B1during %B1 visit%B1of%B1Prime%B1Minister%B1to%B1Oman.html (Accessed 1 September 2022).

77 Samuel Rajiv, "Imparting new dynamism to India's engagements with West Asia", *SPMRF*, 20 March 2018, at https://www.spmrf.org/imparting-new-dynamism-to-indias-engagements-with-west-asia/ (Accessed 26 November 2022).

78 "India and Oman to carry out 13-day military exercise in Rajasthan", *The Hindu*, 31 July 2022, at https://www.thehindu.com/news/national/india-and-oman-to-carry-out-13-day-military-exercise-in-rajasthan/article65706768.ece (Accessed 2 September 2022).

79 Dipanjan Roy Chaudhury, "India, Egypt sign MoU to exchange terrorism information", *Economic Times*, 13 July 2018, at https://economictimes.indiatimes.com/news/defence/india-egypt-sign-mou-to-exchange-terrorism-information/articleshow/53988210.cms? from=mdr (Accessed 1 September 2022).

80 Alvite Ningthoujam, "Military cooperation with MENA Region: An Indo-Egyptian connection", Observer Research Foundation, 27 September 2022, at https://www.orfonline.org/expert-speak/military-cooperation-with-mena-region/ (Accessed 26 November 2022).

81 "Press statement by PM during the visit of President of Egypt to India", PMINDIA, 2 September 2016, at https://www.pmindia.gov.in/en/news_updates/press-statement-by-pm-during-the-visit-of-president-of-egypt-to-india/ (Accessed 28 November 2022).

82 "India Egypt decides to boost defence cooperation", *The Week*, 4 April 2020, at https://www.theweek.in/wire-updates/national/2018/09/23/del27-def-india-egypt.html (Accessed 2 September 2022).

83 "India, Egypt sign MoU to enhance defence cooperation", *New Indian Express*, 20 September 2022, at https://www.newindianexpress.com/nation/2022/sep/20/india-egypt-sign-mou-to-enhance-defence-cooperation-2500158.html (Accessed 14 October 2022).

Index